RAILWAYS
OF THE
TWENTIETH
CENTURY

RAILWAYS
—OF THE—
TWENTIETH
—CENTURY—

Geoffrey Freeman Allen

WW Norton & Company
New York · London

CONTENTS

First published in the United States by
W. W. Norton & Company Inc.
500 Fifth Avenue
New York, NY 10110

**Library of Congress Cataloging in
Publication Data**

Allen, G. Freeman (Geoffrey Freeman)
  Railways of the twentieth century.

  1. Railroads—History. I. Title. II. Title:
Railroads of the 20th century.
TF20.A54   3857.09
ISBN 0-393-01603-X   AACRZ

Printed In Spain by
Graficas Reunidas S.A., Madrid

Perhaps a dozen important terms describing railway operations or objects differ notably from Britain to the United States and Canada. The true *locus classicus* is the British word 'footplate' but because of the glamour and eccentricity of the term, it is known to a good many American rail followers. Footplate is a term of synecdoche to indicate simply the locomotive cab or being in the cab ('On the footplate'). Others are not so obvious. 'Bank' in England means track climbing a hill or mountainside *grade* (the US term), and 'banker' translates into American English as the lowly pusher or helper engine used to help get the train in question up the bank or grade. Some others: wagon in the US is usually a four wheeled vehicle pulled by a horse or a child. In Britain it is any freight car, no matter how heavy or long it may be. The English locomotive driver, which is logical enough, is the US engineer, not quite so logical and pompous besides. In England, a train calls at a station; in the US it stops. 'Shunter' in British English neatly translates into switcher or yard engine in the US.

Some British railway terms are becoming common in America, e.g. 'stock' as a generic term for a matched group of coaches or sleepers. Also Bo–Bo for a diesel or electric engine of two four-wheeled trucks, and Co–Co for one with two six-wheeled trucks. Locomotive trucks convert to bogies in Britain, by the way, and the term must forever conjure up for some the image of Messerschmitt fighters approaching the channel coast in 1940.

One English term staggers the American rail follower's sensibilities. And that is 'switchback' as a description of a railroad curving through mountainous terrain. This happens to satisfy definition 'b' in the *Shorter Oxford English Dictionary*. The author of this book somewhere refers to '210 miles of Erie switchbacks'. In American usage that would mean 210 miles of track that reverses the train via a switch and turnout every half mile or so in order to climb a steep mountainside. Read *that* way it would be a bit of high science fiction fantasy.

H. Stafford Bryant, Jr.

INTRODUCTION

AT THE START of the twentieth century railways commanded the inland transport market. Their only serious challenge was from shipping operators where rail routes were paralleled by canals, navigable rivers or coastal shipping lanes. Where the railways were still in private hands, their competitors were not external but their own kind, and inter-railway struggles were often as vicious as any between rail and other modes half-a-century later. The pressure was still on legislators to protect the traveller and trader from railways' misuse of their dominant standing; that the railways themselves might soon be clamouring for protection from unfair competition was unimaginable.

The shadows of road and air transport were already creeping over the railways between the wars. At that stage the traditional railway had sufficient technological reserve, particularly with electric and newborn diesel traction, to fend off bids for its long-haul traffic in bulk. But with the advantage of small-unit flexibility, road transport was already supplanting the railway as a local carrier. And in the freight market it was free to pick and choose the best-paying business, so that it was already starting to cream off the high-value end of the merchandise market, leaving the railways, still locked in the common carrier legislation enacted in their monopolistic prime, compelled to accept what was left.

Rapid mid-century exploitation of the Second World War's wealth of new air and road vehicle technology so intensified the pre-war trends that in some countries the railway's very survival looked dubious. In much of Africa and South America, in particular, road development pre-empted almost all the cash allocated to ground transport. By the end of the 1960s more than one State railway system in those two areas was imprisoned in a spiral of investment starvation that diminished efficiency, which in turn drove away traffic and thus encouraged fresh penny-pinching. Total collapse was on the cards. Even in the industrialized world the contraction of the railway's role to haulage of coal and other minerals in bulk and to short-hauls of peak passenger flows, notably in the conurbations, looked a possibility. They were the only tasks which road and air were clearly incapable of taking over at acceptable financial and environmental cost.

To claim the last quarter of the century as the 'Age of the Train' may be hyperbole. But at least it is the age in which the train has firmly re-established itself as indispensable and at the same time fully competitive in all its turn-of-the-century activity except transcontinental passenger and rural service.

It might have happened sooner but for many railway managements' slowness to grasp that the new competitive environment demanded a revolution of operating and commercial methods that had been unquestioningly accepted since the late nineteenth century. That reappraisal had begun before energy sources became a global worry in 1973. So had recognition that in some sectors – the huge new consumer goods freight market, for instance – inter-modal techniques offered a better way back into good business than straight confrontation.

Thus when the oil crisis broke, the range of practical, thoroughly economical alternatives to more energy-expensive transport the railway had to offer was much wider than it would have been two decades earlier. And technology was fast advancing the electrified railway's superiority further yet. To cite one example, by 1983 a 160 mph (258 km/h) train would be linking the centers of Paris and Lyons in less overall time than the journey would take by a 314-seater Airbus of the latest build, but for at least 60 per cent less consumption of energy per passenger- and vehicle-mile. Moreover, though railways had been one of the backmarkers in industrial labour cost-shedding, they were now belatedly becoming one of the pacemakers. Rationalization had begun the process. By the 1980s, when over 65,000 bits of information could be stored in a single micro-chip, electronics was accelerating it. With its uniquely disciplined operation over immovable tracks, the railway was the best equipped of any form of transport to benefit from the new age of automation. So, starting with Spain, rail history since 1974 has been dominated by the decision in one country after another to re-draft transport policy with a new emphasis on rail investment and in many cases on rail electrification.

This account of twentieth-century railways, then, is a fascinatingly contrasted three-acter of complacent supremacy, then nervous retreat and finally of tempered confidence. I am deeply grateful to the many friends in the railway industry at home and abroad who have allowed me to see so much of the second half of the action unfold at close quarters.

Blockley, Glos. October 1983   G.F.A.

1
THE YEARS OF SUPREMACY

NEW YORK'S GRAND CENTRAL and Chicago's La Salle Street stations were noticeably busier than usual for the early afternoon on 15 June 1902, but not with passengers. At the start of the twentieth century a new refinement in rail travel was as certain to capture the newspaper headlines as an airline price war in the 1980s, and a *première* to be staged at 2.45 in each of the two stations had excited journalists both locally and internationally – as witnessed by the presence among the throng of newspaper reporters of a representative from the London *Times*. That afternoon the two stations were as much grandstands as places of business. Cynosure of it all was the departure from each end of the New York–Chicago route of the first trains regularly scheduled to cover the 980 miles (approx. 1,577 km) between the two cities in 20 hours – 4 hours less than the fastest service previously on offer. George Daniels, the New York Central's passenger chief, a man with a marketing flair that was at least two decades ahead of its time, had named them the 'Twentieth Century Limited'; and they typified the main thrust of the railways' commercial effort in the Western world at the turn of the century.

The private car was as yet only a rich man's toy, the motor bus in its infancy and the airplane a vision, so for the mass of the population the train was the only practical form of transport for medium- or long-distance journeys. There was no need to court passengers with faster or more comfortable trains. If the élite of the business world and society and, best of all, the flower of Europe's royalty and nobility could be induced to travel more, the publicity they generated would be spur enough in the mass market. So the five cars with which the 'Twentieth Century' started life had room for only 42 passengers and carried a dozen staff to minister to them. It was America's first train to charge an extra fare in addition to berth fees and other supplements (and one of the few able to command such a supplement in subsequent decades).

For that money the 'Century's' passengers had a choice of sleeping accommodation ranging up to palatial staterooms, two of which could be converted by withdrawal of a folding partition into a gilded bridal chamber; a gentlemen's club car with wine bar, barber's shop and white-tiled bathroom; an observation car where ladies could retire while their spouses quaffed, puffed cheroots and swapped scatology in the club car until a fresh list of Wall Street prices, wired from New York, was handed aboard at the next stop; the trainboard services of a library and a stenographer; and a diner the one-dollar dinner of which soon earned a reputation in the haut-monde of Europe as well as in American society. The average menu set off with oysters, then ran through soup, a choice of fish, chicken, ribs of beef and roast goose with such

The mahogany-panelled dining car of the New York Central 'Twentieth Century Limited' in 1902; note the wall-mounted pot plants.

Far left:
The fine Grand Central station building, New York, before it was overshadowed by high-rise commercial development.

A Pennsylvania RR Class E3a 4-4-2 working hard with the 'Pennsylvania Limited' near Philadelphia in the early 1900s.

intriguing side-plates as apple fritters glazed in Kirsch and finished with a selection of desserts and cheeses. Still barely touched by Wagons-Lits and Pullman development on their side of the Atlantic, visiting Europeans were just as awed by the splendour of the 'Century's' diner itself, with its luxuriously moulded mahogany decor, wall-hung pot plants, linen-covered tables and real silverware.

In the first decade of the twentieth century the private enterprise railway's only long-haul passenger competitor was any neighbouring company with a parallel route. Between New York and Chicago the New York Central was in fierce contention with the Pennsylvania, which reacted to advance publicity for the 'Twentieth Century Limited' by hastening to organize its own 20-hour service between the two cities. This, the 'Pennsylvania Special', it managed to inaugurate on the very same day as the rival train's debut. In time the 'Special' was reshaped as the better-known 'Broadway Limited', which battled with the 'Century' for the lucrative and extremely prestigious New York–Chicago business right through to the decimation of the US railroads' passenger business by the airlines after the Second World War.

The store the railways set by the immaculate

functioning of their luxury passenger trains in the early 1900s is epitomized in the treatment of these two 'Limiteds'. Each had operating priority over every other train along their routes, along which standby engines were always posted, steam up, at strategic points to guard against failures. Both were kept constantly refreshed with the latest products of the carbuilder's art; in fact, each company had a standing order with the Pullman Car Co. that its crack New York–Chicago train be supplied with an example of each new car range as soon as the latter was in production.

The New York Central's concern for everyday performance was acute. Each morning the railroad's President insisted that there be on his desk statistics of the overnight 'Century's' passenger loading, its punctuality and gross revenue, plus a nominal roll of the celebrities aboard and any comments they had made to the train staff. Over the years scarcely a night passed without the 'Century's' sailing list (as its card of occupants was officially termed to equate its status with that of an ocean liner) featuring some tycoon or laureate of the arts whose patronage was grist to the publicity mill. Not only did NYC President Alfred H. Smith have all this data wired to him daily when he was abroad but also, so legend has

The observation car of the Great Northern's St Paul–Seattle transcontinental of 1910 (the train covered the 1,829 miles [2,943 km] in 58 hours) is valeted en route; the car housed a buffet, card room, library, lounge and five compartments including a drawing room.

it, conveyed straight to his hand in a forked stick by a native runner when he was on a hunting safari in the African bush. The 'Century' even added a metaphor to everyday language. 'Red carpet treatment' derives from the New York Central's practice throughout the 'Twentieth Century's' career of unfolding from concourse to platform entrance at New York and Chicago, a crimson roll emblazoned with the train's name in gold before each day's 'Century' departure.

Soon more and more railroads emulated the two Eastern systems in the packaging of speed and exquisite luxury for an exclusive market. In 1911, for instance, the Santa Fe put on a once-weekly train, the 'De Luxe', leaving Chicago at 8 pm every Tuesday and reaching Los Angeles at 9 am the following Friday, which was bluntly advertized as being limited to 60 passengers. Each of them was surcharged $25 – quite possibly the equivalent of £200 in today's money values – on top of the fare and other fees. Practically all this train's sleeping accommodation was in individual rooms, dining was epicurean, and a troop of stewards together with a valet, lady's maid, manicurist, barber, librarian and barman were on constant call throughout the trip. More than that, every male passenger was presented with a pigskin

wallet embossed with the train's title in gilt; and at the Californian border uniformed pages would swarm aboard with corsages for each lady. The Great Northern's 'Oriental Limited' from Chicago to Puget Sound was distinguished by its immaculate 5 pm ritual when a steward bearing a silver tea service and a retinue of uniformed maids with trays of delicate sandwiches and patisseries processed the length of the train. The Florida East Coast's 'Florida Special' did even more to justify the 'hotel-on-wheels' cliché by deploying a string quartet amid potted palms to accompany pre-dinner drinks in its lounge.

The topmost echelons of American commerce and society could go one better by having their private car attached to some of these trains – or in the most affluent cases, by making up their own train of such cars, especially after the Interstate Commerce Commission reacted to abuse of railroads' readiness to accommodate the car-owners and early in the century imposed strict curbs on the attachment of private vehicles to public trains. The early 1900s saw these privately-owned vehicles reach the apogee of extravagance and idiosyncracy. The most expensive furniture and draperies, solid gold and silver dinner services and rare artworks as wall-

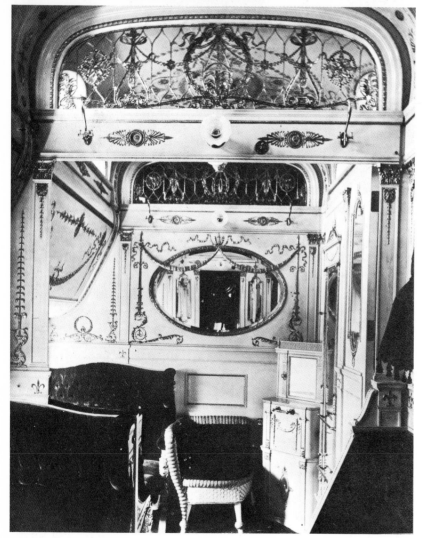

Top:
Service of afternoon tea by a
kimono-clad Japanese maid
was a daily ritual on the
Chicago–St Louis 'Alton
Limited' in the first quarter of
the century.

Above:
At the start of the century the
'Pennsylvania Limited's'
accommodation included this
incredibly florid bridal suite.

hangings were commonplace. 'It saves polish-
ing, you know', remarked one magnate's wife
in sober explanation of her husband's fancy
for gold taps and piping in their car's bathroom.
One owner imported a noted Italian artist to
execute a florid mural on the ceiling of his car,
while Brigham Young, the Mormon leader,
embellished his with a frieze of opulently gold-
plated angels. Pipe organs were fashionable and
frequent adjuncts of the lounge furniture. Probably the most expensively accoutred lounge of all
had quartered oak beams the length of its ceiling,
solid gold lighting fitments and a wood-burning
ornamental fireplace with an electric blower.
Several of these cars included in their staff a
chef recruited at a high premium from an
exclusive restaurant – and in one or two cases
from one in Europe.

Splendidly equipped trains like the 'Twentieth
Century' and others mentioned earlier were the
élite of American trains. In the early years of the
twentieth century the ordinary American rail
passenger was travelling in less comfort than his
British counterpart. British railways might have
been falling behind some of their European
neighbours as well as the Americans in average
express train speed, but the leading British
companies were ahead of the world in their
expanding provision of good-quality, uphol-
stered seating for their third-class customers.
Although British railways were just as enthusiastically, but less extravagantly, singling
out the prime trains on each main route for the
best rolling stock and the quickest timings,
the gulf between these and the rest of the
service was not as wide as on most mainland
European lines.

Before the First World War the most impressive express passenger development in mainland
Europe came from the blossoming of first class-
only, supplementary-fare international services
which stemmed from the 1876 formation of
George Nagelmackers' International Sleeping
Car Company – the Compagnie Internationale
des Wagons-Lits et des Grands Express Euro-
péens, to give the concern its formal title. At the
turn of the century this company could boast an
annual traffic of more than two million passengers in its fleet of 550 sleeping, dining and
saloon cars. For the most part these vehicles
were concentrated in exclusive *trains de luxe*, but
in some cases they ran as individual cars marshalled into ordinary trains. One way or another
they interlinked most European capitals and
many other important cities besides. The complex negotiations involved in establishing these
international services highlighted the fragmented
character of the Continental European railway
network in those days before the aggregation of

individual systems into a unitary state organization. Nagelmackers spent ten years, for example, setting up his 'Nord Express', the inauguration of which in 1896 involved the co-operation of 14 different railway administrations in its itinerary from Liège (where it picked up a through sleeper from Paris), Ostend via Brussels, Cologne, Berlin and Königsberg to the Russian border with Prussia at Wirballen: there the travellers had to change trains because of the discrepancy in gauge. At first the 'Nord Express' ran only once a week, leaving Ostend at 4.30 on a Saturday afternoon and reaching St Petersburg at 3.30 the following Monday afternoon. By the eve of the First World War, however, it operated daily to and from Berlin and twice a week to and from St Petersburg. There was also a daily service between Ostend and Paris in the west and Warsaw and Moscow in the east. That expansion was just one measure of the European *train de luxe*'s appeal in the Edwardian era.

The facilities of these European transcontinentals were not as varied as their American counterparts, nor their furnishing quite as elaborate, but their tone was noticeably higher.

Above:
Wagons-Lits sleeping-cars running through from Paris to the Russian border in the 'Nord Express' at the start of the century.

Top:
The panelling of many Pullman sleeping cars in the US at the turn of the century was opulent: this car, shown with its sections arranged for day use, ran on the Union Pacific.

11

One of the first British Pullmans is the lead car of this Midland Railway express heading north near Elstree in the early 1900s behind a Johnson 4-2-2.

The early European Wagons-Lits cars yielded little to American Pullmans in extravagance of decor; this was a dining car on trans-Siberian service in 1900.

On every trip of the 'St Petersburg–Nice–Cannes Express' one would rub shoulders with the nobility of the Russian and Austrian Imperial courts, and on the 'Rome Express' from Paris (launched in 1897) with lustrous members of the French capital's society. Not to dress for dinner on both trains was a solecism; all else apart, one would have looked so bourgeois alongside the splendid rig of the Wagons-Lits dining car staff in their tail coats, satin knee breeches, long white hose and buckled shoes. Besides, many travellers took with them their valets and maidservants (for whom the train included special, low-priced compartments) to relieve them of the full fatigue of wardrobe preparation and changing. Some, it was said, even had their staff bring the household's silk sheets and monogrammed pillowcases to dignify their berths, despite the fineness of the Wagons-Lits company's bed-linen.

Denied a share in the Wagons-Lits enterprise before the First World War the Pullman company's first European foothold was in Britain, on the Midland Railway. However, the debut of Pullman sleepers on the Midland in the mid-1870s coincided with the first essays of other British companies in the construction of their own sleeping cars, and for the rest of the century the day Pullman's reception by the British was indifferent. One reason for this was the advancing quality of accommodation in the ordinary stock of the leading railways, which made many people resent the supplementary charge incurred to ride Pullman.

The Pullman mode did not become firmly established in Britain until the London Brighton & South Coast Railway, unbowed by the commercial failure of a similar service in the 1880s, re-launched a Sundays-only all-Pullman train between London and Brighton in 1899. This time it succeeded, so much so that in November 1908 the LBSCR was emboldened to transmute the service into Britain's first durable daily all-Pullman service, the 'Southern Belle'. Within a few years patronage justified the doubling of the service on weekdays and its tripling on Sundays. By this time both Nagelmackers and Pullman were dead and a British financier, Lord Davison Dalziel, was able in successive years, 1906–7, to take the chair of the Wagons-Lits company and buy control of the Pullman venture in Britain, thereby setting the stage for an interlocking European development of the two concepts, though this was deferred to the 1920s by the outbreak of war.

For the developed railways of Europe and North America the Edwardian years were the most serene in their history. In Europe the trunk railway map was firmly established, though the

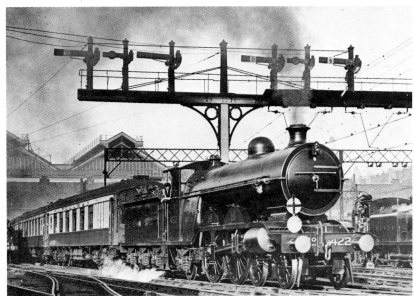

Top:
Pullman luxury, British style – a car of the London Brighton & South Coast Railway fleet early in the twentieth century.

Centre:
London Brighton & South Coast Class H2 Atlantic No 422 starts the 'Southern Belle' out of London's Victoria for the South Coast.

Above:
London Chatham & Dover Class D 4-4-0 No 145 heads the luxury 'Folkestone Car Train' to the Kent Coast.

13

An Austrian 0-8-0 climbs up the southern slope of the Tauern route from Carinthia to Salzburg past the Falkenstein castle early in the twentieth century.

last two transalpine tunnel routes remained to be pierced – a link between Austro-German territory and South-East Europe via the Tauern and Karawanken Tunnels, commenced in 1901 and finished by 1909; and direct access from the area of the Swiss capital to the Simplon Tunnel and Italy via the new Bern–Lötschberg–Simplon Railway and its 9·1-mile (14·6 km) Lötschberg Tunnel, which was finished in 1913.

In the Western US and especially in Canada trunk railways were still building. It needed Canadian Pacific's drive to the Pacific coast in the 1880s and the resultant inducement to settlement of the prairies to fire rapid growth of the country's rail system. To be profitable, however, Canada's other two major railways, Grand Trunk Pacific and Canadian Northern, desperately needed a transcontinental route to compete with Canadian Pacific's. This was eventually completed for the most part as a Government project, forged through the uncharted forests and swamps of Quebec's backwoods and northern Ontario with incredible courage, especially when the forbidding terrain was Arctic for

The two Canadian transcontinental routes near their West Coast terminals about 150 miles from Vancouver: Canadian National's 'Continental Limited' crosses the Canadian Pacific and the Fraser River at Cisco, British Columbia.

weeks on end.

Not long after the second transcontinental was finished in 1914 Canadian Northern collapsed financially, its traffic prospects ruined by the war's check of immigration and of more inland resettlement. In 1917 the Government took it over as the kernel of a state system which became Canadian National in 1918, and which absorbed the financially debilitated Grand Trunk Pacific in 1920. Ever since the private-enterprise Canadian Pacific and nationally-owned Canadian National have ruled the national rail network.

In the USA little cause remained to build new main lines in the States of the Atlantic seaboard or the 'Old North-West', but the South still had some leeway to make good after the Civil War and Reconstruction's wasted years. In the West new trunk route construction was certainly not over; in the first decade of the new century, in fact, the Western States accumulated 28,000 (45,060 km) of the 47,000 miles (75,637 km) of new track laid down throughout the country. The West was staging the last of the epic contests between the American railroad barons. In the dawning years of the new century as much as two-thirds of the nation's 224,000 miles (360,483 km) of rail route were consolidated, in some cases as a result of reasonably scrupulous dealing, but often through buccaneering chicanery, into seven empires.

The cut of a railroad empire-builder: James J. Hill in 1915.

Five were controlled by the grandees of late nineteenth-century finance or railroad promotion – John Pierpont Morgan, William H. Vanderbilt (scion of the New York Central's Commodore), George Gould (son and heir of the unprincipled Jay), Edward H. Harriman and

15

James J. Hill.

The final struggle, marked by all the cut-and-thrust of earlier battles down to pick-and-shovel combat between rival construction gangs, locked Harriman and Hill as between them they carved up the transcontinental routes from the Mid-West to the Pacific. By 1906 Hill commanded both Great Northern and Northern Pacific as well as the Chicago, Burlington & Quincy in the Mid-West. Harriman was master of the Illinois Central, Union Pacific and Southern Pacific, though after his death his empire was shorn of the SP on the grounds that the UP-SP monopoly of much of the Western seaboard violated anti-trust legislation.

Harriman and Hill made peace early in the new century, but then Harriman was confronted with a fresh challenge which he failed to defeat. It arose when the Gould empire's transcontinental ambitions were fulfilled by completion of the 927-mile (1,492 km) Western Pacific from Salt Lake City to Oakland between 1905 and 1909. However, Harriman's ghost had the ultimate laugh, since it took the Second World War to generate worthwhile traffic for the WP. The WP's massive construction costs and its failure at first to abstract much business from the Harriman lines sapped the Gould empire's finances very severely. Finally, the Chicago Milwaukee St Paul & Pacific, better known as the Milwaukee Road, reached the Pacific in the spring of 1909, achieving the extraordinary feat of laying 1,385 miles (2,229 km) of line from South Dakota to Spokane and Seattle in just $2\frac{3}{4}$ years.

Where railways were already firmly established on each side of the Atlantic, they had become efficient, well-disciplined, astutely managed and powerful businesses. Electric tramways or trolley-car systems were prompting a twinge or two of anxiety for the security of urban rail traffic, but otherwise only the age-old rivalry of waterways for freight undermined the railway's supremacy in every sector of medium- and long-haul transportation. Thus railways

well placed to cater for expanding industrialization were reaping a rich reward. Between 1890 and 1910, for instance, the tonnage of the US Illinois Central soared from 6·4 million to 33 million tons (over 6·5 million tonnes to over 33·5 million tonnes). There were reverses to this gleaming coin. The more railway managements recognized that the time had come to co-operate rather than bloody each other's noses, and the more they superseded internecine rate-cutting with pricing agreements, the more public authorities became concerned to safeguard passengers and shippers from unwarranted exploitation of the medium's monopoly of so many transport markets. In the USA each biennial infusion of new Congressional blood seemed to stimulate fresh legislation to regulate the railroads – legislation which would become a highly damaging anachronism in the air and motor transport era of the mid-twentieth century. As late as the end of the new century's first decade the egregious wheeling and dealing of nineteenth-century tycoons like Jay Gould, his confederate Daniel Drew and Commodore Vanderbilt, and of the mismanagement and corruption they inspired, was still so vivid in the memory that President William Howard Taft could damn the railroads as oligarchic monopolies 'exceedingly lawless in spirit'. Under his Presidency the Interstate Commerce Commission was given almost as rigid a control of railroad fares and freight rates as that exercised by the Governments of mainland Europe's nationalized railways in mid-century. Railways must never be allowed to forget that their authorisation to operate obligated them to act as common carriers, obliged to accept any freight without discriminatory charging.

Even in Britain the growing economic power wielded by the big companies as they gathered smaller neighbours under their wing, and as they concluded mutual pricing and joint working pacts, aroused misgivings. Had the First World War not intervened the railways here

The London & North Western was one of the most powerful British companies before the First World War: one of its 'Claughton' 4-6-0s, No 650 *Lord Rathbone*, leaves Carlisle with an express from Glasgow to London.

too might have found themselves circumscribed by tighter regulation. In 1911 a Board of Trade committee appointed to investigate inter-railway agreements and amalgamations had reported that, while it appreciated the economy of co-operative arrangements, 'the protection required by the public . . . must be given by general legislation dealing with any injurious consequences of the cooperative action of particular railways'.

The other important effect of the railways' toughening economic muscle was the defensive organization of their labor forces. The USA experienced its first railroad strike in 1877, when the Pennsylvania and Baltimore & Ohio attempted to ride out a recession on the back of wage cuts. In Britain the nineteenth-century railwayman had more security of employment than most workers and consequently the great majority of managements could get away with a blank refusal to deal with the newborn unions. But in the new century unions grew surer of themselves, and in 1911 pressure for higher wages in the face of escalating food prices and also for recognition was exerted to the point of calling the country's first national rail strike. The Government in the person of Lloyd George was forced to mediate and the railway companies were now compelled to accept the unions as negotiating bodies. That had the effect of trebling railway union membership within three years.

Other controls enforced on the Western World's railways in the late nineteenth century were wholly beneficial. If governments had not stepped in the twentieth century might well have been reached with the railways of individual countries not only following their own bent in operating and signalling practice, but paying very varied degrees of attention to safety precautions. Unless or until they were hit by a catastrophic accident all too many managements deprecated investment in safeguards because these yielded no quantifiable return for the stockholders.

The block system, the basic principle of safe railway working, had emerged in the mid-nineteenth century. Essentially, it divided each running line into signal-protected sections, and ordained that each section be occupied by no more than one train at a time. In the 1850s, too, the English pioneers Austin Chambers and John Saxby had devised the first mechanisms to interlock signalbox point and signal levers so that it was impossible to set up conflicting movements. Soon afterwards Edward Tyer in Britain and Henri Lartigue in France perfected telegraphic apparatus and coded communication routines which enabled signalmen to identify trains to each other and ensured that one signalman could not release a train from his own section into his neighbour's until the latter had verified that he could accept it. So sluggishly did British railways install block working and proper interlocking, however, that in 1889 the Government had to enforce them by Act of Parliament. French railways were no more progressive. Only two of the seven major French systems, the PLM and the Nord, were operating more than 350 route-miles (563 km) on block principles when Government decree made them mandatory mandatory in 1881. Across the Atlantic, similarly, it had needed a quick succession of State orders in the mid-1880s that trains must halt before threading any unprotected flat crossing of tracks to jolt many railroads into expenditure

An early electrically-powered signalling frame at Oakland, Southern Pacific Railroad, USA.

New York's Pennsylvania station under construction in 1908.

on interlocking.

Railways were equally reluctant to standardize their signalling – within countries, that is: to this day European practice differs in detail from country to country, if marginally in some cases, and extraordinarily its standardization is one desirability never mentioned in all the debate on means to simplify freight movement across EEC borders. It was the delays suffered by his military trains in the Franco-Prussian War of 1870, when German drivers were baffled by the signalling of German railways other than their own, which determined Bismarck to make imposition of common practice one of the first tasks in 1875 of his Imperial Railway administration. The French followed suit in 1885, the British in 1892 and at last, in 1897, the American Railway Association secured similar agreement amongst its members.

Away from the cities and urbanized corridors of the USA many main as well as secondary lines were operated purely by timetable and the liaison of train despatchers at strategic points. In the nineteenth century despatchers had inter-communicated by Morse telegraph and many railroads hesitated to supersede that with the telephone, apprehensive that direct speech was easier to garble than a coded message. They chose to ignore the increasingly superficial acquaintance with the Morse code of young recruits to despatching, which often had the latter wildly guessing at the content of machine-

gun-like transmissions from a veteran neighbour. The railroads were into the second decade of the new century before widespread adoption of telephone despatching. That American quirk apart, the basics of safe, disciplined railway operation were firmly established at the start of the century. They could now be refined by exploitation of electricity's possibilities.

Both in Europe and the USA inventors had conceived the critical component of safe twentieth-century railway working, track circuitry. If a weak current were run through running rails, its short-circuiting by the passage of a train's wheels could be made to detect the train's presence in that section to the signalman and also to lock signals and points protecting the movement so that clearance of any endangering route was impossible. From that starting-point it was a comparatively short step to adaptation of track circuitry to revert signals to danger behind a train and hold them that way until the circuited section was clear – the first essays in automatic signalling. The Americans were the front-runners in this development. Traffic control practice on single-line US trunk routes, let alone on rural branches, was still disconcertingly primitive, but the rapidly rising volume of traffic through the big American cities in the eastern half of the country and on some main lines between them spurred the Americans to explore the signalling uses of electric power more quickly than the Europeans. As early as

1902 the Pennsylvania Railroad had installed automatic block signalling on 87 miles (140 km) of its New York Division and in part of its Philadelphia Division. The 'Pennsy', which laid exemplary stress on safety and was in fact the first US railroad to establish a signalling department, was also the American pioneer of electro-pneumatic operation of points and signals – that is, the use of compressed air as the prime mover of signal and point machines at their locations, under the control of valves remotely operated by electricity – in an interlocking plant, or signal box, at Jersey City. Before very long the alternative of all-electric operation was available, but though it was cheaper and simpler to engineer, many companies were more impressed by the superior reliability of the electro-pneumatic method.

Another important by-product of track circuitry was the ability to present a signalman with a continuous reminder of train state throughout the area he controlled. A panoramic diagram of the layout marked off in track-circuited sections could be mounted above his signalling frame and arranged so that the occupation of any circuit by a train was automatically registered at the relevant place on the diagram; in the earliest examples a small bulb was illuminated in each section to indicate that it was free and extinguished when the corresponding track relay was de-energized by the presence of a train; in later years signal engineers sensibly opted for the more positive advice of an illumination when a berth was occupied. Nowadays confidence in these electrical indications is such that in some electronic signalling centers the signalmen are out of sight of the tracks. Throughout their working day the trains they control are visually no more substantial than blocks of light and accompanying alpha-numerical train descriptions jumping soundlessly and automatically from one section to another of their illuminated route diagram in step with the unheard and unseen trains' progress through the signalmen's control area. Yet for the first decade of this century many signal engineers were worried by the indication of track circuit occupation on signalbox diagrams, arguing that it would undermine a signalman's vigilance if he were not forced to keep an eye on the trains themselves. The height of many British signalbox structures erected around this time testify to a corollary of this credo, that a signalman must have the entire track area under his control within eyesight.

The rapidity of power signalling development in the years preceding the First World War can be gauged from the fact that only five all-electric interlocking plants were needed to oversee move-

The main hall of Pennsylvania Station, New York, in the early 1930s, with an airliner of the period on display.

ment into and out of New York's two-level, 67-track Grand Central station completed in 1912. One of these signalling installations had 400 levers, another 360.

The turn of the century was marked by construction of many of the USA's grandest city stations, starting with the 1894 completion of the Union station at St Louis. A Union station, a characteristic of US cities where several railroads met, was independently managed on behalf of the various railroads which used it; that at St Louis catered for 18 different companies. With its 600 ft-wide (182·9 m) but remarkably squat overall roof (the height from ground to the apex of the arch was only 74 ft, 22·5 m) shrouding 32 tracks, the St Louis station of 1894 took the record as the world's biggest – but not for long.

New York's Grand Central was preceded by the gigantic Pennsylvania Railroad scheme, which ended 'Pennsy's' handicap of a terminal no closer to Manhattan than the New Jersey bank of the Hudson River with creation of New York's Pennsylvania station, opened on 27 November 1910. Approaching from the north, the New York Central had only the narrow Harlem River to bridge for access to Manhattan Island. Railroads advancing from the west, like the Pennsylvania, or south had until then balked at the cost of crossing the much wider Hudson and East Rivers and resigned themselves to decanting their passengers into ferry-boats for

The mouth of the Simplon Tunnel in the late 1920s as an international express from Italy emerges to enter Brig behind a Swiss Federal Type Ae4/7 3,210-hp 2-D-2 built in 1927.

the last leg of the journey. Any bridge across either river had to be high enough to allow passage of deep-sea shipping – and not least of US Navy ships.

The Pennsylvania did it the grand way. To minimize train turnrounds in Manhattan it created a through route beneath the city from New Jersey to Long Island (now invaluable for direct Amtrak North-East Corridor service between Boston and Washington) by driving twin tunnels under both the Hudson and East Rivers. Astride this, one block west of Broadway, the Pennsylvania erected the largest through station the world had yet seen, with 11 platforms and 21 tracks, plus extensive subterranean sidings.

Purchase of the 18 acres (7·38 hectares) of Manhattan real estate needed to accommodate the project was a costly enough prelude. But then the railroad had to raze over 100 buildings, including some churches, before it could lay tracks below ground and raise above them a building looking outwardly more like the chancellery of an imperial power than a railway

station. The vaulting roof of its waiting room was 150-ft high (45·7 m) and the floor area 33,000 sq ft (3,066 sq m). In contrast the four waiting rooms of Liverpool Street, at the time London's busiest terminus, handling perhaps twice as many passengers daily as New York's Pennsylvania, aggregated a puny 3,000 ft (914·4 m) of floor space. Sadly the extraordinary ground-level edifice in New York is no more, demolished to make way for more lucrative late-twentieth-century commercial development.

Arguably even more architecturally elegant, the ground-level structure of New York's Grand Central station, opened in February 1912, survives, though it is nowadays dwarfed and its visual impact greatly diminished by the towering blocks that hem it in. There had been a terminal station on the site since 1871 – when it was the biggest in the country – but by the end of the century its capacity was seriously outstripped by traffic growth. Plans to enlarge both the station and its approaches were already in draft when the city authorities imposed a new dimension on them by insisting that rail traction within

Manhattan must be electric. That was the seed of the extraordinary final design, which transformed a 48-acre (19·7 hectares) area of central Manhattan. The approach tracks were dropped below ground and led to a two-level subterranean terminal with adjoining sidings. This allowed Park Avenue to be widened and almost a mile of connecting cross streets to be laid between Lexington and Madison Avenue. In the main line station, immediately below ground level, 42 tracks served 29 platforms with a combined length of just over 5 miles (8 km): below them them 25 more tracks served 17 suburban platforms.

On both levels the outermost group of tracks on each side of the station were not terminal but connected with each other by a semi-circular, single-line loop. Thus a proportion of trains could be run into one side of the station and cleared from their platforms without reversal via the loop and one of the tracks on the far side of the layout. Above all this the splendid terminal building, its Renaissance-style facade surmounted by a florid sculpture of Hercules, Mercury and Minerva, dominated a complex of office buildings, hotels, restaurants and shops. The concourse, 275 ft long, 175 ft wide and 125 ft high (84 × 53 × 38 m), its cerulean-blue ceiling speckled with 2,500 stars executed in gold leaf, was just as monumental as the Pennsylvania station's.

In Europe the civil engineering center of interest at the start of the century was the forging of the final transalpine routes. Completion of Switzerland's first transalpine tunnel, the Gotthard, at last concentrated the minds of the various interests and railways which had been havering for a direct access from western Switzerland to Italy for decades but had signally failed to find common cause on anything but the likeliest route, the Simplon pass. In 1890, German financial interests effected a merger of the two Swiss railways spanning the territory from the Jura through Berne to the threshold of the Simplon pass with the express aim of establishing a base for a Simplon Tunnel project. The following year a scheme for a 12½-mile (20·1 km) tunnel between Brig and Iselle, and a further 12 miles (19·3 km) of track above ground from Iselle to the then limit of the Italian system at Domodossola, was laid before the Swiss Federal Council. In November 1895 Swiss and Italian Government agreed methods of construction, finance and operation. A Hamburg firm, Brandt, Brenau, was contracted and began boring in August 1898. The first euphoric projections had the work forces tunnelling in from each end planning to meet by November 1903, but that did not happen until February 1905. By then the nationalized Swiss Federal Railways had

The electrified Gotthard route in the 1920s, with a Swiss Federal train mounting the northern slope to the mouth of the Gotthard Tunnel at Göschenen.

The southern portal of the
Lötschberg Tunnel at
Goppenstein soon after its
opening, with one of the
Bern-Lötschberg-Simplon's
first electric locomotives.

come into being, at the start of 1902, and in the spring of 1903 had gathered in the company concerned with the tunnel, the Jura-Simplon Railway. So the unforeseen crises that had protracted the tunnel's construction were now a Federal anxiety.

The first trauma was that in the heart of the mountain massif temperature at the working faces soared to 53° Centigrade (127° Fahrenheit), far beyond the 35° Centigrade (95° Fahrenheit) anticipated at worst and thus beyond the power of the ventilating plant to combat. Tolerable working conditions were obtained only by pumping icy water into the bore to keep the working faces continuously sprayed. But hot water several times overwhelmed the injected cold as the tunnellers came unexpectedly upon springs cascading through rock fissures and were all but swept away by deluges that at one juncture poured 15,000 gallons (68,192 litres) a minute into the workings. At another stage tunnellers from the Italian side encountered rock pressures so fierce that even steel reinforcements could not withstand it. The difficulty was eventually overcome; but some ten years after the May 1906 opening of the original, single-line tunnel, when the Swiss were driving an adjoining tunnel to cope with the route's traffic, they found that in this troublesome area the first tunnel had already deformed so dangerously that relining was essential. In this critical zone the two tunnels are each lined to a thickness of almost 4 ft (1·2 m). The second tunnel's construction was just as taxing as the first and lasted nine years to

its completion in 1921.

In 1901 the Austrians started the projection of a second route through the mountains to Trieste and South-East Europe, this time to open up a gateway from the west of the country and at the same time to forge a rail link between the Tyrol and Carinthia. Two major tunnels were involved in the creation of this spectacular route south-eastwards from Salzburg: the Tauern, almost 5⅓ miles (8·6 km) long, beneath the Hohe Tauern mountains, where the line attains its summit of 4,022 ft (1,226 m); and the Karawanken, almost 5 miles (8 km) in length, under the mountains which separate present-day Austria and Yugoslavia.

Last of the transalpine standard-gauge railways – so far: with the oil price-induced trend of international freight back to the railways new routes are no longer a mirage – was the Lötschberg. The Simplon Tunnel was a dog's-leg detour from Berne by rail and in 1899 pressure for a direct route from the area of the Swiss capital to Italy crystallized in a plan to drive up the Kander Valley from Lake Thun, under the Lötschberg pass in the Bernese Alps and then down the northern wall of the Rhone valley to a junction with the Simplon route at Brig. Sensing the concept's value to traffic to and from their own country, French interests were ready to supplement the capital grants the scheme won from the Berne Cantonal and Swiss Federal Governments, and in the summer of 1906 the Berne-Lötschberg–Simplon Railway was formed to build the line. Unlike its transalpine predeces-

The awesome engineering of the Lötschberg line on its descent from the tunnel to the Rhone Valley at Brig: an avalanche shelter protects the railway.

sors, the Lötschberg project was planned as an electric railway from the start. The Lötschberg was the toughest of all the Swiss transalpine enterprises to mount logistically because its summit area was approachable only up steeply shelving gorges. On the south side of the pass, moreover, the wild Lonza valley leading from the southern entrance of the prospective tunnel to the Rhone was one of the most avalanche-prone ravines in the country. Until serried ranks of snow breaks were erected up the mountain-sides the workings were frequently entombed by cascades of snow and rubble reaching as much as 80 ft (24·4 m) in depth. Twelve workers were lost when the construction camp itself was devastated on a February night in 1908.

Much worse followed in the summer of that year. Early one July morning the gangs routinely boring in from the north broke into an un-charted rock fissure of such cavernous size that the tidal wave of its watery content quickly choked almost a mile (1·6 km) of the tunnel; the thunderous surge drowned 26 of the face workers in an instant, destroyed their tunnelling equip-ment and so devastated the workings that the engineers had no option but to seal off the danger area with a 33 ft (10·1 m) thickness of masonry and re-bore on a new line to the east of it. North and south construction forces met in the bowels of the mountains at the end of March 1911 and the whole route, with its spectacular engineering of spiral tunnels to gain height as quickly as the precipitous valley floor on the north side of the 9·08-mile (14·61 km) tunnel, and its breathtaking descent of the Rhone valley's steep northern wall, was opened for business in July 1913.

The Lötschberg tunnel itself was built with

The Bavarian State railway was one of the most determined opponents of German railway unification: its famous Class S3/6 4-6-2 type was perpetuated for a while by the post-First World War Reichsbahn and this example was built in 1927, to become the post-war Deutsche Bundesbahn's class 18.

double track, but funds would not run to double-tracking the rest of the line, with its $7\frac{1}{2}$ miles (12·1 km) more of tunnel and 168 bridges, though the builders made some infrastructure provision against the later addition of a second track. The BLS Railway made a start after the Second World War where the terrain was not too daunting, at the northern end between Spiez and Frütigen, but the rest was beyond its financial resources. In the early 1980s, however, that formidable job was forging ahead following the Swiss Government's post-oil crisis recognition of rising need for extra transalpine rail capacity and its 1976 decision to put Federal money into the widening.

The Swiss, in their 1902 creation of the Swiss Federal Railways, were not the only Europeans to realize around the turn of the century that the now powerful role of railways in social and industrial development demanded better co-ordination of hitherto independent companies. (One should perhaps add that the BLS, discussed in the preceding paragraphs has never been absorbed by the Swiss Federal; it is the biggest of 100 or so concerns, mostly narrow-gauge and localized, which have remained private companies under the financial protection of their Cantonal governments as well as the Federal treasury.)

In Germany the fiercely proud Bavarians, along with the Saxons and Württembergers, had defied Chancellor Bismarck's drive to unite the State railway systems under the sovereignty of his own Prussian State Railway. But on the eve of the First World War the Bavarian network amounted to 5,200 route-miles (8,368 km), whereas the Prussian system was by then master of more than 24,000 (38,623 km) of the total 36,500 route-miles (58,740 km) of German railway. And the standard operating practices which Bismarck's Imperial Railway Office had imposed nationwide were quint-essentially Prussian. Since the Franco-Prussian War German railways had not merely expanded in step with the phenomenal growth of the nation's strength – German population climbed from 41·3 million to 67 million between 1870 and 1913 – but outpaced it. In that same period the State railway systems' route-length had risen from 5,360 (8,626 km) to 36,500 (58,740 km), their invested capital had quadrupled and their gross income had been multiplied sixfold; so had their rolling stock and, very nearly, their locomotive strength. Measured in passenger journeys, rail travel had increased ten times as fast as population growth; rail freight movement had grown in volume five times as rapidly.

The German State governments of the period were as dedicated to securing a worthwhile return on the capital they poured into the railways as any British Treasury mandarin a century later, and since the Prussian State was consistently coming up with a return of 6 to 7 per cent, there was a healthy margin for re-investment, so that German railways approached the First World War better organized and equipped than any of their European neighbours. In express passenger speed the Prussians challenged the best in Britain and in frequency of service they were probably a step ahead on several routes. Over the 100 miles (161 km) between Berlin and Halle, for instance, their 1907

A London terminus on the eve of the First World War: the busy platforms of the London South Western Railway's Waterloo station in May 1912, with suburban trains disgorging passengers at the two extreme lefthand platforms.

timetables showed eight trains each way daily averaging around 50 mph (81 km/h) end-to-end and by the outbreak of the First World War the Berlin–Hamburg schedules listed as many as 11 daily services. Compared with their Austrian, French and Italian neighbours, moreover, the Germans admitted third- as well as second-class passengers to a much higher proportion of their fastest trains and also indulged more of the multi-class trains with restaurant cars.

The impressive solidification of the German system was influential in the Italian decision to nationalize. The inter-city railway network which the Government had fostered with handsome construction grants after Italy's 1862 unification had never made much of a living. Its subsequent consolidation at the Government's behest into three large companies made little financial difference, with the result that a rising tide of traffic in the century's closing years caught the railways desperately short of locomotives, rolling stock and track space to cope with it. With the companies' concessions due for re-negotiation in 1905 and public exasperation at their ramshackle service becoming acute, the Government set up an investigating commission. Although its members advocated a further lease for the railway managements they added a caveat that stricter Government control was required. The companies took note and promptly locked up everything they could for their shareholders, shelving all capital expenditure and freezing staff wages so rigidly that there was a vicious strike at the start of 1905.

In such a climate nationalization was just about the only resort left and the *Ferrovie dello Stato* (FS) was established. Uniquely in Western Europe the FS was made a Government department, so that the Minister of Transport was *ex officio* the chairman of the railway's directorate, the railway's general manager directly subservient to him. The Italians persisted with this stifling arrangement until 1981, when the Minister's automatic right to the chair was ceded, though the continuing civil service status of the FS as a whole was perpetuated as a dampener on commercial enterprise.

The French had been toying with nationalization ideas since 1880. It was the dream of the Minister of Works, de Freycinet, whose passion for rural railways – he set himself to interconnect every town of Prefecture and Sub-Prefecture status in the country – laced France in the 35 years up to the First World War with a huge mileage of bucolic lines that became a running political sore when the motor age flowered between the World Wars. However, although the Government had in 1883 become to all intents and purposes the owner of the major French railway companies' infrastructure, and the railways tenant operators, full state management was confined to the État Railway. That had been created in 1878 to rescue a number of railways, mostly in Western France, which had been financially ravaged by the Franco-Prussian War, but it did not become a major railway power until 1908, when the near-bankrupt Ouest Railway was taken under its wing and extended État suzerainty throughout Western France. But the Nord, Est, PLM, Paris–Orléans and Sud kept their bills paid and nationalization at bay until the late 1930s.

ENTER THE BIG ENGINE ERA

THE CITY FATHERS OF NEW YORK deserve some of the credit for edging railways into the era of the big express passenger engine. One of the stipulations they laid down on approval of the Pennsylvania Railroad's huge Manhattan terminal project was that the new Hudson and East River Tunnels be barred to wooden-bodied rolling stock. The first all-steel US passenger car had been built back in 1889, but metal construction had aroused little enthusiasm thereafter. Now the 'Pennsy' was forced to ordain that from 1906 its future passenger car construction would be entirely all-steel (and the Pullman Company was enjoined to keep its wooden cars out of any PRR trains bound for New York City too). The railroad's 4–4–2s, its standard express passenger type at the century's opening, were already strained by the rising demand for travel which the country's surging prosperity was generating. Now the influx of heavier metal cars forced the operators to double-head or divide still more trains, especially over the ruggedly-graded Pittsburgh–Chicago main line, so as to temper the job to the four-coupled engines' capability. The first US 4–6–2s were already in being on railroads in the Southern and Western States – a batch built by the American Locomotive Co. (ALCO) for the Missouri Pacific back in 1902 was the provenance of the wheel arrangement's 'Pacific' nickname – but those pioneers were general-purpose engines. The pressure on the 'Pennsy' spawned the first express passenger Pacific.

The prototype Class K28 which emerged from ALCO's Pittsburgh works in the spring of 1907 and the K2 series which descended from it were markedly superior to the 4–4–2s. But the 'Pennsy' Pacific did not flower in its ultimate splendour until the appearance of the prototype for the K29s which appeared in November 1911 and then the K4s series, which the K29s begat, from 1914 onwards. The major advance in these later designs was indicated by the 's' in the classification, signifying superheating. Near the end of the previous century Wilhelm Schmidt, a German engineer of Kassel, had at last found a way to realize practically a theory advanced by several earlier locomotive men: that power could be increased or specific work performed at less cost in fuel if steam could be superheated before it entered cylinders, so that energy loss through condensation was reduced. Schmidt achieved the objective by getting more work out of the heat from the firebox. Steam generated around the boiler's main flue tubes was collected in a header, then sent on its way to the cylinders via a honeycomb of small tubes threaded through the boiler flues, so that it reached the pistons in a more gaseous state.

Later patterns of superheater differed from the Schmidt design in detail, but not in basics. Superheating did so much for the 'Pennsy' 4–4–2 format – as it did in Europe, notably, for the 4–4–2s of France's Nord Railway and of Britain's Great Northern, after the latter were superheated by the LNER's Nigel Gresley – that the PRR went on building its final E6s version. The 'Pennsy' was a prudent, thrifty railroad, not given to mass-producing a new design until it had been put to exhaustive proof. The E6s was cheaper to build and operate than a Pacific and had a wider route availability on the PRR of 1914. But when the PRR did commit itself in 1917 to a K4s series, it conceived what became arguably the most remarkable Pacific race in steam locomotive history.

Right through the 1930s, when other roads in the East and Mid-West had moved on to bigger 4–6–4s and those with hillier routes from 4–8–2s to 4–8–4s, the 425 K4s engines turned

Far left:
The ultimate in US Mallet compound articulateds; one of Norfolk & Western's massive Class Y6b 2-8-8-2 is assembled at the railroad's Roanoke works in 1947.

Below:
One of the world's greatest Pacific types: a Class K4s 4-6-2 of the Pennsylvania Railroad.

Bottom:
A typical US Pacific of the pre-First World War years: the New York, New Haven & Hartford RR's No 1093 prepares to leave Boston South station for New York with the new all-steel 'Merchants Limited', the luxury train beloved of Boston's banking and stockbroking élite.

out between 1914 and 1928 remained the
'Pennsy's' front-rank express passenger power.
And by the end of the 1930s these Pacifics were
being set much faster schedules and heavier
trains than they had faced at birth. In 1939 one
K4 was timed to average 84·4 mph (135·8 km/h)
over 78·8 miles (126·8 km) of the main line from
Chicago to Fort Wayne with 914 tons (929
tonnes) in tow; others were known to have hit
90 mph (145 km/h) with as many as 18 steel
cars grossing 1,100 tons (1,118 tonnes) behind
their tenders.

All this was with a locomotive weighing only
136 tons (138·2 tonnes) without its tender and
basically unaltered since the design's first draft
in 1914. (Some K4s, incidentally, were eventually
paired for long-range working with 24,000 gal
– 109,106 litres – tenders scaling 174 tons – 176·8
tonnes – fully loaded, more than the Pacifics they
served!) One critical addition, without which
the ponderous boiler's capacity to keep the
big 27 by 28 in (69 × 71 cm) cylinders fed
on these latter-day assignments would not
have been possible, was a mechanical stoker.
This device, most brands of which employed a
steam-powered revolving screw to wind coal
through a trough from tender to firebox door,
where steam jets under the fireman's control
sprayed it over the firebed, had been perfected by
the end of the new century's first decade. Without it only Superman could have shovelled
enough coal to sustain a proper steaming
rate in the huge boilers some railroad man-

agements were already seeking to use in order to
move the size of trains they were building to cope
with traffic demand. But though the 'Pennsy'
had proved back in 1911 with its prototype K29
that a stoker-fired engine could produce up to 60
per cent more sustained power than one fuelled
manually to the limit of a fireman's stamina,
it was characteristically one of the railroads
which balked at wholesale fitting of mechanical
stokers as improvident luxury. A few K4s
engines only had been given stokers by 1936,
when the recalcitrant companies' hands were
forced by an Interstate Commerce Commission
edict that mechanical stokers must be fitted to
all locomotives exceeding a given weight on
their driving wheels. By the outbreak of the
Second World War the K4s class as a whole was
among the 12,000-odd US locomotives with this
equipment.

The Chesapeake & Ohio was one of the US
systems which had taken up the Pacific wheel
arrangement before the Pennsylvania fully developed its 4–6–2 range. But the C&O main line
through the Alleghany Mountains wound and
climbed steeply to a 2,490 ft (759 m) summit between Covington and White Sulphur Springs,
and as the C&O too adopted all-steel coaching
stock it found itself double-heading too many
trains for its financial comfort. Subsequent
consultation with ALCO suggested that the
answer might be an engine of much the same
size as a 'Pennsy' K4s, but with eight 5 ft 2 in
(157·5 cm) instead of six 6 ft 8 in (203·2 cm)

Railroads with mountainous routes found 4-8-2s with smaller wheels better suited to their territory than 4-6-2s: the most successful of the early 4-8-2s were the series which ALCO began to build for Union Pacific in 1922, one of which heads the UP 'Overland Limited' through Echo Canyon, Utah in the 1950s.

driving wheels. This, the first US 4–8–2 type, appeared in 1911 and naturally stamped the wheel arrangement for ever after as the 'Mountain'. The pioneer C&O Mountains did not impress, however, and the wheel arrangement did not qualify as one of the North American classics until the emergence of bigger-wheeled types on systems such as the Rock Island and Union Pacific after the First World War. UP's crossing of the Continental Divide between Cheyenne, Wyoming, and Ogden, Utah, is a stiffer hurdle than the Alleghenies. The former mounts to summits of 7,107 ft (2,166 m) at Creston and of 8,013 ft (2,442 m) 171 miles (275 km) further on in Wyoming at Sherman, the approaches to which feature grades as steep as 1 in 83. In the Class MT which UP procured from ALCO in 1922–3, a substantially bigger-boilered machine on 6 ft 1 in (185·4 cm) driving wheels by comparison with the C&O Mountain of 1911, it had a locomotive capable of a 3,500 hp output which combined excellent performance on these tough gradients with a nimble turn of speed in the Prairies. That versatility subsequently induced railroads in the East and Mid-West, such as the Illinois Central and New York Central, to acquire 4–8–2s as general-purpose locomotives for more easily-graded routes.

The more dramatic change in the look of American steam power before the First World War, however, was in the freight sector. Here the demand for increased power was far more insistent. The expanding national economy was hungrier for raw materials by the year and the railroads were generally the only feasible means of supply. But the railroads' return on the job was severely pinched by the rate regulation clapped on them in the previous century to forestall any repetition of the monopolistic abuses perpetrated in the heyday of the railroad barons. For a railroad like the Virginian, whose sole *raison d'être* was the haulage of coal from West Virginian mines to the Atlantic seaboard at Norfolk, Virginia, and over a road that struck 14 miles (22·5 km) of 1 in 50 gradient from Mullens to Algonquin, that made motive power policy a very basic affair. All that counted was maximum tractive effort. In other words, ability to get the heaviest possible train on the move and keep it rolling. In this so-called 'drag' era of the American freight train, no one bothered about speed except where trains of perishable goods were concerned. For the rest it was simply a case of hanging as many wagons on the tail of a locomotive as it could manage without falling below 5 mph (8 km/h) on the steepest gradients. How far ambition stretched can be gauged from the train that Erie Railroad assembled to probe the physique of its latest freight mammoth in 1916 – 250 loaded wagons grossing nearly 16,000 tons (16,258 tonnes).

Besides maximizing the payloads moved per engine-hour this ·sledghammer method minimized the cost of operating the single trackage characterizing much of the US trunk network

Top:
A pair of Denver & Rio Grande Western 4-8-2s tackle an 83-car freight near Salida, Colorado, in 1939.

Above:
A Santa Fe 3800 class 2-10-2 built by Baldwin in 1924; with 6 ft 3 in driving wheels and 210-lb (95-kg) boiler pressure it boasted a tractive effort of 81,500 lb (36,968 kg).

output of maximum horsepower. The burly Baltimore & Ohio 2–10–2 of that period was already a 150-ton (152 tonne) machine, stoker-fired, with a 7½ ft-diameter (228·6 cm) boiler to supply its tubby 30 in by 32 in (76 × 81 cm) cylinders and a tractive effort as high as 84,500 lb (38,329 kg).

The progression of conventional freight engine design, however, was almost puny compared with the explosion of articulated locomotive concepts between 1904 and 1912. Finding ten-coupled engines uncomfortable on curves and the load of big boilers on their driving axles damaging to the track of the time, railroad managements and locomotive builders abruptly realized that they had been ignoring a European solution to their difficulty. The scope for enhancing power and adhesion within a given axle-loading and curvature radius specification by articulating two independent engine units had been demonstrated by the engines built to the patent design of the British engineer Robert Fairlie as far back as the 1870s. Over 50 Fairlies were put to very successful work in Mexico during the century's last quarter, but American interest was confined to a single example, and that a diminutive one, exported to the Denver & Rio Grande in 1873. Further stimulus to articulated engine development had come from the perfection of a compound steam expansion system by the Swiss engineer, Anatole Mallet, in 1874. The steady advance of boiler pressures in the first half-century of steam locomotive engineering had brought them to a level at which considerable calorific economy seemed possible if the steam was put to more work during its expansion. The compound process achieved that by protracting the expansion, feeding the steam first to high-pressure cylinders, then conducting it for further use in low-pressure cylinders before it was exhausted to atmosphere. Mallet was quick to appreciate the potential in a marriage of articulation and compounding, but on his own side of the Atlantic its consummation was chiefly on the narrow gauge. Standard-gauge Mallet compound articulateds found a good deal of favour in Eastern Europe, but their appeal elsewhere faded when Austria's Karl Gölsdorf proved that a ten-coupled design of orthodox locomotive layout could be contrived to ride sweetly even over the rather flimsy and often sharply curved track of his own country. The apotheosis of Mallet compound articulated technology was reached in the USA.

The trend-setter was the Baltimore & Ohio, which in 1904 had ALCO build No 2400, an 0–6–6–0, to serve as banking engine in the Alleghany Mountains, where its westbound

outside the inter-city corridors. The fewer the trains needed to clear the tonnage on offer at either end of a line, the fewer the maneuvers required to get opposing traffic streams past each other in intermediate loops. But there was a heavy penalty to be paid in the yards that were eternally clogged while these huge trains were built up or dismantled. The habits ingrained there in the drag era would be hard to eradicate three-quarters of a century later, when deeper penetration of the high-rated merchandise freight market in competition with road transport would become critically dependent on the end-to-end transit speed and reliability of individual wagonloads.

By 1914 US construction of orthodox freight power had already moved into the ten-coupled range, either 2–10–0 or else 2–10–2 where there was an economic case for the higher cost of a trailing-axle layout to accommodate a bigger firebox and allow use of low-grade coal. Wide-firebox engines were equally justified by freight haulage specifications demanding a sustained

coal trains struck a 1 in 44 grade between
Cumberland, Maryland, and Meyersdale, Pennsylvania. This pioneer Mallet had imperfections
that dissuaded the B&O from acquiring more of
its kind until 1911, but its potential mightily
impressed other railroads with a tonnage problem. In 1906 the Great Northern placed the
country's first Mallet series order with the
Baldwin works, starting with five 2–6–6–2s to
serve as helpers where its transcontinental

route – otherwise the easiest of all the Continental Divide crossings – came up against a 1 in
36 grade in the Cascade Range between Leavenworth and Skykomish, Washington, then following with 25 which were the first US Mallets
to be acquired as main-line train hauliers. The
GN Mallets quickly showed themselves as proficient at line haulage as at punching trains up
stiff gradients. Coupled to their superior performance uphill, the ability of their 4 ft 7 in (139·7

cm) driving wheels to keep loads rolling at no less than 30 mph (48 km/h) on easier grades raised the GN's throughput of tonnage between Leavenworth and Spokane by 52 per cent, and for a 34 per cent saving of coal consumption per ton-mile. Another gain was a reduction in coupling breakages, since it was inherently impossible for the two engine units to slip in unison. Consequently a Mallet articulated took smoother hold of a train when its regulator was cracked open.

There were extraordinary facets to the rapid expansion of articulated locomotive fleets over the next ten years or so. Growth in overall locomotive bulk was striking enough, but not nearly so spectacular as that of cylinder diameter. Both railroads and locomotive builders seemed gripped by a compulsion to discover just how big a lower pressure cylinder was practicable.

The ultimate, never exceeded, were the 48 in (121·9 cm) cylinders of ten 2–10–10–2s which ALCO built for the Virginian in 1918. These 305-ton (310 tonne) behemoths were fitted with a bypass valve use of which enabled all four cylinders to be fed with high-pressure steam for extra starting kick. As a result, given the phenomenal girth of the ordinarily low-pressure cylinders (the high-pressure cylinders' diameter was 30 in – 76·2 cm), they packed a short-term tractive effort as high as 176,000 lb (79,834 kg). Working compound the figure was still as much as 147,200 lb (66,770 kg).

To satisfy the clamour for a form of power by then so clearly proven as a cost-cutter of crew and coal bills per ton-mile, Baldwin in 1910 put on the market a Mallet do-it-yourself kit – a front-end unit which a railroad could, as it were, clip on to an existing locomotive of orthodox simple-expansion layout in its own workshops. Other companies did it all themselves, simply cobbling a pair of locomotives together as a makeshift articulated. These self-help exercises were short-lived, however, because such improvisation generally ignored the critical need of a boiler capacity tailored to the compound layout's demands. Most were chronically shy steamers. One of the most determined 'do-it-yourself' practitioners was the Santa Fe. Its affair with compound articulateds was brief, but bizarre while it lasted. With gradients as steep as 1 in 28·5 on the formidable slopes of its trunk route through Colorado's Raton Pass and California's Cajon Pass en route to the Pacific Coast, the Santa Fe was unique among the early articulated operators in fancying Mallets for its passenger as well as its freight traffic. That meant driving wheels of at least 5 ft 9 in (175·3 cm) – they were as big as 6 ft 1 in

(185·4 cm) in the very first Santa Fe 4–4–6–2s of 1909 – and consequently some very elongated engines for the period. So, to avoid any problems of inflexibility on curves, Santa Fe went in for boiler as well as engine unit articulation, cutting the boiler into halves that were held together either by a ball-jointed connecting segment or an accordion-like pleating of annular steel rings. Flexible piping linked the two halves, but the path of steam from the boiler heading to both pairs of cylinders and thence to the exhaust of these grotesque metal caterpillars was so tortuous that one can only marvel they ever moved themselves, let alone a train.

An insatiable appetite for steam defeated Baldwin's effort to expand the Mallet compound into a triple-unit locomotive, which materialized as three 2–8–8–8–2Ts for the Erie and one similar machine for the Virginian in 1916. All these were conceived as super-powerful banking engines. The Virginian engines, which had a smaller firegrate and driving wheels than the Erie trio, were always gasping. They could rarely summon up sufficient steam to muster more than 5 mph (8 km/h) if maximum power was asked of them.

Following the Government's assumption of US railroad control in the First World War the US Railroad Administration rationalized the railroad supply industry by prescribing standard rolling stock designs, among them 12 locomotive types. One of these was a 2–8–8–2 Mallet based very closely on a Norfolk & Western design, which can be taken as representative of the final phase of Mallet compound development in the USA. Total engine wheelbase was now stretched to 58 ft (17·7 m) to accommodate the two sets of 4 ft 9 in (144·8 cm) driving wheels and engine weight alone had climbed to 237 tons (241 tonnes). A boiler of 8 ft 6 in (259·1 cm) diameter, squeezed chimney and domes to pimple height, and a mechanical stoker had the stamina to meet the demands of the 25 in (63·5 cm) low-pressure and 39 in (99·1 cm) high-pressure cylinders under the most relentless driving hand. And some hands were very heavy. The long, severe gradients and enormous trainloads of coal-hauling US railroads like the N&W subjected US locomotives to sustained pounding rarely experienced in Europe. From the late 1920s onwards most railroads rejected the Mallet for simple-expansion articulateds, and the reason for this is discussed in Chapter 7.

Though European railways were not enamoured of Mallet articulateds, their leading locomotive engineers at the start of the century were mostly advocates of compound expansion. The exceptions were the majority of Britain's

locomotive chiefs. The only British railway to operate a thoroughly successful class of compound locomotives, in fact, was the Midland, in the shape of the 4-4-0 created by Samuel Johnson in 1901, perpetuated by his successor Deeley and eventually proliferated to a total of 245 engines by the London Midland & Scottish Railway after its absorption of the Midland in the 1923 Grouping of British main-line railways into four big companies. This British coolness was not insular pigheadedness. A major deterrent was the constriction of the British loading gauge compared with Continental mainland parameters, which cramped the arrangement of a large-diameter low-pressure cylinder (let alone more than one) alongside high-pressure cylinders. Another was the extra cost and complexity of a compound expansion mechanism and its sensitivity both to fine tuning during maintenance and adroit handling on the road for optimal performance. British enginemen never had the grounding in engineering or the inducement of bonuses to master non-standard equipment and to keep it maintained that were accepted practice, for example, in France.

In the twentieth century's first quarter, French locomotive technology was dominated by the de Glehn system of four-cylinder compounding, which took its name from the Alsace Locomotive Works technical director, who evolved and applied it to Nord Railway engines in

conjunction with that company's locomotive chief, du Bousquet. The Nord's compound 'Atlantic' of 1901 was Europe's stellar express passenger performer of the period, exciting attention outside as well as within Europe by the proclivity for speed combined with striking up-grade power in relation to its size, which the class displayed on the prestigious Paris–Calais boat trains.

Top:
One of Great Northern's Class L 2-6-6-2 Mallet compound articulateds built by Baldwin in 1906-7.

Above:
The lead 2-8-8-2 Mallet compound articulated of this pair helping a Denver & Rio Grande Western freight up to Tennessee Pass.

Right up to 1939 these engines, by then fitted with more capacious tenders and treated to such latter-day efficiency aids as a multiple-jet blast-pipe and chimney, were still deployed on tightly-timed, limited-load Paris–Brussels luxury trains like the 'Oiseau Bleu' Pullman and the 'Nord Express'. They were quite capable, too, of keeping 400-ton (406 tonne) Paris–Calais boat trains rolling on level track at 75 mph (121 km/h), the speed ceiling imposed on all French railways since the mid-nineteenth century and not relaxed until 1937, when a very modest increase to 81 mph (130 km/h) was granted over a few well-

aligned stretches of main line. This limitation naturally preoccupied French express passenger locomotive designers with power output, since the faster journey times the expanding travel market demanded were attainable only to the extent that the maximum permissible speed could be held or approached on the flat and up-hill. That specification was becoming harder to fulfil because train weights were advancing as European railways recognized that the ordinary traveller must now be treated to roomier and better furnished coaching stock.

The prowess of the Nord Atlantics persuaded some European railways to persist with the 4-4-2 as their prime express passenger type rather than risk a confrontation with their civil engineers over the impact on track and nine-teenth-century bridgework of bigger-boilered six-coupled designs. But in Britain, France and on the Prussian State in Germany the 4-6-0 was fully accepted by the outbreak of the First World War and in France and Germany the first Euro-pean 4-6-2s had taken the tracks by 1907.

Outside France the most influential loco-motive designer of the Edwardian era was

G. J. Churchward of Britain's Great Western Railway, of which he was Chief Mechanical Engineer. The CME of a British railway was as an emperor to a court chamberlain by comparison with the motive power chiefs of practically all other systems in the world. Responsible only to his board of directors, and with his own works to build his designs, he was master of his company's traction from conception – his own – through drawing-board to manufacture, maintenance and in many cases to the way it was employed in day-to-day service.

Outside Britain the vast majority of railways relied on private firms for locomotive construction. Their traction chiefs had none of the backroom organization of a British CME. Design work was frequently a corporate exercise of the railways' locomotive men, operators, suppliers – and in some instances of professors from seats of engineering learning. British practice had the disadvantage of encouraging some often pigheaded individualism and deterring standardization, the consequences of which were still apparent in the considerable assortment of pre-1923 types that survived for the nationalized British Railways to inherit in 1948. But genius had more room to flower than on many a railway elsewhere, hence Churchward's niche in locomotive history. He took his GWR office in 1902 with a plan to standardize the railway's motive power on six basic types already drafted, starting with a 4-6-0. Such determination to rationalize was innovatory enough for a start, and the bold step up to a 4-6-0 edged a shade higher the eyebrows of engineers on neighbouring railways. The lasting significance of Churchward's pioneer 4-6-0s lay, however, in one of the several features of their design that were new to British practice.

Churchward felt that the hunger for power had preoccupied his contemporaries with the production of steam to the exclusion of concern for its smooth passage through the cylinders to the exhaust, and thus maximization for propulsion of its expansive properties. He therefore took great care to smooth and enlarge steam passages. To allow his engines once on the move to work on an economically early cut-off of steam supply to the cylinders, he also fashioned the latter with an unusually long stroke of 30 in (76·2 cm) in relation to 18 in (45·7 cm) diameter, and with long-travel piston valves of more than previously normal diameter. One of Churchward's virtues, not a common characteristic of the British CME for reasons already discussed, was an open mind. Thus before committing the GWR to his simple-expansion design he had his directors procure three de Glehn Atlantics of Nord pattern from the Alsace works for evalua-

tion against his own products. In performance and economy the match was a draw, but the smoother riding of the French engine, thanks to the more even turning movement of its four-cylinder arrangement, induced Churchward to switch to a four-cylinder layout in his 'Star' class 4-6-0 design of 1907. This class was otherwise very similar to Churchward's earlier two-cylinder 'Saint' 4-6-0s; the boiler was identical on each type. The crowning touch was applied to both classes from 1908 onwards when they were given superheating. In the appreciation and adoption of this Continental device Churchward was again the British pioneer. Throughout the century's first quarter Churchward's 4-6-0s and the bigger 'Castle' 4-6-0 which his successor, Collett, extrapolated from Churchward's first principles had no British peer for ability to sustain a high average speed over an undulating road with 400 tons (406 tonnes) or more of train, and without extravagant fuel consumption. More than one six-coupled express passenger type drafted by less technically imaginative minds on other British railways scored high marks for muscular good looks, but were no

Below:
One of the French de Glehn compound 4-4-2s which Churchward imported for test on the GWR, No 102 *La France*, heads the Birmingham express out of London.

Bottom:
Churchward 'Star' four-cylinder 4-6-0 No 4037 *Queen Charlotte* threads the London suburbs with an afternoon GWR Paddington–Plymouth express.

The historic GWR-LNER
express locomotive exchange
of 1925: GW 'Castle' No 4079
Pendennis Castle climbs past
Finsbury Park with the
LNER 1.30 pm Kings Cross–
Leeds.

The 'Castle's' Pacific rival: on
the same 1925 day, at the
same Finsbury Park location,
Gresley's LNER Pacific No
2550 (later named *Tracery*),
heads the 1.15 pm express
from Kings Cross.

A Nord 'Super-Pacific' heads
the Paris–Calais 'Flèche
d'Or', including through
sleepers from San Remo and
Istanbul, in the 1930s.

advance on the four-coupled predecessors they were intended to outclass when it came to performance and economy.

The ultimate vindication of Churchward's theory, and with it the scene-setting for Britain's most outstanding express passenger steam design phase, came in 1925. The previous year the first GWR Castle, No 4073 *Caerphilly Castle*, had been exhibited at the 1924 Wembley Empire Exhibition alongside the 4–6–2 which Nigel Gresley had created just before Great Northern Railway's 1923 assimilation in the London North Eastern Railway and which Gresley, as the newly-formed LNER's CME, proposed to standardize as its front-rank express power. On the basis of tractive effort theoretically calculated from a standard formula correlating driving wheel diameter, cylinder size and boiler pressure the GWR's publicity machine had been loudly acclaiming the 'Castle' as Britain's most powerful express engine; to which the LNER's publicists had been countering just as stridently that the title was justly its new Pacific's on the score of size and boiler capacity. Juxtaposition of the two engines at Wembley intensified the exchanges and led, according to many accounts, to Gresley's issue of a challenge – let 'Castle' and Pacific duel on each other's normal work to put the issue beyond doubt. But that is almost certainly legend. Behind the propaganda lines the CMEs of the newly-established 'Big Four' were in fact amicably exchanging ideas. Throughout his career Gresley was as receptive to the successful technology of others as Churchward and the likelihood is that he asked for the loan of a 'Castle' to study the fundamentals of such a patently free-running design at close quarters. By whatever means, an exchange was arranged and in 1925 'Castle' and Pacific were put to measured trial on the same trains between Kings Cross and the West Riding and between Paddington and Plymouth. Both home and away the GWR 4–6–0, with its 225 lb (102 kg) pressure boiler and Churchward valve gear, was the clear winner on free-steaming performance and fuel economy. Within a few years Gresley had sagely standardized long-lap piston valves and higher boiler pressure for future LNER Pacific building, and thereafter the Gresley Pacific was on course for its eventual crown as the world's fastest steam locomotive.

Pacific development in France reflected the contrast between British and Continental tradition in the shaping of motive power policy. Except on the PLM, which stuck to its own system of compounding, each railway's Pacific design up to the outbreak of war, starting with the first pair obtained by the Paris–Orléans Railway in 1907, was a de Glehn four-cylinder compound derived fundamentally from the exceptional de Glehn Atlantic. The Nord was nearly a further exception. Until 1912 it was content with a highly successful, comparatively small-wheeled 4–6–0 which du Bousquet had to prefer to satisfy the Nord civil engineers' insistence that their track would not tolerate a heavier axle-load than $16\frac{1}{2}$ tonnes (16·2 tons). By that date British engineers were able to design for 20 tonnes (19·7 tons).

However, these engines, later classified 230D by the nationalized French Railways, proved remarkably effective express passenger hauliers because du Bousquet had prudently enlarged their steam passages to accelerate the flow of steam and match the higher piston speeds resulting from driving wheel diameter reduction. When the Nord's civil engineers took track strengthening in hand du Bousquet prepared a 4–6–4 design and put two prototypes into production, but he died before their completion. The pair were in fact finished but disenchanted his successors, who were drafting their own Pacific when war put a stop to the Nord's track reconstruction.

During the war the French Government, eyeing the fast-approaching date when the operating concessions granted to the railway companies in the nineteenth century would lapse, thought to set the stage for the full-scale nationalization it hankered for by forcing the pace on motive standardization. A proficient new four-cylinder compound 4–6–2 just introduced on the État Railway looked just the right tool for the start of the exercise and Government orders for no fewer than 400 of them were laid in the final years of the war (45 were erected by a British firm, the North British Locomotive Co.). But the Nord, along with the PLM and Paris–Orléans, fended off a permanent allocation of État Pacifics and its traction chief Collin pursued his own design, which materialized as unquestionably the top ranking European express engine of the 1920s.

The Nord 'Super-Pacifics', as French railwaymen justifiably tagged them, emerged in an initial batch of 40 in 1923–4, when the railway's main lines were at last fit for an axleload of $18\frac{1}{2}$ tonnes (18·2 tons). No design of the period was more scientifically considered in every detail. With the benefit of bigger cylinders and 10 per cent more adhesion weight than preceding French Pacifics, plus a 225 lb (102 kg) pressure boiler and most importantly the benefit of abnormally large steam passages which had proved a crucial factor in the Nord 4–6–0's efficiency, the Super-Pacifics spearheaded a rapid advance in the average speed of French expresses. In the mid-1920s the 8 miles (12·9 km) at 1 in 200 from Wood Green to Potters Bar of the LNER exit from Kings Cross would humble a Gresley Pacific towing 500 tons (508 tonnes) to 40 mph (64 km/h) at best by the summit; but on a slope of identical length beginning 9 miles (14·5 km) out of Paris' Gare du Nord a Collin 'Super', stopped by signals at the bank's foot, was timed to accelerate a 550-ton (559 tonne) Calais boat train *from rest* to 57 mph (92 km/h) within the first 5 miles (8·1 km) of the climb – proof enough of the French machine's supremacy. One English observer after another riding the Calais boat trains was dumbfounded by the 'Supers' unfailing ability to hold a steady pace up long slopes with loads of this magnitude – sometimes even to accelerate before they reached the crown of the hill.

The standard German express passenger Pacific took shape after the 1920 amalgamation of the former State railway systems into the unitary Reichsbahn. The Bavarian State apart, the railways of the Kaiser's Germany had been generally content with Atlantics as their principal express passenger power almost to the eve of the war. The energies of the dominant Prussian State, in fact, were bent chiefly to mass production of a sturdy, uncomplicated mixed traffic 4–6–0 with two simple-expansion cylinders rather than to advance in sophisticated multi-cylinder compound design for specialized express duty. Between 1906 and 1921 the Prussians acquired an extraordinary 3,370 of this P8 class, one of the European classics that was also adopted by other railways and which was still widely active well into the second half of the century. Such dedication to an all-purpose machine was largely attributable to the lack of sparkle in German train speed at the time. At the outbreak of the First World War the comparatively few trains timed at 50 mph (81 km/h) or more between stops were largely

The British Southern Railway's leading express passenger type of the inter-war period was the four-cylinder 'Lord Nelson' class: No 858 *Lord Duncan* hurries the Victoria–Dover 'Golden Arrow' down the gradient to Tonbridge.

accounted for by the two dozen which the Prussian State ran daily over the 101 miles (162·5 km) between Berlin and Halle in 110 minutes at a mean speed of 55 mph (89 km/h). Elsewhere pace was hobbled by the close spacing of significant towns that warranted frequent calls – and not least by the determination of many of them to preserve and exercise a right that they had insisted upon at the German railways' construction, to be served by every train on their main line.

Thus when the post-war Reichsbahn cast about for existing types to extend as a stopgap replenishment of its locomotive fleet, which was desperately depleted by war damage, post-war reparations and a backlog of repairs, the only inherited Pacific design that satisfied a national, low axle-load express passenger specification was the Bavarian State's Maffei-built four-cylinder compound Class S3/6. This was a 6 ft 1½ in (186·7 cm) driving-wheel machine,

though in 1912–13 the Bavarians had built 18 of a variant with 6 ft 7 in (200·7 cm) wheels for its Munich–Nuremberg–Würzburg line. That was the only route on which the Bavarian system countenanced a speed of even 70 mph (113 km/h) – further evidence of the mostly pedestrian pace of German rail travel in the Edwardian years. The Reichsbahn had initially expected to find types suitable for national standardization from amongst its heritage of some 350 different classes, subject to some modification, particularly to maximize use of standard components within the group. But none thoroughly satisfied operating specifications that sought equal competence in the flat plains of North Germany and over sharply graded and often tortuous routes in the south and west of the country. So further manufacture of certain reasonably acceptable State railway types had to be pursued as an interim measure while a council of Reichsbahn and manufacturing industry engineers drafted series of new designs.

Eventually there were 29 of them, running the gamut from express passenger Pacifics through 2–10–0, 2–10–2, 2–8–2 and 2–10–2T heavy freight engines to 2–6–2 passenger tank engines. The forerunners, the first Pacifics, did not appear until 1925. Though the designs were in theory a committee exercise, they all had the authoritative stamp of the Reichsbahn's traction chief, R. P. Wagner, another of the giants in European steam's final half-century – and a man with a physical bulk to match his technological stature. Wagner and his aides were imbued with Prussian engineering precepts. And, as may have been inferred from earlier discussion of the P8 4–6–0, the Prussians had been as alert as Churchward in appreciating the potential of a simple-expansion layout complemented by superheating, long-travel valves and well-designed steam passages.

The first standard German Pacific of 1925 was produced in two-cylinder simple Class 01 and four-cylinder compound Class 02 options for practical comparison. The outcome confirmed majority opinion in Berlin that the advances in simple expansion had cancelled out any profit from the higher cost of compounding. The 02s were eventually rebuilt as simple-expansion engines and the entire standard range was erected on the basic theme of high boiler pressure, simple expansion (mostly two- but in some classes three-cylinder), superheating, long-travel valves and high-mounted boilers and running plates to simplify maintenance access to moving parts. The Reichsbahn's standard designs made a profound impression on other European railway managements, several of which – above all those of Poland, Bulgaria, Yugoslavia and Turkey –

The peak of Beyer-Garratt design for the narrow-gauge railways of Africa was the 4-8-2+2-8-4; this was the Class GEA of South African Railways.

had near-replicas of certain German types built in quantity for their own systems.

The Reichsbahn's civil engineers improved their track to such effect that Wagner's team could build their first Pacifics up to a 20-tonne (19·7 ton) axle-loading. In sharp contrast neighbouring Austria's rickety track clamped on its early twentieth-century locomotive designers a 14·5-tonne (14·3 ton) limit, which even by the early 1920s had only been eased to 15·5 tonnes (15·3 tons). In addition Austrian steam had to contend with wretched coal, which posed the tricky problem of accommodating a roomy firebox within this crippling restriction. The only Austrian main line sufficiently free of steep gradients and tortuous curves for sustained speed was the Vienna–Salzburg transversal. For that the Austrian State Railway's redoubtable traction chief from 1891 onwards, Karl Gölsdorf, miraculously contrived a wide-firebox,

6 ft 10¾ in (210·2 cm) driving-wheel express engine, that did not flout the civil engineers' rubrics, by the expedient of inverting the Pacific layout into a 2–6–4. By the outbreak of the First World War, however, railways operating in a mountainous environment like those of Austria and Spain appreciated that the bulk of their express passenger traffic was best served by the greater adhesion weight of an eight-coupled engine, of which the 5 ft 9 in-driving wheel (175·3 cm) 4–8–0 conceived by the Austrian Südbahn for its Semmering Pass main line in 1914 was a pre-eminent example.

The first quarter of the twentieth century ended with the vindication of an idea without which operators of lightly-built lines, those constructed to less than standard gauge especially, would have been overwhelmed by the increased traffic demands. It was the brainchild of a New South Wales Government officer,

H. W. Garratt, who confided it to the British firm of Beyer Peacock, when he was on their Gorton, Manchester premises inspecting locomotives under construction to an NSW order in 1907. Beyer Peacock was impressed, purchased the patented concept and manufactured the first Beyer-Garratt in 1908. Where the Beyer-Garratt scheme scored over other articulated locomotive layouts was in the extra dimension it handed the boiler designer. That was because the boiler did not have to clear driving wheels, but was borne on a separate frame slung like a stretcher between pivots on two widely separated engine units, which carried the engine's fuel and water supplies. There was room in the void between the units for a boiler diameter and bulk of firebox which the loading gauge would have debarred from consideration for a Mallet, but without any penalty of unacceptable axle-loading. And the length

of a Beyer-Garratt was no embarrassment even on the most viciously curved railway, because its adaptability to curvature was dependent solely on the rigidity of the fixed driving wheelbase on one engine unit; the two units moved quite independently on their pivots.

The decisive year for the Beyer-Garratt was 1921. At first its sponsors believed the idea's potential was best realized by building the articulateds as compounds, but in 1921 a simple expansion 2–6–0 + 0–6–2 supplied to the 3 ft 6 in-gauge (106·7 cm) South African Railways dispelled that theory. Evaluated against a local Mallet it proved unmistakeably superior both as a performer and in terms of fuel consumption, setting the scene for subsequent development of the narrow-gauge, simple-expansion Beyer-Garratt as haulier that had the measure of most European heavy freight engines in tractive effort.

3

THE FIRST ELECTRIC RAILWAYS

OCTOBER, 1903 WAS a prophetic month for rail passenger transport, though it would take three-quarters of a century for the prophecy to materialize as everyday practice. That autumn a pair of electrically-powered, standard-gauge coaches were in quick succession whipped up to speeds of 128·5 and 130·5 mph (206·8 and 210 km/h) on a 14½-mile (23·3 km) military railway between Marienfelde and Zossen, in the vicinity of Berlin. It must have been an awesome spectacle. The track had been reconstructed after a brush with catastrophe earlier in the experiments when one of the cars, already so sickly reeling that its pantographs frequently parted company with the conductor wires in an atomic burst of arcing, heeled over enough to

foundered on cost, but that frustration apart the German group's exploits made a significant contribution to the main electrification debating point at the start of the century: whether it was sensible to work straight from the three-phase, industrial supplies of alternating current now becoming available, or whether it was preferable to persist with the direct current traction motors that had been the genesis of electric rail traction in the tramways of the late nineteenth century.

The first electrifications had employed low-voltage dc, which made it safe to use the economical medium of a third rail to supply the current to the traction units. But as sources of high-voltage, three-phase ac at 50 or 60Hz

The first main-line electrification in the US was in 1894-5, after the city of Baltimore had ordered the Baltimore & Ohio RR to stop steam working through the city: the 1440 hp locomotives worked off 675 V dc overhead wires.

Far left:
The rod-driven 2-B + B-2 heading this train preparing to begin the climb from Erstfeld to the Gotthard Tunnel was one of the first series of locomotives built for main-line haulage after the Gotthard route's electrification.

lift one bogie momentarily off the track. But as the previous chapter has indicated, German civil engineering at the time was not widely geared to main-line speeds of even 70 mph (113 km/h), and the vehicles themselves were lumbering, clerestory-roofed 12-wheelers, devoid of any streamlining and quite innocent of any science in the design of running gear for stress-free operation at three-figure pace. As speed climbed their totally unaerodynamic outline churned the imperfectly compacted ballast into a lethal hailstorm of pebbles that hammered the car floors and sprayed the lineside in their wake.

This adventurous German experiment was mounted by an industrial consortium dedicated to the creation of high-speed electric railways. Sadly, the immediate hopes which the tests excited of electrifying the Berlin–Hamburg route for operation by high-speed railcars

(cycles per second) came on stream in the industrialized countries and as newborn electrical engineering companies successfully devised ac motors for stationary plants, interest in the use of this power for rail traction naturally quickened. With a high-voltage supply a specific horsepower could be produced at far less cost in current. In recent times the ratio has been as much as one to ten for comparable 1·5kV dc and 15kV ac rail systems. Had electronics been perfected alongside electric power engineering the three-phase ac motor would almost certainly have been the standard traction tool from the start of main-line electrification. Mechanically it is an engagingly simple machine compared with a dc motor. But until the 1980s, when electronics were at last taming the problem and convincing several European traction chiefs that their next locomotive purchases would be three-phase, it had a critical drawback. This was

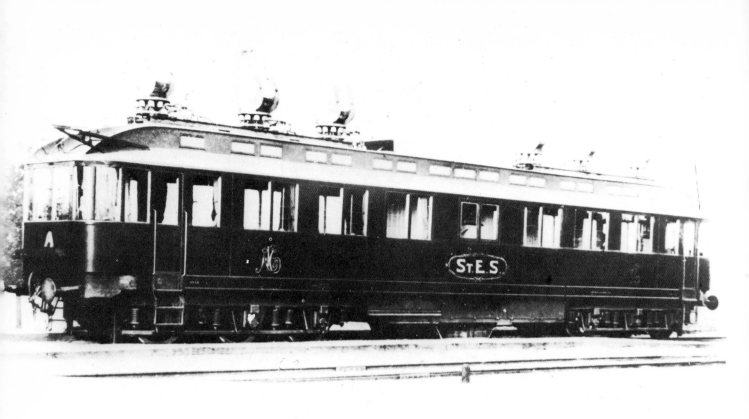

One of the 12-wheeled electric railcars which was pushed up to a speed of 130.5 mph (210.1 km/h) in the Marienfelde–Zossen experiments of 1903.

the difficulty of making its speed variable over the wide range demanded in a rail traction application.

At the start of the century, therefore, some rail electrifiers preferred to develop entirely with dc, transforming and rectifying an ac supply in ground stations so that it reached the conductor in a form assimilable by low-voltage dc traction motors. Dc electrification's prospects would have been severely limited if this technology had been stuck with third-rail transmission, which on safety grounds alone imposed a 650V–750V limit on the traction current. That had to suffice for the electrification which the New York Central was compelled by the city to install in the tunnels leading to its new Grand Central station in New York after the impenetrable murk left by an intensive steam service had been blamed for ignored signals and a disastrous collision beneath Park Avenue early in 1902. However, acceptance of the expense of overhead wire current collection broadened the power horizon. The scope for dc electrification of a long-haul railway became visible in 1911 with the US General Electric Company's conversion of a Southern Pacific line at 1,200V dc. Doubling the voltage quadrupled the distance between sub-stations at which current strength dropped by any specific amount: in other words, more trains or more tonnage could be satisfyingly fed from each sub-station and thus operated without extra capital or running costs. In 1913 came the first essay in

dc electrification of a heavy freight line, the Butte, Anaconda & Pacific, at 2,400V dc. This, granted, was only 25 miles (40 km) long, but two years later the Chicago, Milwaukee, St Paul & Pacific launched a 3,000V dc electrification of its 650-mile (1,046 km) route through the Rockies.

The German sponsors of the high-speed tests near Berlin in 1903 were among the protagonists of three-phase ac traction development, but its most vigorous advocates in the century's first decade were the Swiss firm, Brown Boveri, and the Hungarian concern, Ganz, whose traction engineer Kalman Kando had a particularly profound influence on early rail electrification technology. The initial impact on European rail history, however, was Brown Boveri's. The Simplon Tunnel route had been conceived in the expectation that it would be steam-worked, but very soon there was worrying word from the Gotthard line. As its traffic and train weights increased, so did a smoke problem within the Gotthard Tunnel, despite powerful ventilation machinery. The anxiety this aroused was that, unlike the flat alignment of the Gotthard line underground, the Simplon route was to be crowned by a summit within its tunnel, so that steam engines would need substantial firing inside the bore. Brown Boveri, which had just installed a pioneer three-phase electrification on the Burgdorf-Thun line, promptly offered to supply the Simplon with electric locomotives at its own risk and was accepted. The pair of 1–C–1 locomotives which inaugurated the Simplon route's electric haulage in April 1906 were the first in the world to prove the effectiveness of this form of traction in mixed main-line passenger and freight service.

Italians figured prominently in the late nineteenth century evolution of electrical science – witness, for example, the commemoration of an Italian, Alessandro Volta, in such a basic term as 'volt' – so it is unsurprising that the Italian Government was pressing for main-line electrification before the 1890s were out. Expert Italian opinion advocated the three-phase ac system as having the greater potential in a trunk route application and Ganz, like Brown Boveri, was quick to seed rich-looking ground with an offer to equip a prototype line at its own expense. From that initial scheme, achieved in 1901 on the Colico–Chiavenna branch northeast of Milan, there soon germinated the much more important three-phase electrification of the two exits from Genoa through the Giovi pass, the 1 in 28½ and 1 in 33 slopes of which were hindering the movement of the port's rising traffic. Both lines were electrified by 1911, on the same 3,000V 15Hz basis as the Simplon, with power specially generated at a voltage acceptable to traction motors. The ability of a pair of Ganz's 2,100 hp locomotives to hold 28 mph (45 km/h) with 400 tons (406 tonnes) up slopes that had previously humbled a pair of four-cylinder compound 0–10–0s on 310 tons (315 tonnes) to 17 mph (27 km/h) prompted a rapid extension northward of the catenary, which by 1915 had been carried right through the Mont Cenis tunnel to the boundary with the French at Modane.

Although a 6·6kV three-phase ac system was operative by 1909, on the US Great Northern line through the Cascade range, where 1 in 45 grades and 2,500-ton (2,540 tonne) freight trains had posed the same safety problem in a 2·6-mile (4·2 km) tunnel as on the Simplon route, a majority of would-be electrifiers recoiled from the disadvantages of this mode. The handicap of a limited range of fixed speeds has already been mentioned. Another costly disbenefit was the need of two conductor wires and two current collectors, or pantographs, on each traction unit. That prompted Swiss engineers to devise a way of using for traction only one of the three phases in which industrial ac power is normally distributed. Three-phase output is favoured since thereby currents produced simultaneously but out of step can be transmitted over a single cable. The world's first single-phase ac electrification was installed by Oerlikon on the Swiss Federal's 15-mile (24·1 km) Seebach–Wettingen line in 1904 – another instance of a manufacturer backing the innovation with his own money.

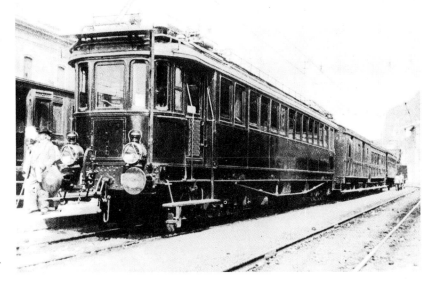

Top: Harlowton, Montana was the eastern extremity of the Rocky Mountain Division which the Chicago, Milwaukee St Paul & Pacific RR electrified at 3 kV dc in 1915.

Above:
Among the first electrifications in Italy, completed in 1902 at 3.4 kV 15.8 Hz three-phase ac, was of the 49¼-mile Valtellina line into the foothills of the Alps from Lecco through Colico to Sondrio: one of its 10 four-motor railcars is seen at Lecco in 1904.

The only three-phase ac main-line electrification in the US was the Great Northern's through the Cascade Mountains in Washington State, completed in 1909: these 1-Co-Co-1s were built for the route after its conversion to 11 kV single-phase ac in the 1920s.

Locomotive for the world's first single-phase ac electrification, between Seebach and Wettingen, Switzerland, installed in 1904.

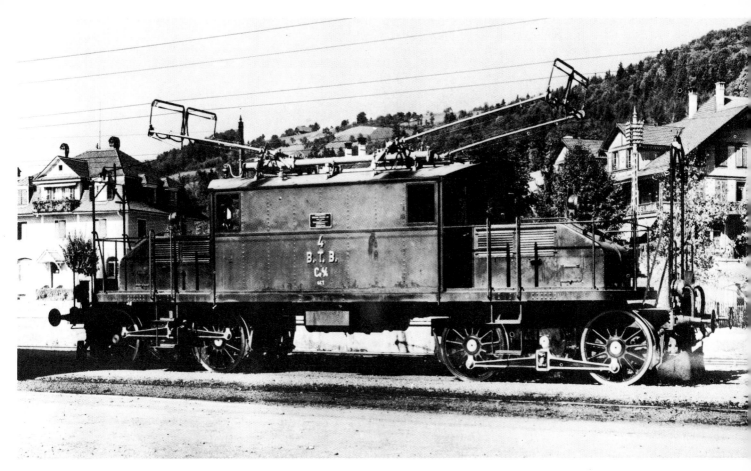

Inexplicably, though the system seems to have worked well, the Swiss Federal was disinclined to take it over and the catenary was dismantled in 1906; but within a few years the technique was taken up by the newly-formed Berne–Lötschberg–Simplon Railway.

Reduction of the current supply to a single-phase frequency of $16\frac{2}{3}$Hz, besides allowing use of a single conductor wire, eliminated many of the technical snags inherent in applying current generated at the industrial frequency to a traditional series-wound motor. Thus single-phase ac electrification combined the advantages of more economical capital and running costs with the speed control flexibility of the series-wound motor, though in the early days railways drawing their current at the full industrial frequency sacrificed some of its efficiency in the sub-station rotary converters which were needed to transmute it to $16\frac{2}{3}$Hz. Here a dc railway got better value from its sub-station rectifiers. Most of the countries which subsequently plumped for single-phase ac, however, were rich in hydro-electric resources which could be cheaply tapped by railway power stations specially arranged to generate at the lower frequency.

On the Gotthard line a pair of steam locomotives had to be thrashed to sustain 20 mph (32 km/h) with 200 tons (203 tonnes) in tow on the long grind up to the tunnel. From their debut

a single one of the 2,000 hp 1-E-1 locomotives which Brown Boveri constructed to Oerlikon designs for the Lötschberg route managed a contented 30 mph (48 km/h) up the new railway's remorseless 1 in 38 grades with 300 tons (305 tonnes). Moreover, the electric locomotive scaled little more than a third of the two steam engines' weight. A year later, in 1914, the Swiss Federal ordered electrification of the Gotthard line on the same 15kV $16\frac{2}{3}$Hz ac system, which it had extended to the greater part of its network by the end of the 1920s. The Simplon route was re-electrified this way in 1930.

The performance of Switzerland's first electrified transalpine routes stimulated electrification schemes elsewhere in Europe that were substantially enlarged in the aftermath of the First World War. Swiss readiness to put the emergent electric traction technology to trunk route proof had been prompted by the country's lack of indigenous coal resources but rich hydro-electric potential. After the 1914–18 war even countries with coal reserves of their own were stretched to satisfy all industrial demand for solid fuel. Much of the German pits' output was sequestered as reparations while France's most productive mines had been severely damaged during the fighting. Shortages were compounded by labour disputes and consequently the price of coal rose sharply, aggravating the concerns of

An early Swiss electric locomotive: built by Brown Boveri for the 750 V 40 Hz three-phase ac Burgdorf-Thun line in 1910, it had a 260 hp squirrel-cage motor on each bogie.

Above:
The Italian State Railways persisted with three-phase ac in the north-west of the country until after the Second World War: 183 of these 76-tonne freight 0-E-0s, which had a top speed of only 30 mph (48 km/h), were built for the three-phase ac lines in 1928-30.

Above right:
Electrification came to Scandinavia in 1915 with Sweden's application of 15 kV 16⅔ Hz ac to the Kiruna–Lulea ore line within the Arctic circle: the rod-driven Class Dm2 1-D+D-1 twin-unit, with a continuous output of 7,155 hp, is one of the present-day types working the lines from Kiruna to Lulea and Narvik.

countries reliant on imports. A case in point was Italy, which the war had left economically debilitated and anxious to curb foreign purchases. Very soon, therefore, the Italian State Railways (FS) set themselves the objective of electrifying over 3,000 miles (4,828 km) of their network by the mid-1920s with the emphasis on their busiest routes so as to cut coal consumption by two-thirds. In the event ambition outran practicality, though by a considerably narrower margin than in France. There a Government decree of 1920 exhorted the Midi, Orléans and PLM Railways to convert a total of 5,500 route-miles (8,851 km) in fairly short order, but at the end of the 1930s the only French trunk routes with electric power were those from Paris via Bordeaux to the Spanish border at Hendaye, and from the capital to Le Mans, on the way to Brittany.

The main-line electrifiers were divided on technique. Most Central European countries surrounding Switzerland, such as Austria, Germany and Hungary, understandably opted for the single-phase ac system, though not always at the same 15kV 16⅔Hz value as the Swiss. This model was also followed in Scandinavia, where Sweden opened the electrification account as early as 1915 on the Lapland line without which the country's prodigious ore fields within the Arctic Circle, in the vicinity of Kiruna, would be starved of world market access. The Swedes initially electrified to their own Baltic port of Lulea, but in 1923 the Norwegians wired their connection to the line which is the more vital

outlet for the ore, since the Norwegian port of Narvik is ice-free all the year, whereas Lulea is unusable for five months of it.

For a time the Italians persisted with three-phase ac and ultimately had 1,240 route-miles (1,996 km) operative on this system in the north-west of the country and from Trento up to the Brenner Pass. By the mid-1920s, however, they were weary of the technique's operational and high-capital cost drawbacks. Starting with the Benevento–Foggia and Naples lines in 1928–31 the FS switched to 3,000V dc, a system already adopted in Brazil, Chile, Spain and South Africa and in the following decade to be taken up by Belgium. The FS lived with two incompatible electric networks until the 1940s, when war damage to the Genoa–La Spezia–Viareggio coastal line made its re-electrification at 3,000V dc the only logical course. That set off a gradual conversion of the rest of the three-phase mileage, which was not complete until the start of the 1970s.

The final variations on the theme were played by France and the Netherlands, which preferred 1·5kV dc. In Britain the London Brighton & South Coast Railway threatened to set a single-phase ac trend with a plan to extend to Brighton the 6·6kV catenary it had begun to instal in its London suburban area, but a Government committee appointed in 1920 to advise on electrification standards with an eye to the impending consolidation of the railways into four groups advocated national adoption of dc systems. Its findings were confirmed by two

subsequent Government committees of the
1920s, the Pringle and the Weir, and in 1926 the
Southern Railway replaced the LBSCR's overhead wires with its standard 660V dc third-rail.
For trunk route electrification outside the SR's
third-rail territory 1·5kV dc overhead wires were
prescribed, but though the advice was accepted
by many British Commonwealth countries none
of the home railways was inclined to finance a
main-line conversion until the mid-1930s, when
the Government's offer of cheap credits for
electrification as a stimulus to economic re-
surgence after the slump encouraged the LNER
to tackle the trans-Pennine route from Sheffield
to Manchester. In the equally desperate recession of 1982, ironically, that electrification was
shut down because post-war changes in industrial traffic flows had denuded it of traffic,
while the nationalized British Rail was at the
same time craving Government support for new
main-line electrification elsewhere – and partly
on the grounds that once more this was a socially
profitable way to spark an industrial revival.

The perfection of electric traction was heaven-
sent for the authorities of cities in the western
world grappling with increasingly acute surface
traffic towards the end of the nineteenth century.
The relief which the first metropolitan railways
won them can be gauged from the first few
years' traffic graph of the part-elevated, part-
underground railway thrust through the heart of
Berlin. This 8-mile (12·9 km) line, opened in 1902,
absorbed 18·8 million passenger-journeys in its
very first year, but within two more it was reporting over 32 million. This, moreover, was at a time
when the city's steam-worked surface lines, the
cross-town Stadtbahn, orbital Ringbahn and
radial suburban routes, were offering such an
intensive service that on one stretch where all of
them converged just over 800 trains could be
counted in a single day's working, which began
around 4 am and continued well into the small
hours. London was the only European city to
start a deep-level network of slimly-dimensioned
Tube railways, all of them financed by private
capital. Elsewhere the preferred method was
'cut-and-cover' – the excavation and subsequent
enclosure of a trench just below the surface,
which had been adopted for construction of
London's District and Metropolitan Railways.
After the enforced mediation of the Board of
Trade in the dispute between these two companies over the merits of dc and three-phase ac –
unanimity was *de rigueur* since both shared the
capital's Inner Circle line – their conversion to
dc electric working had begun in 1903.

Incredibly, some Londoners were not enamoured of the change. 'The steam railways',
complained one critic, 'provided a sort of health

Top:
The London Brighton &
South Coast Railway began a
6.6 kV single-phase
electrification of its London
suburban territory and one of
the ac train-sets is seen at
Victoria.

Centre:
The approach to Clapham
Junction from the London
termini in the 1950s, with a
Portsmouth express multiple-
unit on the South Western
Division main line and two
suburban multiple-units.

Bottom:
A train of the London
Metropolitan Railway's first
electric stock, built in 1905, at
Praed Street: the wooden
bodies were given a varnished
teak finish with cream lining.

resort for people who suffered from asthma, for which the sulphurous and other fumes were supposed to be beneficial, and there were several regular asthmatical customers who daily took turns round the Circle to enjoy the invigorating atmosphere. But today all the sulphur has gone, except in the speech of a few irritable travellers, and has been replaced by an indescribable atmosphere of squashed microbes.' Certainly the suffocating experience of steam-hauled travel below ground had in no way deterred the public. At the conclusion of its steam operation in 1905 the District Railway alone was registering 51 million passenger journeys a year, and that despite erosion of its traffic by the pioneer Tube, the City and South London, and by the most reckless fare-cutting war of bus companies on the streets above.

Paris had nourished the idea of a system akin to London's Metropolitan since the start of the 1880s. But in France central Government was determined to shape conurbation railways as it had the evolution of the main-line map. So for a decade and a half the project was stalled by a clash of principle: the Paris authorities wanted the system to serve a strictly metropolitan purpose, whereas central Government hankered for lines that would interconnect the trunk railways and interchange traffic between them as well as catering for in-town travel. In 1895 the city was allowed to have its way as a reward for agreement to staging a national exhibition in 1900. Metro lines would project no further from the center than the inner rim of the city's historic military perimeter and to guard against any revival of the Government's ambition, as well as to curb construction costs, they would be designed to narrow-gauge parameters. But in passing the Bill for the first Paris Metro scheme the French Parliament slipped in a clause that insisted upon standard gauge. This the astute town council meekly accepted, but it artfully nullified Parliament's intentions by retaining the restrictive loading gauge it had previously approved, so that the Metro would forever be unusable by orthodox standard-gauge rolling stock. Hence the somewhat stunted, slim-waisted cross-section of even today's Paris Metro train-sets by comparison with those of London's Metropolitan and District lines. In sharp distinction to the unfettered free enterprise course followed in London, the Paris city council financed virtually all the fixed works of its Metro. That left the company to which the operation of the system was leased for 35 years little more capital expense than the provision of trains, signalling and some fitting-out of stations. The city pocketed all ticket revenue, from which it paid the operating company an annuity based on traffic volume and ticket sales.

Right from its start, therefore, the Paris Metro, like other Continental systems of the same character, became as accepted a municipally-funded social service as sanitation. But not so London, with consequences for which 1980s users of London Transport are paying dearly in more than one sense of the term. Ironically, pre-echoes of present-day London Transport complaints were to be heard from one of its predecessors, the London Underground Group, as early as the mid-1920s. In 1924 this group (which included the London General Omnibus Company) counted almost 1·5 billion passengers, or nearly 4·5 million a day, yet at the subsequent annual meeting its chairman was rejecting all clamour for fresh Tube extensions. The return on capital had sunk to deplorable levels, he complained, though in those days the reason was not yet the menace of the private car but the effect of uncontrolled public transport expansion. Across the Channel, in contrast, the Paris Metro operating company, by then moving almost half a billion passengers a year over a 58-mile (93 km) network, was living comfortably enough for its shares to command a modest premium and for route expansion to press ahead.

On the other side of the Atlantic New York had set other US cities an example in metropolitan transportation in the late nineteenth century with the country's first urban elevated railway; and it was New York, too, which in 1904 opened America's first true underground electric railway (the pioneering Boston Subway of 1897 had been an underground tramway). By 1904 New York's extraordinary 'El', which totalled 280 single-track miles (451 km) was groaning under an annual load of 250 million passenger journeys. Its busiest Third and Sixth Avenue lines, strutting through the city's prime residential and commercial districts at second-storey level, were running almost a thousand trains a day each in the peak winter season. And that was with steam power: dumpy little 0-4-4 Forney tanks that were set a daily stop-and-start regimen as rigorous as any in today's electric conurbation transport. So closely-spaced were 'El' stations that on average an 'El' train was braking to a halt every 40 seconds. With station allowances sometimes cut to less than five seconds and averaging no more than 10 seconds during the working day, and with trains trailing each other at less than a minute's headway in the rush-hours, it was small wonder that the 'El' had to forego any sort of lineside signalling. Small wonder, either, that rush-hour travelling conditions on the Third and Sixth Avenue routes in particular were bestial, above all as outgoing

and incoming hordes charged each other like hefty American football players at each fleeting station stop.

One New York evening paper, in fact, alleged that a leading US football team's coach forced his squad to shuttle up and down the Third Avenue line every rush-hour as battle training. 'If you expect to win,' the coach supposedly adjured his players, 'you've got to go through the mill. Of course the disabled ones will be sent back, but the ones who come out all right will be able to rush through a brick wall.' The report's credibility was stretched to breaking point, however, with its claim that on the field the team's captain could always rally his men in a crisis by bawling 'All aboard for the City Hall. Let 'em off first – both gates!'

The first of American cities' nineteenth century 'Els' to start electrifying was that of Chicago, the country's second largest with a system of

First of the US 'Els' to electrify was Chicago's: this modern scene at the Wells Street-Wacker Drive intersection indicates that it is the only historic US city elevated railway to retain its original structures almost intact.

230 single-track miles (370 km). That was in 1895, two years after the British city of Liverpool had completed the first overhead railway in the world to employ electric traction *ab initio*; but the Liverpool Overhead, which knitted together the city's port area, was a far more modest enterprise than the big US city 'Els'. American city 'Els' built after 1895 – Boston inaugurated its first overhead line in 1901 and the last in the country, Philadelphia's, was commissioned progressively between 1903–8 – were constructed as electric railways. Chicago's initiative fuelled the mounting exasperation of New Yorkers at the purgatory of travel on their steam 'El'. Their wrath exploded when neighbouring Brooklyn also embarked on a changeover to electric power in 1898. At last, in 1899, the private enterprise owner of the New York 'El', the Manhattan Railway, was goaded to follow suit, but not from any philanthropic or environmentalist motive. The Chicago 'El' was clearly proving more profitable to run with electricity for one thing; more importantly, the New York 'El' was up against the new competition of electric streetcar routes and under further threat from a Manhattan–Bronx electric Subway. Plans for this Subway had taken firm shape in 1894 after the Manhattan Railway had refused to invest in 'El' extensions to improve its service and infuriated public pressure for a new mass transit system had become irresistible. Later that year a public

referendum voted clearly for public control of the new Subway, to the further consternation of the Manhattan Railway. It fought to stifle the project at birth by recanting its refusal to extend but was totally frustrated.

Subway building by cut-and-cover began in 1900 and the first line was opened in 1904. Shortly afterwards the operation of the 'El' lines was leased to the Subway operating company, Interborough Rapid Transit, and the principle of a publicly-owned, operated and co-ordinated New York rapid rail transit system was established. In later years much of the 'El' was converted to underground railway and today Chicago's is the only 'El' which still bestrides the streets much as it did almost a century ago. The New York Subway, a 610V dc system, differed from all other early metropolitan underground railways in one respect. Third tracks had been laid on parts of the 'El' to allow some limited-stop trains to overtake all-stations services, but the trunk of the underground system, the 6 miles (9·7 km) from Brooklyn Bridge to 96th Street, was made continuous four-track to enable the operation of regular express services.

The Subway did not alleviate the city's transport problems. In its very first year the Manhattan–Bronx line's tally of passengers was 106 million (for a standard five cent fare). Three years later the combined Subway and 'El'

The New York Subway's solid but unprepossessing Type R-15 mu stock of 1950.

systems counted over 1·5 million passengers daily on average, and the urgent case for extensions both above and below ground, plus the fact that since 1897 other areas including Brooklyn had incorporated in the Greater New York municipality, brought the Interborough monopoly into acute question. The arguments were resolved in 1913 by a series of complex Dual Contracts under which operation was shared between Interborough and the Brooklyn Rapid Transit (now BMT), with the city retaining overall control and pre-empting half the profits. That cleared the way to a massive extension of the network between 1913 and 1920 – but not massive enough to satisfy a city by then $5\frac{1}{2}$ million people strong. At the same time the financially exhausted operating companies defaulted on their Dual Contracts obligations and travelling conditions so deteriorated – 'Had I treated German prisoners as passengers on the transit lines here are being treated,' thundered a major-general member of the city's Transit Commission, 'I would have been court-martialled' – that in 1925 the city began to build its own Independent Subway or IND. It was the first step to unification under municipal ownership and operation, but that was not consummated until 1940.

Main-line electrification appealed to very few US railroads. Coal was too cheap and plentiful, besides which the economic advantages of electric traction's availability for near-continuous work were vitiated where a single line was traversed by perhaps one mammoth train each way per hour: and that was true for so much US trunk mileage away from the major populated corridors of the East and West Coasts and the Mid-West. Such US electrifications as there were took divergent paths because of a division of technical opinion between the two major suppliers. General Electric put a premium on the flexible performance of dc motors and advocated dc schemes, up to a strength of 3,000V in the Milwaukee Road's Western Extension mentioned earlier (that catenary was scrapped at the end of the 1950s as the route's passenger services dwindled and it was deemed more economical to use diesel power throughout the freight haul to the coast). Westinghouse, on the other hand, was more impressed by the economy of high-voltage ac for long-distance power transmission. Three-phase ac was limited to the 1909 conversion of the Great Northern's Cascade Tunnel crossing of the Stevens Pass, and in the 1920s even that unique installation was altered to the 11kV single-phase ac which dominated US schemes (the GN catenary was also discarded in the mid-1950s). Then Westinghouse pioneered 11kV single-phase ac at 25Hz in 1907 on the New Haven Railroad from the limits of central New York's dc third-rail to New Haven, and it was subsequently adopted

for the Pennsylvania's New York–Washington route in 1915, for fiercely-graded Norfolk & Western and Virginian coal routes in the Appalachians from 1915 to 1925, and for the Boston & Maine's passage of the Hoosac Tunnel. Of these electrifications all but the Pennsylvania and New Haven were dismantled after the Second World War.

City suburban and short-haul interurban railways, on the other hand, the Americans eagerly electrified. Stimulated by the conception of the electric multiple-unit train, thanks to the 1897 invention of one of their countrymen, Frank Sprague, whereby a number of powered vehicles could be controlled from a single cab, urban lines were so rapidly electrified to exploit this new and lively form of mass transportation that by 1930 the US claimed overall the highest electrified route mileage in the world.

In the route-mileage league Britain's lack of interest in main-line electrification had it languishing in eighth place at that juncture. But in one particular it was unsurpassed: the total of electric multiple-unit trains its railways were operating. That was due predominantly to the

enterprise of the Southern Railway under its General Manager Sir Herbert Walker, who was progressively electrifying his entire London commuter network south of the Thames on the low-voltage dc, third-rail system and building thereby the biggest unified operation of its kind in the first half of this century. By 1930 the Southern had already converted 780 route-miles (1,255 km), or almost a fifth of its territory. Testimony enough to Walker's vision and charismatic leadership is the fact that he carried the heavy investment decisions with his Board in a period when economic conditions in the country were unstable and the only obvious stimulus was the escalating price of coal. But Walker had won the Southern post on his track record as General Manager of one of its pre-1923 constituents, the London & South Western. There he initiated and proved the validity of the suburban electrification policy he was now pursuing on the integrated Southern Railway.

Where Walker was ahead of his time was in his appreciation of a market-oriented electric train service's potential to attract business. 'When I put the scheme before my directors,' he

One of the best-known US interurban electric lines was the Chicago North Shore & Milwaukee Railroad, which introduced these buffet bar-equipped 'Electroliners' in 1941 and ran them at up to 85 mph (137 km/h) on very fast schedules.

said of his LSWR experience in remarks to the Institute of Transport in 1921, 'I told them [it] was not put forward with the idea of saving money. The idea . . . was to get greater efficiency, increase traffic and therefore to increase net revenue.' That he achieved by a design of standard operation which both optimized the economic potential of electric traction and maximized public convenience. Each electrified service was given a repetitive, regular-interval timetable which functioned throughout the day, with the superimposition of extra trains in the peak hours. With electric power the marginal cost of sustaining the same frequency in the commercially dead hours of mid-morning and mid-afternoon was worth the chance of generating new business through the timetable's easily-memorized regularity. But only if other components of total operating costs were minimized. That was achieved by exclusive reliance on standard, self-powered multiple-unit train-sets, quickly reversible without any shunting at terminals and easily adjustable in length to suit demand. In short, Walker's philosophy was the seed of the modern Inter-City concept and the market-pricing subsequently developed as its complement.

Environmentally, Walker's electrification drive had its debit. The speed and convenience of the Southern electric service by comparison with standards in suburbia north of the Thames, and the astuteness of its promotion (Walker was the first British railway chief to add a public relations officer to his entourage, and that as early as 1925), magnetized residential development. Suburbia already sprawled much farther to the south of London than elsewhere by the 1930s, when the Southern began to apply the same style of electrification to its short main lines. Thereafter building growth began to scar the Sussex countryside much of the way to its coastal resorts, which themselves gradually assumed the role of dormitories for the City of London.

4
WAR RESHAPES EUROPE'S RAILWAYS

EUROPE WAS PROPELLED into the First World War by its railways both figuratively and literally. The plans which the Russians and Germans in particular had been drafting since the century's start in the ultimate certainty of war were fundamentally reliant on the deployment of their men and material by a gigantic, precisely time-tabled railway operation over a period of days. Thus the signal to set one juggernaut rolling had to be countered immediately by the launch of the other. Both operations were so intensive that neither side could afford brinkmanship. For 16 days at the start of August 1914 the Hohenzollern Bridge over the Rhine at Cologne, for example, carried a westbound train on average every 10 minutes. The Germans' Schlieffen Plan, under which their northern armies were to head for the Belgian coast before veering southward to Paris, was to be mounted with an inaugural rail time-table covering 16 days. Once the Tsar had committed Russia to mobilization, therefore, the Germans had to follow suit at once or else risk getting embroiled with their forces not properly in place. After that it might just have been possible to stop the unfolding of the intricate railway timetables for a diplomatic breathing space, but it would have been immensely difficult.

With the air warfare in its infancy the only railway system to suffer heavy wartime damage was the French, which even outside the battle zones wilted under the 50 per cent of additional traffic the war thrust upon it, especially when some two million incoming American servicemen were added to its load in 1918. The French railways' woes were exacerbated by a progressive decline in their usable stock of vehicles and locomotives, which shipments of War Department engines from Britain and the US were not enough to offset.

The restricted output of new locomotives from French factories was not the problem so much as the great variety of pre-war French steam power. Types acceptable for direction to work beyond the borders of their owning railway were scarce – heavy freight engines especially – and the multiplicity of spares needed to keep every type serviceable was not widely available, so that crippled locomotives accumulated. Hence the sharpening appetite for unification and standardization of the railways' equipment on the part of the French Government, already noted in a preceding chapter.

Germany alone imposed total military control on its railways for the duration. The varying degrees of overall direction applied elsewhere were, however, effective enough to call in question the sense of reverting to the status quo of fragmented railway systems after the Armistice.

In Britain the 130 companies active in 1914 had been brought under state control on the eve of war. The overseer was the Board of Trade, but its direction was exercised through a Railway Executive Committee formed of the ten leading railways' general managers. The original motive was purely military, but in the event the REC coordinated all railway operation and achieved some sensible rationalization, especially in the freight sector. There it secured a great advance in productive use of rolling stock by gradually persuading the major companies to pool their wagons. These could then by used for a fresh load wherever they were discharged, instead of having to be sent back empty to their owning railways; so-called 'number-takers' at interchange yards recorded wagon movements so that wagon revenue was equitably shared at the end of the day. One should add that practically half the wagon stock was excluded from this

A veteran French 0-6-0 moves troops up to the front line in 1917.

Far left:
US War Department locomotives gathered at St Nazaire, France, in 1918: in the foreground, narrow-gauge 2-6-2 tanks for the light railways of the forward areas, in the rear standard-gauge Baldwin-built 2-8-0s.

These unshapely two-axled double-deckers were a characteristic of many Paris suburban services in 1914.

arrangement: that was the privately-owned element, dominated by collieries' and merchants' coal wagons, which remained sacrosanct until the Second World War.

Before 1900 Britain had been so heavily covered with railways, in some areas duplicating or even triplicating the same purpose, that in the last two pre-war decades the companies themselves appreciated there was more profit in collaborative rate and working agreements than in unbridled competition. The three major railways of Eastern England, in fact, had gone beyond pooling deals to formal moves for a merger in 1907–9, but trader anxiety at the resultant concentration of economic power had forced them to retreat. Wartime realization of the improved efficiency of larger-scale railway operation, however, muted the critics. As victory approached trades union pressure for nationalization seemed to be swaying political opinion even to the right of center. In the spring of 1918 Prime Minister Lloyd George assured a Trades Union Congress delegation that he was in 'complete sympathy' with the principle of state ownership; and four days after the Armistice a House of Commons Select Committee recommended flatly that 'the main railway systems of the United Kingdom should be brought under unified ownership and managed as one system if the question of the internal transport facilities is to be considered from the standpoint of economy and efficiency.' Just before that year's December election Winston Churchill, War Minister in the Coalition Cabinet, actually told his Dundee constituents that the Government was at one on nationalization and discounted any belief that

state control would be deferred while a Royal Commission weighed the pros and cons.

But the Cabinet, it transpired, had reached no such agreement. In 1919 a phalanx of industry, Chambers of Commerce and railway managements lobbied the nationalization idea into limbo. The Government had to make do with the creation of a Ministry of Transport and retention of control over the railways for two more years while it mulled over a new railway policy. Some sort of consolidation was inevitable, because without it several railways that had proved strategically vital in the war, such as the Highland in Scotland, were likely to collapse financially. None had received a pro rata payment for their wartime effort. The Government had merely guaranteed each company an income equivalent to its net receipts in 1913. That was totally inadequate for recuperation of the excessive wear and tear inflicted by wartime traffic; so, too, was the extra sum grudgingly conceded later in 1921, as a once-for-all compensation.

The Government eventually elected, in its Railways Act of 1921, to amalgamate the 120 or so companies of significance into four large private enterprise Groups, the London Midland & Scottish, London & North Eastern, Great Western and Southern, which became operative at the start of 1923. Like the railways of France, each had a territorial monopoly, so that although scope for competition persisted over some trunk routes from London to the provinces it was eliminated locally. The nearest the Act came to nationalization was in a clause which empowered the Minister of Transport to require any railway company 'to conform gradually to measures of general standardisation of ways, plant and equipment' and 'to adopt schemes for co-operative working or common uses of rolling stock, manufactories, plant and other facilities'. In the ensuing 20 years the four Groups complied individually within their own communities; but the Ministry's exercise of its powers over the whole British railway scene was limited to safety measures.

On the European mainland the assertive role of nineteenth century governments in railway network development had already culminated in nationalization, as in Italy, or else it had the stage well set for a final act of unification. In some countries, such as Sweden and Belgium, a State railway already in being was progressively taking over private companies; in Belgium that process reached the point of nationalization in 1926. Elsewhere railways had been consolidated into a few major companies, as Britain had just done. Since 1890, for example, Holland had been partitioned between a State railway and the private Netherlands Railway; they were combined as the state-owned Nederlandse Spoorwegen (NS) in 1938. Spanish railway operation was dominated by four companies, which survived considerable financial strains until the depredations of the Spanish Civil War made a State takeover ineluctable in 1943, when the national system, RENFE, was created.

France had been trying to edge its railways into full state ownership since the Franco-Prussian war of 1870, which had ruthlessly exposed the weaknesses of fragmented railway management in a transportation crisis. In 1883 the railways were in fact taken halfway down the nationalization road by new financial contracts which made them effectively operating tenants of state-owned assets. But this arrangement benefited the companies so handsomely that in the early 1900s the most enterprising of them headed the European railway profitability table, with an average operating ratio – that is, of expenditure to income – of only 53 per cent. The war shattered such profitability. No company was financially unscathed, but those that had been in the front line were ravaged. Enactment of an eight-hour working day in 1919 and its corollary of a requirement for additional staff squeezed their resources still more. Inevitably the companies reacted by depressing wages, whereat many of their railwaymen attempted a national strike to secure nationalization. But the effort was ineffectual because most workers in the war-devastated areas rejected the strike call, worried that a rail stoppage would be disastrous for the revival of normal working life in their neighbourhoods. Shy of taking the final nationalization step, the Government patched over this

economic crisis in 1921 by requiring the more affluent and less severely war-damaged railways to siphon off a higher proportion of their profits into a sinking fund for the aid of the less fortunate systems. Together with increased state subsidies this system held up until the end of the 1920s, when erosion of rail traffic by road transport drove every company into steadily worsening deficit.

In the first half of the 1930s France as a whole was beset by grave economic and political crisis. With one Radical Government after another tottering at intervals of a few months, in 1933–4 President Lebrun summoned one of his predecessors, Doumergue, to form an administration of National Unity. Granted sweeping powers by the French Assembly to reform the country's economy, Doumergue attacked the railways' drain of the Exchequer by cutting 5–10 per cent off railwaymen's pensions and wages, and by decreeing a co-ordination of road and rail transport that aimed to shut some 6,000 miles (9,656 km) of the secondary and branch lines so fecklessly built under the Frey-cinet Plan of the late 1870s to link every town of Prefecture or Sous-Prefecture status in the country with a standard-gauge track. The powers which had been enacted in 1921 to raise fares and freight rates if the railways fell into deficit, on the other hand, this and later Governments refused to exercise throughout the 1930s, even though French charges were below the European average as well as lagging behind the general price index. No French politician dared to prejudice industrial recovery from the decade's global depression.

Evidence of the 1923 Grouping of Britain's railways the newborn LMS tries one of the Lancashire & Yorkshire Railway's four-cylinder Hughes 4-6-0s, No 1674, seen heading out of Euston past Kenton, as front-rank power for Anglo-Scottish expresses.

Pride of the Caledonian
Railway's West Coast Anglo-
Scottish Route power was the
graceful inside-cylinder
McIntosh 'Cardean' 4-6-0, of
which five were built in 1905:
No 903 *Cardean* herself
descends Beattock bank with
a southbound express.

**British Express Passenger Steam
at the end of World War I**

Above:
The North Eastern Railway
favoured 4-4-2s for its front-
rank express duties: one of
Worsdell's Class V, No 698,
takes water from Wiske Moor
troughs heading a Newcastle–
Liverpool express.

Left:
The London & North
Western's biggest – and not
conspicuously successful –
type was the four-cylinder
'Claughton' 4-6-0, of which
130 were built between 1913
and 1921: No 5908 *Alfred
Fletcher* heads a Belfast boat
train past Kenton in early
LMS days.

Above:
Most of the companies soon to be merged into the Southern Railway relied exclusively on four-coupled express passenger power: No 163, one of the South Eastern & Chatham's bigger-boilered 1919-20 rebuilds of a 1905-9 design, heads a Kent Coast express out of London.

Above left:
Between 1917 and 1920 J. G. Robinson built six four-cylinder 4-6-0s for the Great Central: No 1167 *Lloyd George* takes a Marylebone–Manchester express through the London suburbs.

Left:
Churchward's first mass-production 4-6-0 design for the GWR was the two-cylinder 'Saint': No 2904 *Lady Godiva* storms through Twyford with a Paddington-Plymouth express.

The co-ordination plan soon faltered, for reasons to be discussed in Chapter 5, and the administrations which succeeded Doumergue's were too harassed on other economic fronts to coerce the delinquents. So the railways plummeted deeper into deficit, which was drastically inflated when a discontented nation voted Leon Blum's Popular Front into office in 1936. This coalition of the Left immediately launched a new order of management-worker relationships which was easier to envisage than to implement. For the railways the first outcome was an enforced and very costly recruitment of 50,000 more staff through the institution of the 40-hour week and a 6 hours 40 minutes working day as a move to mop up unemployment. By the start of 1937 only two companies were managing to cover even direct train running costs with revenue: one was the Nord, the other the PO-Midi, the amalgam of two companies which had to all intents and purposes merged in 1934 to gain some relief from financial exhaustion. Under a left-wing Government nationalization was the predictable next step, and an easily achievable one under the powers which the

Popular Front regime had arrogated to itself to combat the effects of the economic depression. It was executed in August 1937 by Blum's successor, Chautemps, and the Société des Chemins de Fer Francais (SNCF) came into being at the start of 1938.

US railroads, their reputations scarred by their subjection of efficient national service to profiteering during the Spanish-American war of 1898, had taken tentative steps to co-ordinate their operation when European demand for US-manufactured war supplies applied the first pressures. Inhibited by anti-trust legislation and duty to their shareholders, however, they had done little more than identify an agenda when the country entered the war in April 1917. At that time, under legislation passed in 1916, a Railroads War Board of railroad chiefs, akin to Britain's Railway Executive Committee but with fewer members, was formed with a mandate to mould the railroads into a continent-wide network operationally. But the Board lacked the executive teeth to impose its will on individual managements, who were apprehensive that hard-won traffic surrendered to a rival route in the

Robinson's sturdy heavy freight 2-8-0 design for the Great Central Railway, premiered in 1911, was selected as a standard, war-theatre type by the British Ministry of Munitions: over 500 were built, many of which returned from France to serve on other railways than the GCR, like No 3031, still in GWR service on a Hereford-bound freight in 1952.

name of wartime efficiency might never be retrieved when peace returned. Thus shortages of freight cars which were already worrying as tonnage climbed 14 per cent above any previous year's total in 1916 had by 1917 become critical. In November 1917 wagonloads delayed for lack of vehicles to shift them topped 158,000, the equivalent of a 1,170-mile-long (1,883 km) train; moreover, locomotives were in short supply, fixed plant was running down and staff were restive over poor pay. To cap it all, an abnormally severe blast of winter weather hit the country just before Christmas and more than one railroad's service threatened to disintegrate.

On 26 December President Wilson ordered a Government takeover, effective as early as 28 December. A United States Railroad Administration (USRA) was formed and intelligent controls were rapidly enforced – but not without a sensible first step towards improvement of staff wages and working conditions. Railroads were compelled to send freight by the shortest route to destination, both to ease congestion and also to secure more productive use of locomotives and rolling stock, so as to solve some of the scarcity problems. Operating capacity was also increased by drastic rationalization of passenger services, which the railroads had been expanding to reap the dollars on offer from a rising market. Rail passenger traffic had grown by 12 per cent in 1916 alone, and in 1918 it climbed a further 8 per cent, but as a result of USRA's action that increase had to be satisfied by an operation totalling some 67 million fewer passenger-train miles (107·8 million km) than in 1917, a cut of about 10 per cent. Besides formulat- a range of standard locomotive designs which all railroads were told to accept rather than build their own, USRA also instituted common practice in several other areas of equipment and maintenance.

US railroads' financial as well as physical exhaustion by the war effort was aggravated by the size of USRA's wage award and its attendant changes in working conditions. That, plus rapid inflation of material costs and USRA's reluctance to permit a rate increase until June 1918, kept the railroads $900 millions short of covering their operating costs from revenue in the 26 months of USRA's rule. Consequently in 1920 their average operating ratio had deteriorated to a perilous 94·3 per cent, compared with 70·4 per cent in 1917. And the Government's compensation for wear and tear, when it was eventually disgorged after protracted haggling, totalled only $222 millions compared with claims aggregating $677 millions. To rescue the most impoverished companies as well as to preserve the patently efficient practices enforced by USRA

the railroad unions sought support for public ownership, but public opinion was more impressed by the railroad managements' emphatic opposition to the idea. So in March 1920 the railroads were returned to full private control and sent on their way with licence to raise their charges substantially (their freight rates by as much as 40 per cent in the case of Eastern railroads). And with alacrity all the unifying work of USRA was undone.

As for the defeated Powers, the terms of the 1919 Treaty of Versailles were draconian. The national Reichsbahn in which Germany's 1920 Weimar Constitution vested the country's railways was much less than the sum of the pre-war State systems. The 1,224 miles (1,970 km) of railway in Alsace-Lorraine had to be returned to France, confronting the French with an operating problem, as they had been methodically reorganized and resignalled for German righthand running; the French ultimately built some flying junctions as the least expensive way to pass trains unchecked to and from the adjoining areas where left-hand working was standard. Over 2,940 miles (4,731 km) in the east had to be ceded to Poland; the Belgians took almost 100 miles (161 km) in Eupen and Malmédy, the Danes over 150 miles (241 km) in Schleswig. Besides being obliged to surrender sufficient locomotives and rolling stock to operate these reclaimed railways the Germans had to make good all the Allied equipment they had appropriated (and in most cases run into total disrepair) or destroyed. Claims under the latter totalled no fewer than 5,000 locomotives, 15,000 passenger coaches and 135,000 freight wagons. Every item the Germans surrendered in restitution had to be of the latest design, in perfect order. Allied inspectors at the handover points made sure the locomotives fulfilled the specification by putting them through trial runs. The bulk of these transactions was not completed until 1920 because a certain amount of the material offered was rejected. The final reshuffle was not approved until 1924.

Desperately short of quality equipment and of coal, and with a good deal of its fixed plant decrepit, the Reichsbahn started life with a rail system close to operational collapse in many areas. But recovery of German industry was a high priority and restoration of railway efficiency was deemed to be its pre-requisite; thus large-scale railway investment was quickly put in hand. At the same time rail freight rates and fares were pegged for industry's benefit, so that by 1923 the Reichsbahn was spending a phenomenal seven times as much as it was earning. Unification of the system and its urgent need of new traction and rolling stock were a stimulus to make the

most of such an opportunity by perfecting new technology. That was how the Reichsbahn was soon surefootedly on course to its dominant mid-1930s standing in world rail practice and performance. However, the prodigality of German rail investment was tamed in the second half of the 1920s. After the nation's 1922 default on reparations payments and the succeeding Franco-Belgian seizure of its industrial heartland in the Rühr, which precipitated the 1923 collapse of the Deutschmark to a billionth of its par value, the railways were one of the German activities put under a lien by the Dawes Plan. The Reichsbahn was taken out of supreme German control, turned into a limited company – the Reichsbahn Gesellschaft – under the supreme authority of a Reparations Commission, forced to make an annual contribution to reparations payments and compelled to raise its charges substantially so that this obligation would be covered. The Reichsbahn was not returned to exclusive German management until 1930.

The railway system most drastically reformed by the Allied Powers was without question the Austrian. The Versailles Treaty's restructure of the Central and South-East European map sheared away no less than 72 per cent of the pre-war Austrian rail mileage; and with it went an equivalent amount of locomotives and rolling stock. The rump of the Austrian system was left so denuded of equipment that even in 1920 it could not muster more than 10 express trains daily into and out of the seven termini which Vienna still boasted in those days. The wretched Viennese were often condemned to wait a whole day for a seat on a long-distance train; and when their turn did finally come it would like as not be for a place in an archaic

four-wheeler in a deplorable state of decay, stripped of its lighting, most windows smashed and seats crumbling, since all the best vehicles had been sequestered for the transferred territories. At the start of the 1920s it was recognized that the pillage of Austrian equipment had been overdone and an equitable number of locomotives and vehicles was returned, though the majority were in a miserable state. The need was so critical that few were given more than make-do-and-mend treatment before they were put back into Austrian traffic, while the precarious state of the national economy with an inflation rate little less astronomical than Germany's (the railways' freight rates in 1924 were nominally 16,800 times those of 1914!) deferred any new construction until 1923.

The contraction of the Austrian railway system posed problems of re-orientation that would take decades of heavy investment and engineering to solve. They were to be aggravated by the further territorial adjustments following the Second World War, and they still handicap the Austrians in the 1980s. Under the Austro-Hungarian Empire the railway network had developed along a north and north-east to south axis with Vienna at the center; now the focus was primarily east to west, a flow to which the railway facilities of Vienna itself were particularly ill-suited. Main lines, such as the Arlberg, built as single-track would now be confronted with traffic flows far heavier than had been envisaged before the war; in contrast, other once vital arterial routes had been made irremediably unviable not only by truncation but because that surgery had severed them from their main sources of industrial freight. Hopelessly crippled by loss of main-line mileage was

To make good its post-war loss of indigenous coal sources the Austrian Federal Railway (OBB) electrified: this is a modern scene on the Semmering route, with a double-headed freight fronted by the OBB's latest Bo-Bo type, the Class 1044.

the Südbahn. This was the last of Austria's privately-owned railways, which alone had fended off the State Railways' pre-war bid to rule a nationwide system. Its woes compounded by serious wartime damage, the Südbahn was now sliding into bankruptcy. Concerned to preserve untroubled through rail routes to South-Eastern Europe, the Allied Powers tried to restore at least its operating authority over the full extent of its pre-war main-line domain. But Austria's neighbours refused. Months of haggling culminated in 1923 agreement to partition the Südbahn between the Italian, Yugoslavian and Austrian State Railways. The Hungarian sector of the railway, however, was allowed to preserve an independent existence as the Danube–Save–Adriatic Railway until 1932.

The Austrian State Railway was run as a Government department and thus a prey both to political manipulation and stultifying bureaucracy. This was no sort of a régime to grapple effectively with the system's grievous post-war problems and under Allied prodding Austria reconstituted its railway administration in October 1923 as a separate, commercially-oriented undertaking, though one with considerable statutory obligations. Titled the Austrian Federal Railway (OBB), it took official control at the start of 1924.

Amongst all the other Versailles Treaty deprivations Austria had been cut off from its previously indigenous sources of good-quality steam coal. That deprivation, together with belief that another form of traction would enlarge single-track operating capacity sufficiently to avoid the dauntingly expensive and difficult double-tracking of its mountain pass routes, determined the OBB to pursue electri-

fication. By 1935 it had converted four main lines that had become key trunk routes since the war: the Arlberg, the Brenner, the Salzkammergut and the Tauern. The conversion from Salzburg to the Brenner Pass took the OBB's 15kV single-phase ac up to the fringe of the Italians' 3kV three-phase ac catenary. These days Austrian or German electric locomotives can be exchanged for Italian 3kV dc power (conversion from three-phase ac reached the pass in 1965) in the Brenner station without technical difficulty. In the 1930s the two systems could not be brought into such close contact. The OBB therefore installed a Brennersee station only a mile (1·6 km) short of the pass on the Austrian side at which, absurdly, international trains had to undergo a cumbersome changeover to steam for the last, short climb to the frontier.

The OBB was never out of the financial wood during the inter-war period. Its financial fragility was underlined in 1933 when the slump drove it to the crisis point of paying its men their month's wages in instalments. A procession of experts from Britain, the League of Nations and elsewhere were invited to study and advise how the system might be reshaped for greater stability, but none had any inspired solution to the fundamental problem. How could a railway that was once some 28,750 miles (46,267 km) in extent, the third largest in Europe, but now reduced to 4,150 miles (6,679 km), quickly and at endurable cost be re-adapted to a traffic pattern its original builders had never foreseen? In essence the question still confronts the OBB of the 1980s.

5

PASSENGER TRAVEL BETWEEN THE WARS

US RAILROADS WERE THE FIRST to feel the full draught of new forms of overland transportation. The wind had been gathering since 1908, when Henry Ford unveiled his Model T. Once he had devised for its production an assembly-line system which began rolling in 1914, the days of the railroad's monopoly were numbered. The price of a new auto tumbled to less than $400 within three years, bringing purchase within the means of a far wider bracket of the population and setting up a strident clamour nationwide for decent roads on which to drive. With almost 5 million autos already active by 1917, Congress had to launch a Federal highway programme and the stage was set for the motor age. The air age too was in sight, though it would not open fully until the 1930s, for the US Post Office launched a Washington–New York air mail service as early as 1918.

Despite the spectacular growth of rail freight traffic from the 1890s onwards, passengers still generated about a quarter of the railroads' income in 1916, the peak year for volume of American rail travel. Some railroad men were not ecstatic at this ratio. They resented the pas-senger as a nuisance who occupied track space which could be put to more lucrative use for the booming freight business. The most prestigious of them was the Great Northern and Northern Pacific empire-builder James J. Hill, who excoriated the passenger train as the equivalent of the male teat – 'neither useful nor ornamental'. Even in 1916 no more than 2 per cent of all kinds of business traveller were using other than trains for inter-city journeys. The more affluent of them were riding the plush all-parlour trains that made the news, but the great mass of commercial and pleasure travel was by ordinary train, which was much slower-paced than contemporary European expresses and more basically furnished, or by electric interurban. These were the people whom the Model T and, from the early 1920s, new inter-city bus services exploiting the Federal highways began to seduce.

During the 1920s the US population increased by 13·5 per cent, but the railroads' aggregate passenger-mileage and passenger revenue slumped 42–43 per cent. At the end of the decade Americans were doing five times as much travel in their family auto as by train and the picture

Day travel in a US Pullman, here on the Santa Fe, in the 1920s: by night upper berth beds were let down from the cupboard recesses above the seats.

grew bleaker still as the Great Depression followed the Wall Street crash of 1929. Worse still for the long-term future of the American passenger train was the effect of dwindling business on profits; by 1929 the average operating ratio of the railroads' passenger operation – that is, direct running costs in relation to revenue, excluding fixed costs – had regressed to an unhealthy 90 per cent, whereas in sharp contrast the freight ratio had been slightly improved to 67 per cent. Earliest sufferers were the electric interurban railways. Since the turn of the century they had exploded to a national route-length of 15,580 miles (25,073 km). As late as 1916 one major interurban promoter had believed that 'the fad of automobile riding will gradually wear off and the time will soon be here when a very large part of the people will cease to think of automobile rides.' But some 4,000 interurban miles (6,437 km) were driven out of business in the 1920s and 5,000 miles (8,047 km) more in the Depression years; at the outbreak of the Second World War fewer than 3,000 miles (4,828 km) survived and most of these would be eliminated by 1960.

The main-line railroads took it all pretty complacently in the 1920s. A few branch lines were shut and timetables thinned here and there, but it took realization that the new inter-city buses had seized a quarter of the mass market and the threat to their premium-fare business of the country's first scheduled air service in 1927, between New York and Boston, to prod the companies into new enterprise. One obvious course of action was to better the lot of the non-Pullman customer, the coach-class passenger. Some crack, previously-all Pullman trains in the Eastern US such as the 'Pennsylvania Limited' and 'Wolverine' were made mixed Pullman-and-coach formations. That started a trend which culminated, in June 1949, in the adulteration of the country's last surviving all-Pullman, the New Haven's New York–Boston 'Merchants Limited', an exclusive travelling club for the Brahmins of Boston banking and stockbroking which offered eight different and highly select vintages of champagne on its wine list. The standards of coach-class accommodation on long-haul trains were smartly improved. Bench seats were superseded by individually-backed furniture and as early as 1932 the Chesapeake & Ohio, in its new Washington–Cincinnati 'George Washington', was courting the coach-class trade with a spacious two-and-one open saloon layout in well-upholstered seating that was barely distinguishable from the comfort bought for a Pullman supplement elsewhere in the train. By then, moreover, air-conditioning was coming into vogue, pioneered by the Baltimore & Ohio, and coach-class passengers were getting the use of observation cars, previously the prerogative of Pullman travellers.

The coach-class passenger was shown the ultimate respect in 1935, when Union Pacific premiered the country's first all-coach-class transcontinental with sleeper accommodation, the Chicago–Los Angeles 'Challenger'. Besides benefiting from a schedule as fast as that of the crack 'Los Angeles Limited', 'Challenger' customers had full air-conditioning. They were served with three table d'hôte meals daily for an all-in price of only 90 cents, supplied with free pillows if they had not bought space in the special tourist-fare sleeping cars, and finally cherished with a car reserved as a retreat for mothers and their children, where the first railway stewardess-nurse service was available. This highly successful venture soon prompted the UP to put on a companion 'San Francisco Challenger'.

None too soon, the railroads also began to resume the accelerations which the war had snuffed out. Never mind the burgeoning air competition, the bus lines were now claiming to make Chicago from New York within 27 hours, far more cheaply than the train, whereas the New York Central had not budged since the war from a best timing of 20 hours between the two cities. At last, in 1932, that was pulled back to 18 hours, but only for the Central's and Pennsylvania's crack 'Twentieth Century' and 'Broadway Limited'. Because a $10 supplementary fare was levied on these flag trains the railroads tried for a time to peg the rest of the New York–Chicago service to schedules three hours slower, but the competitive pressures of the coach-class market soon forced them to close the gap by

Above:
Lunch is served in the diner of one of the Baltimore & Ohio's 'Limiteds' in 1924.

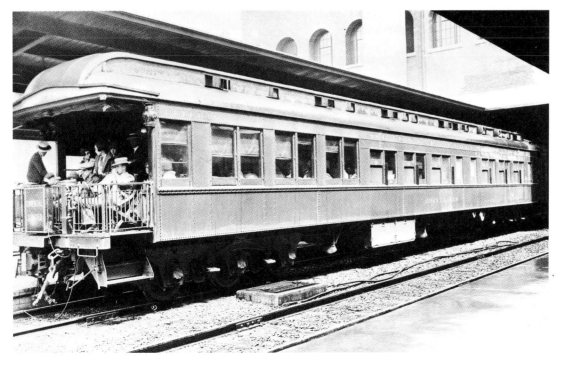

Left:
The open-ended observation car of the Great Northern's transcontinental 'Oriental Limited' in 1922: besides the rear-end lounge and buffet the vehicle housed a smoking/card room and four compartments.

The Baltimore & Ohio
pioneered air-conditioning in
its Baltimore–Washington
and Chicago 'Capitol
Limited' train-sets of 1932, of
which this was a diner: note
the pseudo Hepplewhite
chairs and Sheraton
sideboard (at the car's rear)
and the ornate Georgian-
style leaded windows.

stages to just one hour. The eastern railroads as a whole reacted much more defensively to the slump than those to the west, especially in the curtailment of their timetables. Consolidation of previously separate services into single, all-purpose trains had proud expresses like the New York Central's 'Commodore Vanderbilt' making extra stops at numerous small towns in New York State, Indiana and Ohio, while on the same railroad's Detroit–Windsor–Buffalo route conductors complained that it was impossible to check tickets satisfactorily on combined trains frequently running to a length of 20–23 cars (and a load of as much as 1,400–1,600 tons – 1,423–1,626 tonnes, incidentally).

Nor would the eastern railroads countenance any reduction of the coach-class fare to counter-act the recession's drain of traffic until 1936. Then, under pressure of the Baltimore & Ohio, it was dropped from the high rate of 3·6 cents a mile (1·6 km) set in 1920 to 2 cents. Whereupon the gross passenger revenues of the five big eastern systems climbed 16 per cent over the next three years.

In 1933 only 43 US trains were timed over any part of their journeys at average speeds in excess of 60 mph (97 km) start-to-stop. The table was headed by a couple of 64·5 mph (103·8 km/h) sprints over a mere 11·9 miles (19·2 km) between stops on the Camden–Atlantic City route in

New Jersey, where the Reading Railroad was sustaining the traditions of an express service that had been easily the world's fastest at the turn of the century. The continent's fastest trains in 1933 were to be sampled in Canada. There Canadian Pacific and Canadian National were battling it out for the Montreal–Toronto traffic with speed – Canadian Pacific's 4–6–4s were being asked to hustle 550–600 ton (559–610 tonne) trains over the 124 miles (200 km) from Smith's Falls to Montreal West in 108 minutes for a start-to-stop average of 68·9 mph (110·9 km/h). But the Canadian companies called a truce that same year, pooling their traffic and easing their exacting schedules substantially.

In the US a new inter-city rail era, both in style and in speed, dawned the following spring, on 26 May 1934, when a sleekly streamlined, diesel-powered three-car unit winged across the continent from Denver to Chicago non-stop at an average of 77·6 mph (124·9 km/h) for the entire 1,015·4 miles (1,634·1 km). The implications of this prototype's – the 'Pioneer Zephyr' – exploit for world rail traction are discussed in the following chapter. Here we note only its transformation of the US inter-city and long-haul passenger train.

The state of the diesel engine art in the mid-1930s dictated that the first streamliners be short, self-powered train-sets designed with overriding

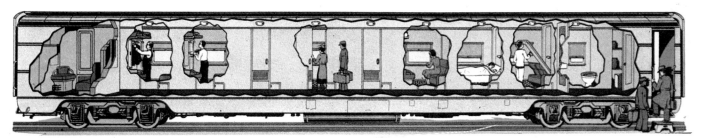

Above:
Two of the types of sleeping accommodation available in the Pullmans of US 'Limiteds' in the mid-1930s.

Left:
The changing style of the 'Limited' interior: one of the lounge-bar cars styled by Henry Dreyfuss for the 'Twentieth Century Limited' of 1938.

Top:
The 'Los Angeles Challenger'
of Union Pacific crosses Utah
in 1940 behind 4-8-2 No 7023.

Above:
The steam 'Limited' becomes
the steam 'streamliner': the
Pennsylvania 'Broadway

Limited' of 1938 heads out of
Chicago behind a Class K4s
Pacific specially styled by
Raymond Loewy.

Another example of 1930s steam streamlining: Chesapeake & Ohio's 'Fast Flying Virginian' hurries through Kentucky behind a streamlined 4-6-4 rebuilt from a Pacific.

concern for light weight so as to keep a high average speed up and down gradients within the power plant's capacity. By November 1936, however, the pioneering Chicago Burlington & Quincy was operating the makings of a locomotive-hauled train in its new 'Denver Zephyr' sets, where the power plant was concentrated in a 3,000 hp twin-unit fronting ten passenger cars. In these new streamliners, which were set a daily 16-hour overnight schedule between Chicago

and Denver that dramatically clipped almost 10 hours from the previous best steam timing, the accommodation hinted at the splendours to come. An Art Deco-style cocktail bar supplemented the elegant diner; there was a wide choice of sleeping accommodation (the first in any train to be equipped with electric razor points); and the formation was tailed by a spacious observation car.

Canadian National 4-6-4 No 5701 pulls out of Montreal with an express for Chicago via Toronto and Detroit.

The diesel 'Pioneer Zephyr' on its stunning Chicago–Denver non-stop run of 26 May 1934.

By 1937 General Motors' evolution of the main-line diesel locomotive was well advanced and the head-end power available to cope with updated, high-speed versions of the sumptuous steam limiteds. In the spring of 1937 Santa Fe unveiled the country's first all-Pullman diesel streamliner and the most celebrated transcontinental of all, the Chicago–Los Angeles 'Super-Chief'. Built, like the 'Zephyrs', by Budd, and thoughtfully designed within by a group of eminent architects and stylists, its restaurant, observation lounge, bar and wide choice of overnight accommodation – every room richly panelled in wood veneers from the four quarters of the world – were very reasonable replicas of the hotel accommodation to which the Hollywood *haut monde* who frequented it were accustomed.

So was the train-board service, especially in the diner. 'Bedsheet-size menus printed in turquoise blue and gold,' to quote the late Lucius Beebe, 'listed Guaymas shrimps, limestone lettuce, out-of-season strawberries, Cranshaw melon, Rocky Mountain trout, Westphalia hams, Mexican quail in aspic, fresh caviar (for just $1.75!) and rare cheeses from France and Holland . . . Dinner-jacketed *maitres d'hotel* confected *omelette aux confitures* at table for John Ford and the Contessa di Frasso and as many breakfasts were served in bed as in the diner.' The champagne list was not content with Veuve Clicquot, Mumms Extra Dry and Bollinger, but 'for the extra fastidious and well-heeled' ran to Dom Perignon Cuvée too.

It was the railroads of the West like Santa Fe, Burlington, Union Pacific, Chicago & North Western and Southern Pacific, followed by those of the south, which set the new diesel streamliner trend in the later 1930s. And their enterprise paid off. A consultancy which analyzed the performance of 70 of the new high-speed diesel trains in 1938 found that all of them had stimulated new business and generated substantially more net revenue than their steam predecessors. Top of the league were the Burlington's 'Denver Zephyrs', which were chalking up a surplus as high as 75 per cent of their direct running costs, but the 'City of San Francisco', a joint Union Pacific-Chicago & North Western-Southern Pacific exercise, was running the 'Zephyrs' close.

Striking evidence of the instant appeal of the new streamliners, even at the top end of the

market, came from Santa Fe. Inaugurated as a once-weekly transcontinental, its 'Super-Chief' had taken $238,580 gross in its first six months. Early in 1938 inexorably rising demand had compelled the railroad to step up frequency to twice weekly and in the first half of that year the train's takings had leapt to over $488,000 gross. In 1938, incidentally, Santa Fe also complemented the 'Super-Chief' with the all-coach 'El Capitan' on a similar schedule. Lucrative as the streamliners proved in the chief inter-city corridors and on the main transcontinental routes they could not redress the losses on US passenger operation as a whole. All the improvements did was to stop further rot and hold the overall deficit on total costs at around $250 millions a year from 1936 up to Pearl Harbor. Even in the streamliners the railroads were storing up trouble for the future. The more elaborately they furnished the trains and the more lavish the on-board service they presented, the more daunting they would find both renewal and staffing costs in the post-war inflationary era. Even in 1937 similarly lucullan standards of on-train catering to those described for the 'Super-Chief' were running the Pennsylvania

into an annual loss on its dining cars of more than $1 million. In 1949 the deficit in this department was four times as debilitating.

A new dimension was added to North American streamliner travel in 1945 with the creation of the 'Vista-dome', a bi-level car with a raised lounge beneath an elevated, glass-panelled cowl that gave the occupants uninterrupted overhead and panoramic viewing of the scenery. A General Motors executive riding a diesel's cab through the Rockies had the inspiration, but the enterprising company which had Budd build the first versions for public service was again the Burlington.

In its ultimate development during the early 1950s the 'Vista-dome' became the 'Super-Dome', a 100-ton (102 tonne) mammoth in which the glazed-roof upper saloon extended the full length of the car. In the version applied to the Great Northern's 'Empire Builder' in 1955 the upper floor of the 'Super-Dome' seated 74 on settees angled towards the side-windows for comfortable viewing; the lower floor housed an enticing 35-seater lounge-bar and writing-room, conveniently linked by electric dumb-waiter with the solarium above for drinks and snacks

The rapid advance of the diesel streamliner: Union Pacific's 'City of Denver', introduced in 1936 with two 1200-hp power units on a 16-hour, 8-stop schedule between Chicago and Denver', 1,048 miles (1,687 km) – the country's fastest over such a distance – had as early as 1939 swollen to a format of three power cars and 12 cars.

service at both levels. The history of the Chicago–Portland and Seattle 'Empire Builder' in the late 1940s and 1950s exemplifies the huge burdens of amortization and staff costs which the railroads were accumulating as they strove to defend their business from each other as well as rival modes of transport. The first post-war re-equipment of the train in 1947 – five train-sets were needed to provide a daily transcontinental service – set the Great Northern and its Burlington partner back $7 millions; only four years later another end-to-end re-equipment was deemed necessary at a cost of $12 millions; and then the 1955 purchase of six full-length domes added $6 millions more to the 'Empire Builder's' post-war capital account.

At that juncture the 'Empire Builder' was a 15-car train grossing more than 1,100 tons (1,118 tonnes), but with room for only 323 passengers because of its lavish provision of observation lounge, dome lounge, coffee-shop, bar, dining space and selection of sleeping space. To serve the maximum payload of fare-paying customers the train carried a staff of 25, and that figure excludes the numerous locomotive crews employed to satisfy union agreements prescribing only 150 miles' (241 km) driving as the limit of a day's work at basic rates.

Top:
Diesel debut on Santa Fe's 'Super-Chief': two Electro-Motive 1,800-hp diesel-electric demonstration Bo-Bos bring the train into Pasadena, California on 14 May 1936.

Above:
In the 1950s the 'Super Chief's' many luxuries included a private diner, the Turquoise Room, on the lower floor of one of the train's dome cars.

The momentum of acceleration set off by the first diesel trains was phenomenal. It was not checked by Pearl Harbor and barely restrained even in 1943, when US railroads were overwhelmed by troop and war material movement. One operating theory maintained that the faster the passenger trains could be got over the road, the longer tracks would be clear for freight traffic.

In the mid-1930s the three railroads competing between Chicago and St Paul, for instance – the Chicago & North Western, Burlington and Milwaukee – each ran only one fast train each way daily in either direction on a timing of about $9\frac{1}{4}$ hours for the 409 or 428 miles (658 or 689 km) according to route, whereas in 1949 the trio were operating a total of seven diesel streamliners in each direction averaging only 6 hours 29 minutes for the journey. By the mid-1950s US timetables were offering over 160,000 miles (257,488 km) of daily start-to-stop timings at 60 mph (97 km/h) and more, involving 3,264 different trains. The list was headed by the world's fastest schedule of 41 minutes for 57·7 miles (92·9 km) in the flat terrain of the Mid-West between Prairie du Chien and La Crosse which the Burlington set for the 'Twin Cities Zephyr' and the 'Empire Builder'. That represented a start-to-stop average speed of 84·4 mph (135·8 km/h).

Above:
The ultimate in dome cars
was the full-length dome: this
was one of Santa Fe's.

Top:
A sample of the extravagant
furnishing of the ultimate US
diesel streamliners: the
ranch-style coffee-lounge bar
of Great Northern's 'Empire
Builder'.

In Europe it was the resumption of luxury train service development which attracted most attention in the 1920s. Early in the decade a handful of trains on either side of the English Channel just managed to crack the 60 mph (97 km/h) average speed barrier between stops, but the majority of the fastest trains in Britain were timed at a mean speed of only 50–55 mph (81–89 km/h), those on the European mainland slightly less. By the end of the decade these averages had been lifted a mere 5 mph (8 km/h) or so, though in the summer of 1929 Britain's Great Western Railway had grasped the ease with which it could seize the world's blue ribbon on Brunel's superbly engineered main line from Swindon to Paddington and had pushed up the timing of an otherwise unremarkable afternoon train from Cheltenham to Paddington to a 66·1 mph (106·4 km/h) average over these 77·3 almost level miles (124·4 km).

British railways did more than those on the Continent to democratize their express passenger timetables in the 1920s. As early as 1922, Birmingham was accessible from London by two routes, the GWR and LNWR, offering a total of 30 weekday trains with a combined average speed of just under 55 mph (89 km/h) throughout, whereas over a French route of comparable distance, between Paris and Troyes, the Est Railway scheduled only 11 trains averaging 50 mph (81 km/h) between them. The Est ran 10 trains between Paris and Basle, 326·3 miles (525·1 km), at an average of 38·2 mph (61·5 km/h), but the traveller from London to Carlisle could pick from a total of 27 over 299–304 miles (481–489 km), according to route, and their combined average speed was 46·4 mph (74·7 km/h). Another significant Anglo-French contrast of 1922 was in the provision of train catering. In that year one could count 556 daily restaurant car operations in the British timetables. In France, where the Wagons-Lits company had the exclusive dining-car concession, a level of cuisine was fashioned mostly for the upper end of the travel market and priced accordingly; as a result, restaurant cars were listed for only 158 daily trains.

The success of the Wagons-Lits company and the stimulus to expand its operation was patent, however, in the breadth of its sleeping-car operation in France. None of the British companies running overnight from London to the North offered a service to compare with that of the PLM. Every night the PLM was despatching 14 sleeping-car trains from Paris Gare de Lyons to the Riviera, the Alps and Italy.

From December 1922 those Gare de Lyons departures included a train that heralded the new, inter-war style of the European *train de luxe*, the 'Paris–Mediterranean'. This and its companion, the 'Calais–Mediterranean', simultaneously inaugurated to cater for the still prodigious market for premium-fare travel from Britain to the mainland, were the debutants of the Wagons-Lits company's first all-steel sleeping cars, liveried in gold-lined dark blue instead of the previous wooden-bodied cars' teak. Each car embodied both single and two-berth compartments – exclusively first-class on this prestigious service – which were exquisitely finished internally with mahogany panelling that extended to the lavatories; in some of those built adjoining pairs of rooms shared an intervening dressing-room with wash-basin, which left room in each compartment for a comfortable armchair facing the berths. The status of travel by Wagons-Lits *train de luxe* in the 1920s, the natural medium for European diplomats to go about their business and for the nobility and *nouveaux-riches* to take their vacationing pleasure, was obvious from the glittering company which assembled on Nice station to greet the first arrivals of the new trains. Everyone who counted in the Côte d'Azur's administration was mobilized as a matter of course, but the Crown Prince of Sweden and the Duke of Connaught, wintering on the coast at the time, joined many of the Riviera society's élite who felt it incumbent on them to repair to the station of their own accord to salute the incoming trains. The external colour of the new cars quickly earned these new trains the tag by which they are far better known, 'Train Bleu', though the title was not given the official stamp until 1949.

In the depression years the Calais train contracted to just two sleepers, run to Paris in the 'Flèche d'Or' and worked from the Gare du Nord via the French capital's Ceinture line for attachment to the 'Train Bleu' at Gare de Lyons. But though its British trade declined, the 'Train Bleu' remained the acme of French travelling fashion throughout the inter-war years. In the height of the season it was an odds-on bet that at least some of the 'beautiful' people draped around the French capital's Ritz bar one night would the next be congregated in the Pullman-style lounge bar which the 'Train Bleu' acquired after a few years in service. There cocktails and gossip ritually flowed for the first hour after the train's departure from Paris before the *maître d'hôtel* deferentially beckoned guests to a six-course *tour de force* in the adjoining diner.

Pullman and Wagons-Lits, as recorded in an earlier chapter, were now intimately associated in Europe under Lord Davison Dalziel. The 1920s were marked by his energetic expansion of Pullman services, many of them as exclusively Pullman trains, on both sides of the Channel. At

Headed by a four-unit diesel
the Great Northern's 'Empire
Builder', with dome cars
conspicuous in mid-train,
negotiates the Montana
Rockies en route to the
Pacific Coast in the 1950s.

One of the most extravagant
flights of the US streamliner
train designer's flights of
fancy was the 'Little Nugget',
a pastiche of the saloon of
earlier days, in club car Union
Pacific's 1937 'City of Los
Angeles'; its decor featured a
star-studded blue ceiling, red
velvet drapes, lace curtains,
marble-topped tables,
flowered blue wallpaper, gas
chandeliers, and – to the right
of the bar – a mechanical,
warbling 'bird in a gilded
cage.'

81

Seating in the first-class
compartments of the 1938
'Flying Scotsman' was only
two-a-side, with the extra
comfort of loose cushions and
footstools.

the same time Wagons-Lits business was developed both territorially and quantitatively, in the latter case to a significant degree by the construction from 1924 of sleeping cars specifically for the second-class passengers who had been admitted to the double-berth compartments of certain services since 1919. All this had by 1925 swollen Dalziel's rolling stock resources (Britain excluded) to a total of 1,739 cars of all kinds in commission, plus a total of 179 more sleepers, 85 diners and 96 Pullmans under construction. And his companies' rail activity covered not only the greater part of Europe, but also the Middle East, North Africa and even the Far East, where the 'Trans-Siberian Express' had begun making a regular nine-day journey from Moscow to Kharbin and thence into China in 1903. The Russian Revolution of 1917 annulled that operation, with the Wagons-Lits company stripped totally uncompensated of all its rolling stock and other assets in Russia. But from 1919 it operated the 'Trans-Manchurian Express' from Tchita to Vladivostock, complementing this later with services from Harbin to Changchun and from Nanking to Peking, where it had its own hotel. At the end of the 1930s the

company was still running 20 cars in the Far East.

In Britain Pullman service developed on two principal fronts, on the LNER routes from London Kings Cross to the North and Scotland, and on the SR's lines from London to the Channel ports and the South Coast resorts. The LNER's foray into Pullman operation was rather involuntary. At its 1923 formation it inherited a stock of Pullman cars and an unexpired contract to run them from one of its constituents, the Great Eastern. The cars had been thrust on the GER by the American General Manager it appointed in 1914, Henry Thornton, who sanguinely expected the country folk of East Anglia to relish the conceits of supplementary-fare travel as eagerly as his native New Yorkers. It was a rare aberration in an otherwise brilliant railway executive. The newborn LNER naturally switched the majority of the cars to the likelier markets of its main line from Kings Cross; and by the mid-1920s it had found them a commercially rewarding niche in the timetables from Kings Cross to the West Riding, Newcastle, Edinburgh and Glasgow as the 'Queen of Scots' and the 'West Riding Pullman'

82

(renamed the 'Yorkshire Pullman' from 1935). This pair of trains clung to a profitable market until the 1960s.

The prosperity of the 'Queen of Scots' was a striking testimony to the magnetism of Pullman travel in some sectors of the market. Because it was routed via Harrogate to cater for the then fashionable Yorkshire spa, it spun out far more time over its London–Edinburgh run than the 'Flying Scotsman'. Yet even when the latter was re-equipped in the 1930s with regal two-a-side first-class compartment stock and decked out with cocktail bar and hairdressing saloon the 'Queen's' regular Anglo-Scottish clientele did not decamp to the faster and arguably much more comfortable train. Opulent compartment seating and a flashy bar car were no substitute for the obsequious attention of a Pullman car crew at one's table throughout the trip.

On the European mainland the successful post-war launch of Pullman trains from Rome to Genoa/Turin, Venice/Trieste and Naples was followed by the international 'Milan–Nice Pullman', in the winter of 1925, then in 1926 of the all-Pullman 'Sud Express' making the day's journey from Paris to the Spanish frontier's

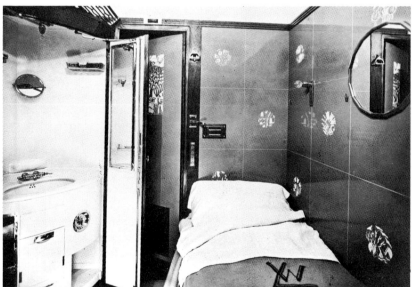

Top:
PLM 4-8-2 starts the northbound 'Calais–Mediterranean' *de luxe* train out of Menton for Paris.

Above:
A first-class Wagons-Lits berth in the 'Train Bleu' of the 1930s.

First-class Pullman travel in a Continental European *train de luxe* in the 1930s.

break-of-gauge, where passengers changed to a broad-gauge sleeping- and restaurant-car 'Sud Express' for the remainder of their journeys to Madrid or Lisbon. The next step was to link the budding Continental Pullman network with its British counterpart. That was also achieved in 1926 with the inauguration of the all-Pullman 'Flèche d'Or' between Calais and Paris and a complementary all-Pullman train between London Victoria and Dover. The latter, inscrutably, was not named 'Golden Arrow' until 1929; some say the Southern's refusal to match the French train's name immediately was pure chauvinistic antipathy to honouring a foreign enterprise, since the 'golden' epithet was a tribute to the Wagons-Lits company in its jubilee year. European timetables were sprinkled annually with a number of new Pullman trains in the remaining 1920s, though a few were short-lived commercial fiascos. Pullman train operation even extended to Egypt, where the Wagons-Lits company had had a foothold since the late nineteenth century. The successful operation of single cars during the earlier 1920s prompted the November 1929 creation of a thrice-weekly all-Pullman service, the 'Sunshine Express', between Cairo and Luxor. This built up a handsome Anglo-American tourist trade in the 1930s: the done thing was to make the round trip between the two cities by Nile steamer one way and the Pullman the other. The 'Sunshine Express' died with the Second World War, but the Wagons-Lits company was still running sleeping-cars in Egypt until the early 1960s.

The Wagons-Lits company was debarred from operating internal German services. Foiled in its post-war intrigues to destroy Mitropa, the similar company in which the Kaiser's Government had vested all Wagon-Lits' German-based vehicles and assets in 1915, it had had to be content with a spheres-of-influence pact with its rival. Besides allowing Wagons-Lits cars on international itineraries to transit the Reichsbahn, this agreement conversely permitted Mitropa to run through to Dutch, Austrian, Swiss and Scandinavian destinations. The most spectacular outcome of the latter provision was Mitropa's 1928 opening up of an alternative luxury route from England to one of the British market's most cherished holiday havens, Switzerland, via the Hook of Holland, Cologne and the Rhine Valley to Basle. Pullman-like in its concept and furnishing, the 'Rheingold' stung Wagons-Lits into a counter-attack within four weeks. The riposte was a new train also drawing its British clientele from London's Liverpool Street and Harwich, then a night boat across the North Sea: the 'Edelweiss Pullman' from Antwerp, which gained Basle via Luxembourg and Strasbourg. The Swiss Federal gave the rivals strictly impartial treatment. At Basle it amalgamated their respective Zurich and Lucerne portions into a pair of combined trains, eye-catching in their juxtaposition of the blue-and-cream mainland Pullman and purple-and-white 'Rheingold' liveries.

Behind the façade of these showy services, European railways were by now losing a worrying amount of ground in the mass travel market to road transport. Rural railways in particular were being sapped of passengers and freight. And the Germans had thrown a new shadow over the long-haul passenger business as they led Europe's air transport from purely international service into domestic inter-city operation. In the first few post-war years the German Reichsbahn's total passengers climbed almost 40 per cent to nearly 2·2 billion in 1925, but between 1925 and 1929 the graph reversed to a level of 2 billion at the decade's end. In those same four years the total of private cars and buses operating in the country soared more than 150 per cent, the number of passengers taking the bus by 250 per cent. Britain and the rest of North-West Europe reported similar trends. By the start of the 1930s most countries had taken legislative steps to protect trunk railway services from damagingly direct bus competition, though Britain and France were major exceptions; it has been reckoned that by the end of the inter-war period bus services had drained Britain's railways of over 200 million passenger journeys a year.

When the French did face up to the mounting

losses unbridled road competition was inflicting on their railways, they attempted a draconian solution. As recorded earlier, the Doumergue Government of 1934, set about a transport co-ordination programme that had the explicit aim of suppressing long-distance road freight and passenger traffic on the one hand, but on the other of yielding almost all rural movement to the road. Under the second head some 6,000 route-miles (9,656 km) of the secondary and branch lines so recklessly installed under the Freycinet Plan were to be abandoned. Raoul Dautry, the outstanding General Manager of the État Railway, got the scheme off to a quick and very promising start. Within weeks of its official promulgation he announced agreement with road interests in the Rouen-Le Havre-Dieppe area to a passenger plan providing for the take-over of traffic on 300 miles (483 km) of branch line, which would be shut down. So would nearly all intermediate stations on the main lines in the territory. That would end the senseless com-petition of slow stopping trains with, for ex-ample, three dozen daily bus services along the main road from Rouen to Le Havre. For their part, the bus operators undertook to reshape their rural operations as feeders to the surviving railheads. As to freight, French road hauliers were to be restricted to an operational orbit of about 20 miles (32 km) from the principal towns – but not at once. Dautry charitably accepted the hauliers' submission that they be allowed to carry on plying from Le Havre and Rouen to Paris, Lille, Lyons and other provincial cities

until they had amortized the capital cost of their lorry fleets.

It was a dangerous precedent, all too easily exploited to sabotage the freight side of the co-ordination plan. By the end of 1934 some 1,250 route-miles (2,012 km) of rural railways had been closed under seven Regional agreements involv-ing the État, Nord, PLM and PO-Midi Railways, but that was the limit of achievement. The rationalization of long-haul freight service was blocked by effective filibustering from the road interests, which the Government vainly tried to silence in 1935 with an unworkable proposal to transfer to each road haulier secondary rail freight to the precise value of any trunk road tonnage of his that the railways claimed to be logically theirs. Moreover, the Government itself hamstrung progress by insisting on simultan-eous, nationwide advance and refusing to endorse piecemeal such local pacts as had been struck. Local civic objection to this centrally-dictated reshaping of rural transport made the confusion even worse. And through it all the railways were still kept fettered to uneconomic fares and freight rates as one means of encourag-ing recovery from the slump.

Consequently the railways' already shattering losses in 1935 worsened by a further 15 per cent in the first half of 1936. That summer the Popular Front Government of the Left swept into power. As already recorded, its natural response was nationalization. Once that had been effected the Popular Front regime mounted a fresh co-ordination drive which resumed the transfer of rural passenger movement from rail to road in 1938. By that year's end it had also created a tarification framework which at least precluded road hauliers from selectively creaming off the railways' most lucrative freight traffics by rate-cutting. But the railways were left, as they were throughout Europe, with their unique common carrier obligations to accept all traffic offered, remunerative or not; and, of course, shouldering far more of their infrastructure costs than their rivals. As for the ambitious 1934 plan for total co-ordination, that was a dead letter. Had it been forced through, it could have been the model for an economic, rational employment inter-modally of Western Europe's overland transport resources which would have had the Continent far better prepared for the growing energy crisis of the second half of the twentieth century.

To meet the challenges of the 1930s the railways had to look for new cost-cutting methods and for improved service quality. For some – Italy especially, where Mussolini had decreed a national policy of autarchy, which amongst other things demanded less reliance on imported coal – this was a stimulus to electrify. It was also an encouragement to invest in reversible oil-engined railcars, chiefly for low-volume rural lines where their cheaper operating costs would make the most impact, but in certain cases for trunk passenger work as well; the early European development under this head is described in Chapter 6.

British railways courted the rapidly enlarging

mass market for leisure travel with cheap excursion fares. So did the Italian State system, which although a Government department seems to have had much more licence to bargain for optional business than its European mainland neighbours in the early 1930s. Seats on the Italian equivalent of the British day and half-day excursion trains to popular resorts, the *treni popolari*, were priced at only 20 per cent of the normal fare for the return journey.

The most striking passenger service developments, however, were in the quality of coaching stock infused into the standard express trains on the main trunk routes and above all in the pursuit of higher end-to-end speed. In Britain the Great Western had crossed the 70 mph (113 km/h) average speed mark in the autumn of 1932 when it recaptured the 'world's fastest train' title from Canadian Pacific by accelerating its afternoon Cheltenham–London train already mentioned, by now known as the 'Cheltenham Flyer', to cover the 77·3 miles (124·4 km) of flat country between Swindon and Paddington at a start-to-stop average of 71·4 mph (114·9 km/h). More significant for the future, though, was the number of trains on the European mainland by then being operated at little less pace over longer distances, less friendly gradients and with heavier loads. Front-runner was France's Nord Railway, which by the summer of 1933 had its chief Paris–Brussels expresses timed over the 147·7 miles (237·7 km) from Paris to Jeumont, on the threshold of Belgium, at 66·1 mph (106·4 km/h) start-to-stop, and that within a national speed

GWR 'Castle' 4-6-0 No 5006 *Tregenna Castle* sets the 'Cheltenham Flyer' rolling on its onetime world's fastest schedule from Swindon to Paddington.

limit of 75 mph (121 km/h). And in Germany the morning, steam-hauled business trains over the 178·1 miles (286·6 km) between Berlin and Hamburg were set non-stop schedules of 163 minutes eastbound and 165 minutes westbound, representing averages of 65·8 mph (105·9 km/h) and 64·8 mph (104·3 km/h) respectively.

Such disregard of major intermediate towns and cities would have been unthinkable in pre-First World War Germany. But with air travel emerging as a competitive factor, though as yet far less vexing than the cheaply-priced road coach, many railways were driven to reshape their timetables for longer non-stop runs between the principal wellsprings of their express passenger traffic. The corollary was frequently an expansion of the timetable as a whole, to provide adequate service for the towns neglected by the limited-stop trains. The world record for regular non-stop running with steam was acquired in 1928 by Britain's LNER. With the provision for its Pacifics of tenders with a slender side corridor through which, at the halfway point of the journey, an engine crew riding in the train could change places with one on the footplate, it began that year to operate its lavishly furnished 'Flying Scotsman' non-stop over the 392·8 miles (632·1 km) between Kings Cross and Edinburgh every summer.

To revert to the Berlin–Hamburg service in the summer of 1933, this was overall the fastest rail passenger operation in the world over 150 miles (241 km) or more, boasting 12 trains daily between the two cities at a combined average speed of 58·2 mph (93·7 km/h). That was largely because one train was averaging 77·4 mph (124·6 km/h) on its westbound morning run, then returning in mid-afternoon at a mean start-to-stop speed of 76·3 mph (122·8 km/h) for the 178·1 miles (286·6 km).

But not with steam power. High-speed diesel traction had taken the European stage in the shape of a 78 tonne (76·8 ton), streamlined, two-car articulated train-set, the 'Fliegende Hamburger', a title quite innocent of the burlesque its English 'Flying Hamburger' translation conjures up nowadays. And in France the fastest timing that summer was claimed by a two-car Bugatti railcar set booked to cover the 136·2 miles (219·2 km) between Paris and Deauville at an average of 68·1 mph (109·6 km/h). The following year a similar 800 hp set was scheduled over the 318·2 miles (512·1 km) between Paris and Lyons in 4 hours 50 minutes, representing an overall average speed of 65·3 mph (105·1 km/h).

The German diesel streamliners dominated the European express passenger scene in the mid-1930s. They cannot have been cheap to operate since their payload was very restricted. Even the

three-car units adopted from 1935 onwards seated only 139 in a dual-class format, but that was cut close to 100 when the diesel streamliner service was made first-class only in 1938. The seating capacity of a French Bugatti two-car set was only 81. Moreover, all routes plied by the German diesel trains had to be specially equipped with Indusi automatic train control, and the trains' operating paths meticulously protected to guarantee their punctuality.

Nevertheless, the Reichsbahn progressively interlaced all Germany's major population centers with each other and with Berlin in a network of 'Fliegende' services offering the commercial world practical out-and-home-in-day business travel possibilities. As early as 1935 the diesel streamliners held the first 13 places in the league table of the world's fastest scheduled trains.

High German speed was not the sole preserve of diesel traction in the second half of the 1930s. In 1936 the streamlined Class 05 4-6-4s which will be discussed in Chapter 7 were allocated to new morning and evening five-car trains between Berlin and Hamburg with which they had to average 73·7 mph (118·6 km/h) eastbound and 74·2 mph (119·4 km/h) westbound non-stop. And on the eve of the Second World War, when

Pullmans in Switzerland: the train combining the Lucerne portions of the 'Edelweiss Pullman' from Antwerp and of the German Mitropa company's 'Rheingold' from Hook of Holland pauses at Arth-Goldau behind a Swiss Federal 2-D+D-2 electric locomotive in 1930.

Top:
The first-class restaurant cars of the 1938 'Flying Scotsman' were decked out in Louis XIV style, with pelmeted curtains and loose individual armchairs.

Above:
Stanier streamlined Pacific No 6222 *Queen Mary* heads the Glasgow–London 'Coronation Scot' streamliner of the LMS near Preston.

the Reichsbahn set about electrifying from Munich to Berlin (a project which the war halted at Dessau), it conceived for a high-speed Munich–Leipzig–Berlin service the Class E19 1–Do–1 electric locomotive with a continuous power rating of 5,360 hp and a designed top speed of 140 mph (225 km). On test in 1939 one of the two prototypes hustled a four-car, 400 tonne (394 ton) train up to 125 mph (201 km/h) within $4\frac{3}{4}$ minutes of a standing start – but the war deprived the design of any opportunity to exploit its potential in public service.

The Berlin-Hamburg schedules set for the Reichsbahn's 05 4–6–4s excelled the best attained with British steam. So for that matter did an unexpected Belgian entry into the world speed stakes in 1939 with a service of three-car flyers hauled by a specially-built series of streamlined 6 ft $10\frac{1}{2}$ in-driving wheel (209·6 cm) Atlantics. Six years earlier the Belgians had put the finishing touches to a direct, well-aligned route from Ostend to Brussels and over the 57·4 miles (92·4 km) of it from Brussels Midi to Bruges these high-stepping 4–4–2s and their feather-weight loads were timed at a start-to-stop average of 74·9 mph (120·5 km/h).

In Britain the LNER, more addicted to singling out a few trains for spectacular acceleration than the neighbouring LMS, soon determined to adopt the Reichsbahn's model of high-speed morning and evening business service by limited-load train between major provincial cities and national capital. The German builders of the Reichsbahn's flyers were invited to offer proposals for the equipment, but not with total conviction. Apart from reservations about moving into main-line diesel traction when coal was home-produced and cheap, the LNER Board fretted that the constricted facilities of the German train-sets might affront a British business clientele by now taking for granted spacious compartments and separate restaurant car space with accompanying full kitchen. So when their Chief Mechanical Engineer, Nigel Gresley, affirmed that he could produce steam power to better the Newcastle–Kings Cross schedules envisaged in the German diesel firms' prospectus, the LNER promptly opted to build fully streamlined steam train-sets.

They were not quite the European front-runners in this genre. In 1935 the French PLM streamlined – rather grotesquely – two existing 4–4–2s of its 221A class and matched them with a pair of specially-built and aerodynamically-shaped four-car train-sets. After trials in which speeds verging on 100 mph (161 km) were logged, the two rakes were installed in public Paris–Lyons service in July 1935. But their 5-hour time allowance for the 318·2-mile (512·1 km)

An ETR 200 series electric train-set of the Italian State Railways, the type which averaged 102 mph (164 km/h) from Florence to Milan in a record-breaking run of July 1939.

journey in each direction was less adventurous than the schedules set for the streamliner which the LNER premiered just over two months later. And the French trains were unveiled with nothing like the éclat of the LNER's record-breaking streamliner launch.

The pioneer LNER train, the 'Silver Jubilee', exploded into the British headlines with a press preview on 27 September 1935 in which Gresley's inaugural streamlined Class A4 Pacific, No 2509 *Silver Link*, despatched 25 miles (40 km) on end at 100 mph (161 km/h) or more, in a burst crowned by a new British speed record of 112·5 mph (181·1 km/h). Three days later the train entered daily Newcastle–London service on a 4-hour schedule for the 268·3 miles (431·8 km) with one intermediate stop.

The 'Jubilee' was an instantaneous and continuing commercial success in terms of daily seat occupation factors. But almost certainly neither the 'Jubilee', nor its 1937 LNER complements, the Kings Cross–Edinburgh 'Coronation' – Britain's fastest-ever daily steam train, with a 71·9 mph (115·7 km/h) timing from London to York – and Kings Cross–Leeds/ Bradford 'West Riding', nor the LMS Euston–Glasgow 'Coronation Scot' ever covered out of revenue the total costs they incurred. Operation of a handful of trains at average speeds widely outstripping the pace of all other traffic was too disruptive of railway working.

The last pre-war word on rail passenger speed issued from Italy. Before the First World War travel on Italian trunk routes had been purgatorially slow. From Naples to Milan, for instance, took at best 17 hours and that only if the train ran to time: but punctuality was more observed in planning than in actual performance. Between the wars, however, the Fascist regime revolutionized the trunk routes, so much so that by the

1939 summer the same journey of 523 miles (842 km) could be achieved in 8 hours.

Under Mussolini the country's inter-city passenger services were transformed not only by acceleration, which generally halved the end-to-times of the best trains, but by massive expansion of train frequencies, up to as much as 114 per cent between Rome and Naples. This was accomplished largely by widespread electrification, but also by the first steps to supersede some of the viciously curved and graded main lines constructed in the nineteenth century with new, well-aligned bypasses. The first of these *Direttissima* had been built along the coast from Rome to Naples, the second from Florence to Bologna, cutting through the Apennine Mountains in a new 11½-mile (18·5 km) tunnel.

To bolster Mussolini's claim of Italy's technical supremacy on land, sea and air an extraordinary demonstration was staged over this second *Direttissima* on 20 July 1939. With the route's traction current voltage temporarily boosted from 3kV to 4kV for extra power, a three-car articulated inter-city train-set, No ETR201, was sent hurtling northward from Florence to achieve the fastest rail journey on world record until the Japanese opened their first Shinkansen a quarter-of-a-century later. Though the *Direttissima* climbs to its Apennine Tunnel on almost 11 miles (17·7 km) of continuous 1 in 106 gradient, the unit bore its exultant party of Ministerial and Italian press guests to Milan at a start-to-stop average of 102 mph (164·2 km/h) for the whole 195·8 miles (315·1 km). Once in the flatlands of the broad Po Valley pace rose to an average of 109·2 mph (175·7 km/h) throughout the 124 miles (199·6 km) from Lavino, north of Bologna, to Rovoredo, on the outskirts of Milan, and during this stretch speed peaked at 126 mph (202·8 km/h).

6

AMERICA LEADS THE DIESEL REVOLUTION

MID-TWENTIETH CENTURY railway development owes almost as much to Dr Rudolph Diesel as that of the previous century did to the Stephensons. Railways historians do not venerate 1895 as they do 1825 or 1830, the opening years of the Stephensons' pioneering railways, but they should. That was the year Diesel first produced power from the kind of compression ignition engine which bears his name. One of Britain's Admiralty establishments was running a little 9 hp oil-engined locomotive as early as 1896, but the internal combustion engine gave little inkling of its potential rail conquest until well after the First World War. One reason was that its technologists took decades to solve the problem of specific weight: power comparable to that of a main-line steam locomotive was for years unobtainable without recourse to an intolerably heavy and cumbersome power plant. Even if they had progressed faster, the designers would still have been balked by the lack of a proven system to transmit the engine's output to the roadwheels without wilting. Nevertheless, before the First World War the evidence of the internal combustion engine's economic potential in its reduction of time off work for servicing and lower fuel costs by comparison with steam was sufficiently persuasive to encourage its rail use within the low power limits at that time available.

The savings to be had from its application to lightly-trafficked branch lines were immediately appealing, though initially this did not involve the diesel engine. In 1905, in the US, the Union Pacific essayed a petrol-engined railcar, a 100 hp, 31 ft-long (9·5 m) vehicle with a mechanical drive, which performed promisingly enough to spawn a company that turned out 155 similar cars

for various railroads between then and 1917. A year later General Electric produced for the Delaware & Hudson the first petrol-engined railcar with electric transmission – that is, with the engine driving a generator delivering current to electric traction motors. Known in North American parlance naturally as a 'gas-electric', this type of railcar was very much in vogue after the First World War, when 700 of what by then had rather enigmatically earned the nickname of 'Doodlebugs' were active up and down the country's rural lines.

It was the Swedes who in 1913, after some experience with petrol-fuelled railcars, first successfully operated a diesel-engined railcar. The difference between the combustion process in a petrol and a diesel engine, of course, is that in

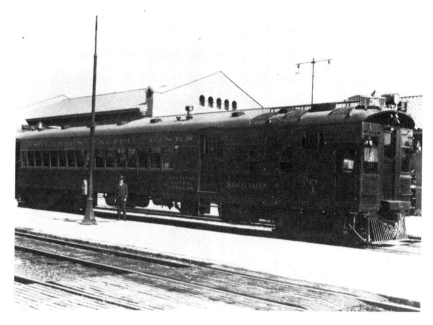

At first GM's Electro-Motive Division indulged railroad customers' fancy for a little individual styling in their diesel locomotives' outline and fitments, but in the late 1940s the company standardized its 2,000-hp Type E7 for mass production as passenger power: a cab-and-booster E7 combination of the Gulf Mobile & Ohio leaves Chicago in 1952.

The engine is installed in one 2-D-2 unit of Canadian National's cumbersome, 334-ton diesel-electric twin-unit locomotive of 1928, total output of which was only 2,660 hp.

The Burlington's first two 'Zephyr' train-sets, already enlarged from three to four cars, pose at Chicago in 1935.

the former ignition is sparked, whereas in the latter it is entirely the result of compression. Because that compression is so excessive there is a correspondingly complete expansion of the hot products of combustion: hence the greater power obtainable from a diesel engine for a given size and fuel cost in a heavy load application such as rail traction. A minor benefit is that stored diesel fuel is not so volatile as petrol. A perennial complaint about the US 'Doodlebugs' was their vulnerability to fire.

Right up to mid-century engineers were still striving to perfect a mechanical power transmission capable of absorbing high power outputs without breaking. Apart from costing less in price and weight than an electric system, the mechanical did not waste so much of the prime mover diesel engine's power in the course of transmission; moreover, it avoided the need of electrical expertise to keep the traction unit serviceable. But by the 1920s it was clear that electric transmission's penalties of extra bulk and absorption of 15–20 per cent of the diesel engine's output at the shaft were more than offset by its reliability and potential capacity. It was to become the preferred system throughout world diesel traction, challenged only by variations on the hydraulic theme in which the principal medium is one or more oil-filled torque converters inserted between engine and a final mechanical drive. The only major railroading country to favour hydraulic transmissions exclusively however, was to be Germany.

During the 1920s the diesel-electric locomotive came on stage both in Europe and North America, but principally as a modestly-powered shunting machine because the art of compacting power plant and transmission had yet to be mastered. The first thoroughly successful American machine, a 300 hp shunter created for the Central Railroad of New Jersey in 1924–5 by a consortium of ALCO, General Electric (for the electrical gear) and Ingersoll-Rand (suppliers of the diesel engine), scaled a creditable 55 tons (56 tonnes). But when Baldwins shortly afterwards built a 1,000 hp prototype, subsequently acquired by the Reading Railroad, locomotive weight jumped to almost 123 tons (125 tonnes). And to attain 2,660 hp Canadian National had to indulge as much as 334 tons (339 tonnes) of locomotive bulk in its experimental twin-engined, articulated twin-unit No 9000 of 1928.

The breakthrough which set North American railroad dieselization rolling in the 1940s stemmed from General Motors' acquisition in 1930 of the Electromotive & Winton Engine Companies, the latter a specialist in diesel engines. Restructured as GM's Electromotive Division, these concerns immediately applied themselves to dedicated research and development which by 1933 had perfected an engine, branded 201A, capable of 600 hp for a mere quarter of the bulk and fifth of the weight of previous plant with the same output. The secret was a marriage of welded constructional method with use of new lighter-weight alloy steels and adoption of a two-cycle combustion process.

The new engine was displayed at the 1933 Chicago Century of Progress Exhibition, where it riveted especially two railroad managements, those of Union Pacific and the Burlington, who were worrying how best to hitch their systems to the new streamlined-styling bandwagon. Vogue was by no means their preoccupying concern. By now Henry Ford's Model T was the cherished possession of countless American families and over the longer hauls bus competition was bleeding the rail passenger business severely. The Burlington had seen its passenger revenues collapse from $28·5 millions to $6·7 millions between 1923 and 1933, its passenger volume slump from 18 millions to 7 millions during the same period, and it desperately needed to counter-attack spectacularly. Within a year of the 201A's unveiling each railroad had a striking streamlined, self-powered train-set embodying the new GM traction technology. Initially it was the Burlington unit, the 'Pioneer Zephyr', which excited more attention, both for its form and for its flair in performance. Structurally the 'Zephyr' three-car set premiered the lightweight stainless steel alloy bodywork which the Budd firm of Philadelphia was just adapting to rail passenger car building after its successful employment in automobile construction, and which would subsequently find a worldwide as well as a wide-ranging North American market. As for performance, the 'Pioneer Zephyr' tore the existing US transcontinental speed record to shreds within two months of delivery from the builders.

Until then the 1,015 miles (1,633 km) between Chicago and Denver had never been covered in less than 18 hr 53 min, and that by a featherweight special back in 1897. In 1934 the fastest steam service was $26\frac{3}{4}$ hr, inclusive of 40 intermediate stops, in the small hours of 26 May 1934 the 'Pioneer Zephyr' was flagged out of Denver's Union Station targeted to reach Chicago in 15 hours, which was unimaginable enough. But by dint of covering the whole distance at a phenomenal start-to-stop average of 77·6 mph (124·9 km/h) – a non-stop feat still unsurpassed over such a distance – the 'Zephyr' made it in two seconds under 13 hr 5 min. In the flatlands of Colorado and Nebraska the average was 90 mph (145 km/h) for 129·5 continuous miles (208·4 km), during which speed peaked at 112·5 mph

Above:
Union Pacific's pioneering three-car diesel streamliner, the M-10000, which at the start of 1935 was installed in daily service between Kansas City and Salina as the 'City of Salina.'

Right:
The popularity of the diesel streamliners is underlined by this scene at Southern Pacific's Oakland Pier station in 1940: the 'City of San Francisco' is running in two parts, the main train of latest equipment on the left, the second section on the right formed of one of the historic M-10001/2 units, identifiable by its unique rear-end fairing.

(181·1 km/h). And it was all done on only 418 gallons (1,900 litres) of fuel oil, the bill for which in those halcyon days was a scarcely credible $16!

Union Pacific's three-car counterpart, the aluminium alloy M-10000, did not immediately vie with this exploit, but it was no less a crowd-puller on its preliminary exhibition tour of the country and commanded a near-100 per cent load factor on almost every trip when it was installed in public service between Kansas City and Salina. That encouraged UP to immediately order a six-car, 1,200 hp-engined unit including Pullman sleepers, the M-10001, which on 22 October 1934 did earn a comparable honour in the record books.

This time it was coast-to-coast, over the whole 3,259 miles (5,245 km) from Los Angeles to New York, a journey which then spread over 84 hr by the leading steam train of the period and which had never been accomplished by rail in less than 71 hr 27 min, again by a special, in 1906. M-10001 spanned the continent in 56 hr 55 min, inclusive of a 40 min halt in Chicago. A fortnight later M-10001 was installed in public service as the 'City of Portland' on a 39¾ hr schedule for the 2,272 miles (3,656 km) between Chicago and its namesake which at a stroke slashed 18 hr from the previous steam standard for the route.

Other railroads scurried to their order books and similar trains such as the Boston & Maine's 'Flying Yankee' and the New Haven's 'Comet' were soon in gestation. But it was already obvious that the ticket-office drawing power of the new diesel streamliners would overwhelm the capacity of a three-car set like the 'Pioneer Zephyr'. After space had been pre-empted for power plant, mail, baggage and buffet-grill, the 'Zephyr' could seat only 72 customers.

By 1936, in the 11-car UP 'City of Los Angeles' and 'City of San Francisco' sets and in the 12-car

Top:
By 1936 Union Pacific's 'City of San Francisco' had already expanded to a format of a twin-unit power car with a total output of 2,400 hp and nine trailers.

Above:
The original twin-unit 'Fliegende Hamburger' diesel streamliner of the pre-war German Reichsbahn, powered by a pair of 410 hp high-rpm engines.

Burlington 'City of Denver', the format was perceptibly progressing to one of locomotives and trailers. The units were still self-contained, but their two leading vehicles were pure diesel-electric power cars of the 900 or 1,200 hp output which GM's engine development now made practicable. The 'Denver Zephyr', moreover, translated to the streamliners all the customary facilities of the period's steam-hauled Pullman transcontinentals, as remarked in the previous chapter. Even with 11-car streamliners UP was frequently turning away business in 1936. In that year the new trains were the prime stimulus of a one-third improvement in the railroad's passenger revenue (an advance which significantly went against the trend on most other lines), so 17-car rakes were commissioned for 1937–8.

The new trains spearheaded the steady acceleration of long-haul passenger services to which US railroads were now – and none too soon – dedicated to defend their traffic from the competition. In 1930 American timetables disclosed only 29 daily runs, aggregating a mere 1,106 miles (1,780 km), timed at an average speed of 60 mph (97 km/h) or more. By the end of 1935 the totals had soared to 413 and 19,279 (31,026) respectively and diesel traction was already claiming some 10 per cent of the gross, though at that stage the fastest sectional timings of the Burlington 'Zephyrs', those over the 54·6 miles (87·9 km) from East Dubuque to Prairie du Chien exacting an average of 74·5 mph (119·9 km/h), were just edged out of top spot in the table by steam. On the Pennsylvania, the steam-hauled 'Union' was required to maintain 75·6 mph (121·7 km/h) over the 40·8 miles (65·7 km) from Valparaiso to Plymouth and the 'Detroit Arrow' 75·4 mph (121·3 km/h) from Plymouth to Fort Wayne. By then, incidentally, the Pennsylvania alone was running more mile-a-minute or better mileage daily than all British railways put together; and 13 US daily services eclipsed for pace the Great Western's 'Cheltenham Flyer', so recently vaunted as the world's fastest train.

That global crown, however, was still in Europe, lately assumed by the other 1930s protagonist of diesel traction development, Ger-

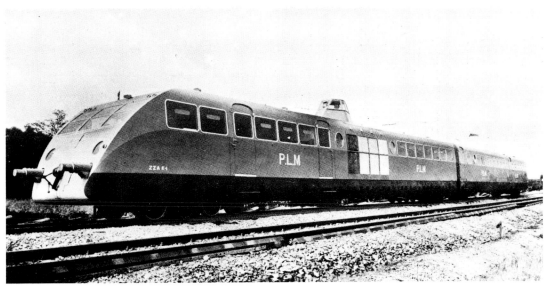

Top:
This ungainly-looking
Daimler-engined railcar,
seen at Vienna's South
station, was tried on the
Austrian Federal Railway in
the 1930s.

Left:
A Bugatti twin-unit railcar,
with each car on four-axle
bogies, employed by France's
PLM Railway in the mid-
1930s.

many. Well before UP and the Burlington across the Atlantic had glimpsed GM's new 201A engine and ordered their pioneer diesel streamliners, the Germans were convinced that their native diesel engine and carbuilding art had brought within reach the world rail speed crown they craved for the greater glory of the Third Reich. Back in 1931 the Reichsbahn had commissioned a twin-car set from the Görlitz works of Wagon und Maschinenbau AG and the following year this articulated unit, horsed with a brace of 12-cylinder, high rpm 410 hp Maybach engines and aerodynamically shaped with the benefit of exhaustive research at the Zeppelin works in Friedrichshafen, was ready for protracted proving trials. Those satisfyingly completed, the 78 tonne (76·8 ton), 102-seater set was committed to public operation between Berlin and Hamburg as the 'Fliegende Hamburger', as briefly noted in the previous chapter.

With this service the Reichsbahn immediately seized the world title. On a schedule of 138 min for the 178·1 miles (286·6 km) the 'Fliegende Hamburger' was prescribed an unsurpassed average speed of 77·4 mph (124·6 km/h). What is more, it was the first public train in the world required to run daily at up to 100 mph (161 km/h), since its timing was otherwise untenable because of the speed restrictions enforced over some parts of its itinerary.

The instantaneous commercial triumph of the 'Fliegende Hamburger' and the diesel unit's impressive economy in running costs soon determined the Reichsbahn to standardize the concept. Fresh train-set orders were deferred until 1935, however, as the Reichsbahn sensibly insisted that each putative high-speed route must first be fully equipped with inductive automatic train control and have its track fettled up to a special standard of repair. As remarked in the previous chapter, comfort was not a hallmark of the inaugural 'Fliegende Hamburger', which though it was exclusively first-class packed 102 seats and a cramped four-seater bar into its two cars. Most of the first production series of German units, known as the 'Hamburg' type, were also two-car but these were more generously laid out to accommodate only 76; they were also arranged so that a pair could be coupled into a multiple-unit and driven from the leading cab. Four of the 1935 batch, however, were three-car. Classified 'Leipzig', these also foreshadowed later German practice by embodying hydraulic transmissions; all other pre-war 'Fliegende' units were diesel-electric.

In their final series of inter-city train-sets the Reichsbahn discarded articulation to allow for longer car bodies and more seating space. The ultimate 'Köln' type of 1938 introduced a format of two independent 600 hp power cars enclosing a trailer; 102 exclusively first-class seats were arranged three-a-side in compartments as opposed to the saloon configuration of earlier series, and instead of the tray-meal service at seats to which the first sets had been confined, the Köln sets featured a separate dining saloon in one of their power cars.

As early as the summer of 1935 the Reichsbahn's diesel flyer schedules were topped by a 115 min booking for the evening non-stop service over the 157·8 miles (254 km) from Berlin (Zoo) to Hannover that exacted an average of 82·3 mph (132·5 km/h) throughout. No less striking and compelling testimony to diesel traction's superior stamina was the distance some of the 'Fliegende' diesels were set to run at consistently high speed in a day's work: the 'Fliegende Kölner', for example, had a day's out-and-back stint totalling 719 miles (1,157 km),

to be covered at an average of 71·2 mph (114·6 km/h). By 1939 the Reichsbahn monopolized the first 32 places in the European daily speed table with timings ranging from 75·1 mph (120·9 km/h) up to 83·3 mph (134·1 km/h), the latter over the 109·7 miles (176·5 km) between Hamm and Hannover.

In the course of the 1930s practically all European railways took up the internal combustion-engined railcar as a cost-saving tool for rural branch or secondary cross-country route service, especially in countries without the benefit of indigenous coal. But in others, such as Britain, acquisitions were limited or on some railways were still in the experimental stage by the Second World War's outbreak.

At the end of the 1930s the biggest – and decidedly the most diverse – European railcar fleet was that of France's railways, which was some 700 strong on the newly nationalized system alone and over 1,100 if one also took into account the country's private and departmental companies. The French opened their account in 1931 with branch-line cars that both resembled physically and were technically adaptations of petrol-engined road bus designs, one version by Renault and the other by Michelin. The latter were also the product of two years' research inspired by André Michelin himself and pursued after his death by his son Marcel to prove the superior adhesion characteristics of pneumatic-tyred wheels in rail use, and hence their benefit to acceleration, braking and economy of traction. The hazards of a puncture on the move were mitigated by multiplying a vehicle's axles, so that if one tyre blew that wheel's load would be safely taken up by others: thus the prototype 20 hp 24-seater Michelin car was mounted on as many as five axles.

By 1936, three years after the first French essays in main-line express operation with bogie railcars between Paris and Deauville, and Lisieux and Trouville, had taught the companies that this type of vehicle could successfully fulfil a much wider role, the Michelin railcar had graduated into a unit with high-speed capability. The 400 hp single-unit main-line car acquired by the PLM that year was a grotesque animal. No less than 99 ft 4 in (30·3 m) long, the body was a rigid structure from end to end, with a powered bogie of four axles – all driven, the outer ones through chains – in the center and at each end four-axle bogies with necessarily so much lateral play relative to the frames that the throwover of the body on curves was a formidable $21\frac{1}{2}$ in (54·6 cm). Lightweight steel and duralumin construction pegged the car's tare weight to a remarkable 16 tons (16·3 tonnes). The con-

currently-produced, twin-engined 500 hp Michelin for the État was an articulated three-unit,
again with four-axle bogies, in this case four of
them; the inner two were powered and articulated to the 50 ft 10 in (15·5 m) trailers a power
unit just under half the non-powered cars' length.
Before leaving Michelin it is worth recording
that a 1937 proposal to develop pneumatic-tyred
locomotive-hauled stock for the Paris–Strasbourg service, because there traffic was outstripping railcar capacity, though at the time
not pursued, was resurrected by the SNCF after
the war. Three six-car sets of stainless steel cars,
each mounted on two five-axle bogies, were built
in 1947, and 12 vintage Class 230-K 4–6–0s were
meretriciously and hideously streamlined to
work with them. Indeed, these engines' immedi-

Dieselization comes to one of
the world's most celebrated
trains: a pair of Electro-
Motive E7s moves the New
York Central's 'Twentieth
Century Limited' out of
Chicago's La Salle Street
station.

ate nickname of 'The Whales' was rather a slur
on the mammals. The rubber-tyred sets served
the Paris–Strasbourg route until 1952 and the
Paris–Basle from then until 1956, when they
were retired.

Four-wheeled bogies, but steel-tyred, were
also a characteristic of the Bugatti railcars.
Distinguished for their unprepossessing, flat-

fronted streamlining and conning-tower cabs, these were constructed in single, two- and three-car versions with varying power between 1933 and 1938, and were also operated chiefly by the État and PLM. Best-looking of the French 1930s express railcar sets were unquestionably the 820 hp, Maybach-engined three-car units which the Nord installed between Paris, Lille and Tourcoing in 1934. Some long-serving post-Second World War French railcars copied the Bugatti's conning tower cab arrangement, which gave them, in terms of conventional railway aesthetics, such a surreal outline that they were always known as the 'Picassos'.

Claims of peak speeds well over 100 mph (161 km/h) were made for various of the French express railcar units during private trials, as they were for the German diesel sets, but the public performance of the French cars was circumscribed by the Government-imposed limit of 120 km/h (74·6 mph) throughout the French system until the mid-1930s. Then it was relaxed for the express railcars, but very modestly, to 130 km/h (80·8 mph). Consequently the French could not aspire to the end-to-end average speeds of the Reichsbahn's flyers, but given their constraints the average of 73 mph (117·5 km/h) tabled for their fastest service in 1939, over the 219·1 miles (352·6 km) from Nancy to Paris, was extremely creditable.

Though the Italians were eagerly electrifying in the late 1930s they too were energetic protagonists of the diesel railcar and sustained some of their mile-a-minute service with this equipment in the decade's closing years. For the important Turin–Milan–Venice–Trieste transversal, not on the immediate electrification agenda, they attempted a three-car unit that would emulate the Reichsbahn's flyers, but the two Type ATR100 articulated sets built in 1936–7 to this specification by Fiat, each with a pair of 400 hp engines, were flawed. Their interior appointments, which even ran to air-conditioning, were elegant enough, but though the prototype was tested at up to 107 mph (172·2 km/h) the units proved too fallible for regular operation at the intended 100 mph (161 km/h). Persistent engine, transmission and braking snags with the two prototypes delayed construction of a further eight until 1939, and by then the whole squadron was restricted to a maximum of 115 km/h (71·5 mph). Well over 80 per cent of the Italian railway's railcars of the period were war casualties, chiefly because they were stripped of their engines for military purposes, then herded into yards soon to be laid to waste by Allied aircraft.

So it was that, except in Russia, where shortage of convenient water supplies in the country's wilder areas was a powerful inducement to develop the use of diesel locomotives, this form of traction had made negligible European headway by the war's outbreak. True, the diesel's potential economy in operation by comparison with steam was by now irrefutably documented; and besides that dieselization was a very appealing alternative to the huge first cost of electrification in an era when most railways' balance-sheets were ravaged by the depression. But the power/weight ratios offered by the Continent's diesel traction engineers were still uninviting. Virtually the only machine built in Europe before 1939 which offered some hope of matching a high-power steam locomotive's capability within a minimally acceptable bulk was the 4,400 hp twin-unit 2C2+2C2 diesel-electric prototype procured by France's PLM in 1937 as a medium for the haulage of 450-ton (457 tonne) expresses from Paris to Marseilles and the Côte d'Azur at an end-to-end average of more than 60 mph (97 km/h). If nothing else this machine powerfully demonstrated the diesel's resilience to continuous work by its regular, unchanged haulage of 600-tonne (591 ton) *rapides* throughout the 690 miles (1,110 km) between Paris and Menton.

By 1937, however, the diesel locomotive revolution was already rolling in the US. In 1935 GM's Electro-Motive Division came up with a 900 hp, 12-cylinder version of its 201A engine, two of which could be fitted into a diesel-electric locomotive on two two-axle bogies grossing no more than 107 tons (109 tonnes). The prototype was turned out as a semi-permanently-coupled, double-ended twin-unit with a total output of 3,600 hp for a gross of only 214 tons (218 tonnes), and demonstrations on various railroads soon made plain that this was a machine which could comfortably maintain steam timings on trains of 12–14 cars at anything from 40 to 60 percent less cost in fuel, let alone savings in reduced servicing requirements. Within the year Electromotive had rung up its first production sales, to the Baltimore & Ohio and the Santa Fe. Now Electro-Motive took a crucial decision that materially influenced not only the advance of US railroad dieselization but the US diesel locomotive industry's subsequent dominance of world markets for diesel traction. Just about the only standard element in the early diesel streamliners had been the power plant itself, and that only in certain cases. For the rest each railroad had indulged its own design fancy, in almost every case incurring horrendous custom-building expense as they strove to style their trains more distinctively than their rivals.

Such fecklessness, Electro-Motive determined, would not be allowed to distort the costs of

A final credit to the FT: its more even weight distribution admitted it to tracks which could only bear steam locomotives up to about 75 per cent of the FT's gross tonnage.

Such was the FT's impact on its host railroads that 13 of the 20 it had visited commissioned production models in short order, almost all of them for severely graded routes. The first of these was active on Santa Fe by 1940. If the US had not entered the war the pace of subsequent freight, as well as passenger dieselization might have been more rapid than it now became, because from 1942 the War Production Board not only controlled the supply of locomotives, compelling railroads to accept designs selected for standardization, but also the output of manufacturers. Thus besides putting an embargo on construction of specifically passenger power the Board confined main-line diesel manufacture to the biggest builder, Electromotive, and debarred the other major firms by then taking a slice of the market, Baldwin and ALCO-GE (ALCO left that partnership in 1953), from turning out machines of more than 1,000 hp. Nevertheless 1,095 FTs were built.

In the post-war development of the F range it was the F7 of 1949, with the V-16 567B engine now uprated to 1,500 hp, which became the star

In the early 1960s all three major US builders produced ultra-high-horsepower diesel-electrics at Union Pacific request: these three 5,500-hp Bo-Bo-Bo-Bos, each powered by a pair of 16-cylinder engines, were ALCO's 'Century 855' entry, but were the only ones built by that manufacturer.

thundering Santa Fe 2–10–2 with 1,100 tons (1,118 tonnes) or by a Southern Pacific cab-in-front 4–8–8–2 with 1,350 tons (1,372 tonnes).

Through the whole 11 months not one failure in traffic was marked against the FT, which ended its tour with a fuel bill half that of the various steam locomotives which it challenged, taking ton-mileage performed as the baseline.

of the series – became, in fact, the best-selling streamlined cabbed-body diesel type in history. No fewer than 3,716 were eventually acquired by 49 different US railroads (and 27 bought 314 FP7s, a version with some detail changes for passenger work). Altogether 7,374 units in the F range were turned out by Electro-Motive between 1939 and 1957.

The first of Electro-Motive's mass-production 'hood' models was the 1,500-hp GP7 Bo-Bo: this Santa Fe trio, photographed in 1980 by which time they had been rebuilt, were some of the 2,660 sold to US railroads.

However, the tally of Fs was left well behind by Electro-Motive's total sale of its GP (for General Purpose) series of so-called road-switchers – more than 10,500 between 1949 and the mid-1970s. The idea of adapting the diesel yard shunter into a machine capable of modest main-line duty originated with an ALCO-GE 1,000 hp type of 1941 and for a time it looked as though this partnership might have the road-switcher market almost to itself. Not that it was much of a market until the war's end: most rail-roads were unconvinced of the need for such a unit and they were apprehensive, too, that the unions might bridle at driving a clutch of road-switchers multiple-unit and insist that each locomotive had its own crew, though in the event this never became an issue. Until the late 1940s,

therefore, Electro-Motive was content to keep a toehold in the market by producing a 1,500 hp BL (for Branch Line) diesel that somewhat resembled a foreshortened version of one of its Fs. But when interest quickened in the ALCO-GE product Electro-Motive knew the time had come to make a determined and fully-worked-out play for the trade. Electro-Motive's chief designer once summarized his GP philosophy this way: 'I had two dreams,' he wrote. 'The first was to make the locomotive so ugly that no railroad would want it on the main line or any-where near its headquarters, but would want it out as far as possible in the back country, where it could do really useful work. My second dream was to make it so simple in construction and so devoid of Christmas-tree ornaments and other

Top:
American export: a 2750 hp
Class Dx Co-Co of New
Zealand Railways, built by
General Electric, heads the
overnight Auckland–
Wellington 'Northerner'.

Above:
British Rail was the only
national system to undertake
simultaneous large-scale
operation of diesel-electric
and diesel-hydraulic main-
line types: the diesel-
hydraulics were concentrated
on BR Western Region,
where the most powerful type
was the 2700-hp Class 52 C-C,
of which No D1007 *Western
Talisman* passes Acocks
Green, in the West Midlands,
with the up 'Cambrian Coast
Express' in 1963.

Diesel-hydraulic traction still dominates the German railways: on East Germany's Reichsbahn (DR) several 2,000-3,000-hp diesel-electric types of Soviet build are now in DR service, but the 2,000-hp Type V180 diesel-hydraulic B-B, seen here on a Budapest–Berlin express of Hungarian cars, remains an express passenger haulier on non-electrified routes.

whimsy that the price would be materially below that of our standard main-line freight locomotives.'

The ugliness materialized in what is now termed the 'hood' outline – a narrow, rectangular cross-section bonnet housing the power plant and auxiliaries that extends the length of the locomotive, but which is narrower than the latter's main-frame width so that there is room for a walkway each side of it to facilitate maintenance, and with a full-width cab offering perfect fore-and-aft vision slightly offset from one end. The only major variation in this outline, which was subsequently adopted by railways practically the world over, came in the 1960s when numerous customers preferred to have the bonnets of their 'hoods' cut down at the shorter end; that way they obtained full-width cab windows on the side where the locomotive crew were nearest to the coupler.

It took only five years to sell 2,660 of the 1,500 hp GP7 to 74 US railroads, then only

another five, from 1954 to 1959, to dispose of 3,601 of the succeeding 1,750 hp GP9. Eventually 2,500 hp was obtained from the turbocharged 567 series V-16 engine and that powered the popular GP35 of the early 1960s. This, like all GPs, was a four-axle Bo–Bo, but by the 1950s numerous railroads were asking for a six-motor Co–Co 'hood' that would have the extra adhesion to roll heavy freight tonnage but would still be as kind to indifferent track as the Bo–Bo roadswitcher. Via interim models incorporating the final version of the 567 engine this pressure led in the mid-1960s to the era of the high-horse-power 'hood', exemplified by Electro-Motive's SD (for Special Duty) range. With a new V-20 645 series engine, the output of a single unit could now be hoisted, in the SD45, to 3,600 hp. One or two railroads aspired to even more powerful machines, notably Union Pacific, which marked its centenary by ordering from Electro-Motive some 98½ ft-long (30 m) 6,600 hp monsters housing two 645 engines and mounted

on a pair of four-axle bogies, its 'Centennials'. But the vast majority of managements were content with 3,000 to 3,500 hp as a ceiling. Above that operational flexibility could be sacrificed, unless one was prepared for the extra horsepower to be under-utilized now and then, besides, there was evidence that extreme horsepowers incurred a debit of disproportionate maintenance costs.

This account has focussed on the output of General Motors' Electro-Motive Division, or EMD as it is often known, because it was, and remains, the mainspring of US railroad dieselization. All but one of EMD's other major competitors, ALCO, the Baldwin-Lima-Hamilton consortium and Fairbanks-Morse, had left the locomotive business by 1969 and today GE is the only other substantial force in the US so far as manufacture of new locomotives is concerned. I should add that GE is an increasingly potent rival; in 1982 its order books were as full as EMD's. Across the border EMD has another powerful world market contender in Canada's Bombardier-MLW, and within the US several firms are active in the remanufacture of locomotives – that is, the refurbishing of still serviceable chassis with new power plant, these days a

very substantial business because of the drive to curb capital expenditure.

Finally, I have concentrated on dieselization as it was experienced in the US for two further reasons. First, it was the scale, pace and effectiveness of the revolution there which after the war swayed the traction policies of almost every railway around the world not already committed to expensive electrification. The speed of US change in the 1940s was staggering. In 1938 only 314 diesel-electric locomotives were at work on US railroads, but thereafter, taking the figures at two-year intervals, the total climbed through stages of 797, 1,667, 3,049, 4,441 and 8,089 to an aggregate of 11,980 in 1950. In that first year of the new decade only a dozen new steam locomotives were built for the Class 1 railroads, whereas at the start of the 1940s the annual output was around 400. And by 1952 the 40,041 steam locomotives serving US railroads in 1940 had already been cut to 15,869.

Second, the basic of US main-line diesel locomotive design – rugged chassis construction, comparatively uncomplicated medium-speed diesel engines and electric transmission – informed the later dieselization policy of almost all other railways and their suppliers. The out-

The Eastern European diesel look: the T478 diesel-electric Bo-Bo is a modern mixed traffic model of 1,960 hp, built by Skoda, in service on Czechoslovak Railways since 1978.

Australia now has a substantial home locomotive industry, building mostly around US diesel engines: these 2,500-hp Class 80 diesel-electric Co-Cos of New South Wales State Rail Authority, built locally by Comeng, have US Alco 251 engines and Mitsubishi transmissions from Japan.

standing iconoclasts, as indicated earlier, were the Germans. In West Germany the post-war Deutsche Bundesbahn and the diesel locomotive industry were convinced of the countervailing advantages of combining compact, high-speed engines with hydraulic transmission: a superior power/weight ratio in any output range, because of the power plant's lesser bulk; and consequently, in theory at any rate, the recipe for lighter locomotives on fewer axles that should be less costly to build, less expensive to maintain. There was also the promise of high and sustained tractive effort over a wider speed range, which was one of the inherent characteristics of the

hydraulic transmission.

The DB's main-line locomotives were and still are exclusively of this kind and on its home ground the high-speed engine/hydraulic transmission marriage has served as efficiently and reliably as anyone's diesel-electrics. But the Germans made no converts among other major railways so far as locomotives were concerned, though low-powered diesel-hydraulic railcars are a global commonplace.

Two US systems with viciously-graded routes over the Rockies, the Denver & Rio Grande Western and the Southern Pacific, were persuaded to import batches of 4,000 hp

German-built diesel-hydraulics in the 1960s, but they found the foreigners' delicate machinery too susceptible to malfunction in the harsh conditions of American freight working and laid the locomotives aside within a few years.

Only in Britain, on British Rail's Western Region, were German-pattern diesel-hydraulics operated in quantity, alongside conventional diesel-electrics of comparable power and purpose to allow a reasonable judgement to be made of respective merits. After only four years the unequivocal verdict was that while the diesel-hydraulics were cleverly designed locomotives,

their high-speed engines were intricate machines which expensively protracted many maintenance and repair operations; that the transmissions and their gearbox drives were not resilient enough; and finally that the first cost of a diesel-electric was lowering below that of a diesel-hydraulic. With that BR, too, went exclusively diesel-electric in its main-line fleet.

The popular US railroad trunk freight workhorse of the early 1980s: a trio of Electro-Motive 3000 hp SD40-2 diesel-electric Co-Cos wind a Union Pacific freight through Echo Canyon, Utah.

BARELY WAS EUROPE ACCUSTOMED to the bulk of a Pacific at the front end of an express train than one or two railways moved up a locomotive size. The 1925 election of Spain's Norte Railway for a comparatively small-wheeled 4–8–2, forerunner of what became typically Spanish express passenger power for steam's remaining decades, was quite understandable, for Spanish main lines were frequently fierce switchbacks where the extra adhesion of a fourth coupled axle would be an asset. But that same year both the Est and PLM Railways of France rolled out big-wheel 4–8–2s; and three years later, inverting the layout to accommodate the roomy firebox essential for effective combustion of the country's execrable coal, the Austrians unveiled a 2–8–4 with 6 ft $4\frac{1}{2}$ in (194·3 cm) driving wheels. Was the Pacific an ephemeral phase of development? Could the inexorable commercial pressure for more speed with trains growing progressively heavier because of public demand for better-quality accommodation be met only by ever bigger boilers and the chassis to go with them? On both counts the answer was no. That the demands were satisfied more economically on many railways was in large measure a tribute to the genius of France's André Chapelon.

In the mid-1920s, when he was a research engineer with the Paris–Orléans Railway, Chapelon was asked to investigate why his company's new Pacifics were bafflingly incapable of bettering the work of the 4–4–2s they succeeded. Deciding that the problem was deep-seated, Chapelon soon embarked on a methodical re-examination of the basic processes of converting heat into locomotive energy; and from this, with the support of practical dynamometer car tests of existing locomotives on the road, he concluded that contemporary locomotive design was heading up a blind alley. The free running at speed and higher power expected from bigger and bigger locomotives was not forthcoming because orthodox design practice was incapable of optimizing the boiler's potential. Only when the engines were on loose rein was full value obtained from the coal and water consumed. As soon as they were pushed for extra speed they disappointed because the traditional layout of steam passages choked on the boiler's increased output and dissipated a good deal of the steam's power before it reached the piston heads. Some of Chapelon's predecessors, in particular Churchward of Britain's GWR, had grasped the importance of improving steam circulation. But none had previously undertaken such a scientific study of the question or devised such a detailed programme of re-design as a solution.

The Chapelon theory, broadly speaking, propounded two interdependent lines of action. To maximize the steam output for a given coal and water consumption, a higher degree of superheating must be applied and more efficient draughting contrived. The latter was secured by fitting a double instead of a single blastpipe and chimney, a concept in which Chapelon refined the work of a Finnish engineer named Kylala –

A Chapelon rebuilt Pacific of French Railways, the 231-H formed of original Paris–Orléans and Nord Railway types, heads a Nîmes–Paris express out of St-Germain des Fosses in 1952.

Far left:
The first of the Reichsbahn's streamlined Class 05 4-6-4s emerges from the Borsig works in 1935.

The remarkable French Railways Class 240-P which Chapelon rebuilt from a former Paris–Orléans Pacific type.

mixed traffic 4–8–0s – their driving wheels were only 5 ft 10½ in (179·1 cm) in diameter – which Chapelon reconstructed from a dozen P-O Pacifics in 1932–4 must not be overlooked. These engines were nominally rebuilds, though by the time all Chapelon's precepts had been embodied in the redraft most of the original 4–6–2 components must have been discarded.

Of the many striking demonstrations of up-hill power obtained from these compound 4–8–0s, in which an extra axle added the benefit of greater adhesion weight to those of Chapelon's thermodynamic practice, the most impressive was probably that staged with a 635 ton (645 tonne) train between Calais and Paris in 1935. For this trial the statutory French 75 mph (121 km/h) speed limit of the period was waived, though one wonders who had expected a machine with such moderately-sized driving wheels to take much advantage of the licence. But almost at once, after lifting the 635 tons up the 6¾-mile (10·9 km), 1 in 125 Caffiers bank out of Calais at a minimum of 51 mph (82 km/h), the 4–8–0 touched 85 mph (137 km/h) on the descent to Boulogne. Later in the trip the engine actually accelerated its train from 76 to almost 80 mph (122–129 km/h) on the long 1 in 333 ascent beyond Amiens, then sprinted up to 89 mph (143 km/h) on a favourable slope to Creil, held 68–71 mph (109–114 km/h) all the way up the ensuing 1 in 200 Survilliers bank and finally hit 91 mph (147 km/h) on the 1 in 200 downhill to the Paris suburbs. Not the least spectacular of the Chapelon 4–8–0s feats that day was its maintenance of a 79·7 mph (128·3 km/h) average throughout 46·6 miles (75 km) of level track beyond Étaples, an achievement similarly-dimensioned Pacifics with considerably larger driving wheels never bettered. In 1940 the SNCF transformed 25 more P-O Pacifics in the same fashion, but with the additional refinement of mechanical stokers: they were the SNCF's Class 240P.

In Britain, the LNER's Nigel Gresley was powerfully influenced by Chapelon's thought in the design of his streamlined three-cylinder simple Class A4 4–6–2 for the LNER streamlined trains of 1935–9, the dazzling debut of which was described in Chapter 5. As recorded there, the first of the A4 line, No 2509 *Silver Link*, was whipped up to a new British speed record of 112·5 mph (181·1 km/h) on its pre-public service demonstration of the 'Silver Jubilee' to the press in September 1935. Even more telling testimony to the locomotive's design and workmanship, perhaps, was the fact that three days later and with the Pacific still little more than a fortnight from completion at Doncaster works it began unrelieved duty, Mondays to Fridays, on the up and down 'Silver Jubilee' for two weeks. So in

hence the 'Kylchap' name by which the Chapelon system was subsequently known. Alongside these changes in the steam production process Chapelon prescribed a smoothing and doubling of the size of steam passages throughout, coupled with an increase of piston valve size and travel. Further research convinced the French that the new layout was best complemented by the poppet type of valve, cam-operated by otherwise conventional Walschaerts gear, but some railways did not regard this as an essential concomitant of Chapelon practice. A 50 per cent uplift in performance and striking improvement in fuel economy were the instant results from a prototype rebuilding of one of the previously sluggish P-O Pacifics to the Chapelon specification. Thereafter Chapelon theory imbued not only all French steam locomotive practice but that of many other countries' engineers too. No more European eight-coupled express passenger designs were taken to mass production until 1934.

Chapelon had evolved his theory primarily for the compound expansion system which predominated in French railways' express passenger locomotive studs, but in most respects it was just as valid for simple expansion designs. Considering the subsequent prowess of Chapelon-inspired compounds in France, both rebuilds of existing types and brand-new classes, it is nevertheless surprising that engineers in other countries were not persuaded to re-assess compound propulsion in their adaptations of the rest of Chapelon's principles.

Although it is true that until 1934 European interest in eight-coupled express passenger design was confined to the French PLM's production of its one-off Class 241C 4–8–2 in 1930, the epic performances of some essentially

The third and last of the LNER's pre-war streamliners, the 'West Riding Limited', is headed out of Kings Cross, London, by the pioneer Gresley A4 Pacific, No 2509 Silver Link.

that period, without any failure, *Silver Link* ran just over 4,500 miles (7,242 km) at an average of 70 mph (113 km/h), an assignment way beyond the demands previously imposed on a British locomotive. Indeed, no lost time as a result of engine defects was booked against any of the inaugural quartet of A4s, Nos 2509–12, during their first 100,000 miles (160,930 km) of 'Silver Jubilee' haulage. Contemplating the protracted 'de-bugging' to which practically all modern traction is subjected before it is entrusted with public service, one has to concede that the resilience of the steam locomotive went a long way to offset its comparative crudity, its thermal inefficiency and its extravagant servicing needs.

The first A4s were not fitted with Kylchap double blastpipes and chimneys because steaming had not been fully satisfactory in a 1934 design which Gresley had modelled very closely on Chapelon's 4–8–0s, down to the use of poppet valves and double chimney – but not of compounding. This was his prototype Class P2 2–8–2, the only eight-coupled express passenger type ever built in Britain. The three-cylinder simple No 2001 *Cock o' the North* and the other five of the type (which were not poppet-valve engines) were conceived specifically for the LNER's difficult Edinburgh–Aberdeen route. For this, unfortunately, their bulk proved unsuited. On test with a 19-coach, 650-ton (661 tonne) train between Kings Cross and Grantham, however, the *Cock* showed that it had much of the Chapelon 4–8–0s' capacity for sustained speed with a massive load irrespective of gradients. Had the design been refined to eradicate its few flaws it could have served the LNER's heavy expresses admirably between Newcastle and London, and then become an invaluable wartime asset when the truncation

of passenger timetables for military traffic compelled operation of trains up to 20 or more coaches long. But Gresley had other pre-occupations. And, after his death, his successor Edward Thompson had the 2–8–2s reconstructed as mis-shapen and lustreless Pacifics.

The operational flexibility of a comparatively small-wheeled locomotive, provided it could manufacture and process steam smoothly enough for the higher speed ranges, was becoming apparent to numerous European railways during the 1930s. In Britain the outcome was long-run production of two-cylinder 4–6–0s with 6 ft (182·9 cm) driving wheels – the GWR 'Halls' and Stanier's LMS Class 5 4–6–0s, the 'Black Fives' – and of Gresley's three-cylinder, 6 ft 2 in-wheel (188 cm) Class V2 2–6–2s for the LNER, which early in the 1940s also adopted the two-cylinder 4–6–0 format in its 6 ft 2 in-wheel Class B1. All were machines capable of 80 mph-plus (129 km/h) on express passenger duty, moderately loaded except in the case of the bigger V2, which was purpose-built as a Pacific's match except on the tightest LNER schedules. But all were equally proficient as freight hauliers, except on really heavy mineral trains.

During and after the war both LNER and SR acquired 6 ft 2 in-wheel (188 cm) three-cylinder Pacifics, the latter the most innovative machines put into series production for a British railway in modern times. Designed by Oliver Bulleid, these idiosyncratically streamlined engines – 'air-smoothed' was the technical description of the boiler's graceless sheath – were prodigious performers. But they were high fuel consumers in their original form, which in addition incurred abnormal upkeep costs because of such eccentricities as a chain-driven valve gear immersed in an oil-bath. This complexity was an anathema to

113

Gresley's Class P2 2-802 No 2001 *Cock o' the North* crosses the Forth Bridge with an Aberdeen–Edinburgh train.

the motive power chiefs of the new, nationalized British Railways administration of 1948. Having persuaded their masters to go against the trend to dieselization or electrification everywhere else in Europe and allow steam one more chapter, the BR men designed a range of 12 classes that with one exception (an express passenger 4–6–2 of which only a prototype was ever built) were ruggedly simple two-cylinder, mixed traffic types, not excluding the two mixed traffic Pacific classes in the family. Inevitably they later rebuilt the Bulleid engines as more conventional locomotives with orthodox valve gear.

On the European mainland the French Nord and PLM Railways amassed large fleets of mixed traffic 2–8–2s in the 1930s. After the war the SNCF modernized them, but simultaneously accumulated an even bigger stud of two of its own brands, the four-cylinder compound Class 141P and the two-cylinder simple Class 141R. Over 1,300 141Rs, a 5 ft 5 in-wheeled type (165·1 cm), were acquired from US and Canadian builders. Many of these arrived equipped with mechanical stokers, but when coal was at a premium in the immediate post-war years the SNCF converted a considerable number to burn oil.

Another country which after the war favoured the eight-coupled locomotive as a maid-of-all-work was Czechoslovakia. There a family of three-cylinder simple and compound 6 ft-wheel (182·9 cm) 4–8–2s originating in 1934 bred a two-cylinder simple version with slightly smaller wheels in 1948. This and the concluding three-cylinder 1954 versions of the Czech 4–8–2 breed, all with Kylchap double exhausts, mechanical stokers and other refinements derived eclectically from ultimate French, German and American practice, ranked amongst the most sophisticated products of European steam's final era.

The designs which dominated the closing acts of European steam, though, were naturally those created to satisfy the inexorable commercial demand for enhanced passenger train performance to fend off air and road competition for long-haul traffic. Not that the stimuli were exclusively external. Chauvinism in many more activities than sport had been fuelled by the autarchic regimes of Germany and Italy. And in Britain the survival of private railway companies added the spice of intramural rivalry.

The first European impetus to the design of a purpose-built high-speed steam locomotive came from the trade association of German locomotive builders. On Christmas Eve 1931 this body advised the Reichsbahn that it was independently embarking on preliminary studies of such a machine, convinced that need of it would soon be inescapable, and invited the Reichsbahn's traction and rolling stock bureau to collaborate. The Reichsbahn's initial reaction was lukewarm. It was alive to the need of more pace to combat the new threat from the air at the upper end of the passenger market, but felt it had that threat covered with its emerging plan for lightweight diesel streamliners. The railway therefore limited its interest to support for a design exercise with construction of a single prototype as the ultimate but as yet undated end-product. Wagner, the Reichsbahn's motive power chief, was convinced from the start that the specification was best met by a 4–6–4 development, with bigger firebox and enlarged boiler heating surfaces, of the Class 01 and 03 Pacifics taking shape in the Reichsbahn's standard range. That was what eventually materialized, but not until folios of the competitive designs which Wagner's colleagues and superiors preferred to solicit from the six major German builders had been sifted and dismissed. They were an exotic collection, including a basically Stephensonian 4–6–4 with 8 ft $2\frac{1}{2}$ in (250·2 cm) driving wheels, a steam turbine or two and numerous cab-in-front creations, since one school of thought was convinced that at the higher speeds in mind the engine crew must have a panoramic forward view.

So well over two years elapsed before a Borsig proposal closely reflecting Wagner's original thought was committed to metal in 1934. By then so much had been spent in research and development that the Reichsbahn upped the building order to three locomotives, though it promptly nullified some of the economics of this by ordering the third as a cab-in front type, mechanically fired with pulverized coal to solve the inverted layout's handicap of a lengthy feed from tender to firebox at the front end. The aim was to determine whether the advantages of a front-end cab outweighed its accompanying complications. They did not. No 05.003 made no mark on history and was soon rebuilt.

Not so Nos 05.001 and 05.002. The second of these comprehensive streamlined three-cylinder 4-6-4s with 7 ft 6½ in (229·9 cm) driving wheels, a high 285 lb (129 kg) boiler pressure and very spacious firegate was spurred up to a world steam speed record of 124·5 mph (200·4 km/h) on all but level track near Berlin in May 1936. That was a well-prepared and publicized demonstration with a four-coach load of Third Reich functionaries, staged to add a technological glitter to the show of physical strength put on by Hitler's re-occupation of the Rhineland the previous March.

The two made just as much impression on the new pair of morning and evening Berlin–Hamburg expresses to which they were assigned in October 1935. These five-car trains, put on to supplement the limited seating of the diesel streamliners, were at first timed over the 178·1 miles (286·6 km) between the two cities at an average of 76·3 mph (122·8 km/h) eastbound and 77·4 mph (124·6 km/h) westbound, but with maximum speed limited to 90 mph (145 km/h) that was too demanding and in 1936 the schedules were eased out to a still spectacular 73·7 and 74·2 mph (118·6 and 119·4 km/h).

By 1939 the Reichsbahn had lifted the steam speed limit up a notch to 150 km/h (93 mph) on suitably signalled and upgraded trunk routes and had embarked on mass-production of streamlined Pacifics, 55 of Class 01.10 and 60 of Class 03.10 (two huge streamlined 4-8-4s, Class 06, were also produced). In the last pre-war summer, however, steam-hauled Reichsbahn trains were less dazzlingly timed than they had been in the middle of the decade. Even the Berlin–Hamburg flyers were marginally decelerated.

That allowed the Belgians a brief tenure of the title to operation of the Continent's fastest daily train. In the spring of 1939 the Belgian National Railways (SNCB) installed a twice-daily service of three-car trains over its easily-graded, well-aligned route between Brussels and Ostend which was scheduled over the 57·4 miles (92·4 km) from the Belgian capital to Bruges at an average of 74·9 mph (120·5 km/h) start to stop. For their traction the SNCB created a sextet of 6 ft 10½ in-wheel (209·6 cm) 4-4-2s, looking like some malformed flying fish with large smoke deflector plates set apart from a bulbous stream-lined casing that completely concealed their chimneys. One of these Atlantics was logged at 102·5 mph (165 km/h) on the service's maximum permitted load of five cars.

The 71·9 mph (115·7 km/h) average of the LNER's 'Coronation' streamliner between London and its York call en route to Edinburgh was the fastest attainable on British main lines, with their profusion of intersecting traffic flows and element of slow-moving and at best partially-continuous braked freight trains. Nevertheless, in the 1939 summer British steam was responsible for just over half the European daily mileage timed at 60 mph (97 km/h) or over with this form of traction; and for almost a quarter of the Continent's entire operation in that speed range.

In 1939 a new LMS 'Coronation Scot' train and Stanier Pacific No 6229 (it exchanged nameplates and numbers with No 6220 Coronation for the event) were shipped across the Atlantic for exhibition at the New York World's Fair; during their US travels LMS engine and train posed with the Baltimore & Ohio 'Royal Blue' train and its Pacific on Relay Viaduct.

Just before the war, too, Britain grabbed the world's steam speed record and never surrendered it.

That record was partly a riposte to the Reichsbahn's 1936 exploit, partly the *coup de grâce* in a long-running East Coast-West Coast contest which the 1923 amalgamation of the nineteenth century 'Race to the North' companies into the LNER and LMS had not muted. Of the other two post-1923 'Big Four', the SR, with its short and mostly unsuitable main lines, all of them encumbered with dense local traffic in the Greater London area, was no high-speed contender. And the GWR, which preferred to extend the Churchward 4–6–0 lineage to a burly four-cylinder 'King' class rather than move up to a 4–6–2, had tired of spotlighting the 'Cheltenham Flyer' and from 1935 onwards was more wisely concerned to uplift the standard speed of its expresses; by 1939, in fact, the proportion of GWR trains timed at an average of 58 mph (93 km/h) or more start to stop was Britain's highest.

A year after the 'Silver Jubilee's' flamboyant premiere the high-speed service's commercial magnetism was so clearly established that both LNER and LMS decided to launch similar trains between London and Scotland. To probe the A4 Pacific's capacity on the heavier Anglo-Scottish train in mind, the LNER laid on a measured evaluation of No 2512 *Silver Fox*'s performance on the 'Jubilee' for 27 August 1936 and, as a sideshow, bid the Pacific's driver attempt a new speed record down Stoke Bank, the well-aligned 12-mile (19·3 km) descent between Grantham and Peterborough that blessed the LNER with the finest rail racing-ground in the country. A marginally higher peak than the previous year's, 113 mph (182 km/h), was reached – but only just, and at some cost. None too artistically driven, *Silver Fox* had overheated so traumatically that

its middle big-end was allowed to flail and explode the front of the middle cylinder. It limped on to London like a wounded bull, high pressure steam jetting *fortissimo* from below the buffer-beam at each wheel revolution.

In November that year the LMS staged a London–Glasgow test trip that was more impressive, though the top speed registered was only 95 mph (153 km/h). The engine was No 6201 *Princess Elizabeth*, one of Stanier's initial series of four cylinder Pacifics that were essentially an embodiment of the design practices he had imbibed in his previous career at the GWR's Swindon works before recruitment as Chief Mechanical Engineer of the LMS. Stamina rather than extraordinary pace was asked of the *Princess* in this examination. No 6201 responded by working a seven-coach train from Euston to Glasgow, 401·3 miles (645·8 km), at an average of 68 mph (109 km/h) throughout on the first day, then returning the next with eight coaches at a mean speed of 70 mph (113 km/h), topping the formidable Shap and Beattock climbs north of Crewe at almost a mile (1·6 km) a minute.

For the resultant LMS Euston–Glasgow 'Coronation Scot' streamliner of 1937 Stanier designed Britain's biggest Pacific, the so-called 'Princess Coronation' type. This was a four-cylinder, 6 ft 9 in (205·7 cm) wheel machine with a bigger boiler and firebox than Gresley's A4 to endow it with sufficient power for the severe gradients north of Crewe as well as sustained speed capability elsewhere. Though the 'Coronation Scot' was to run to a more indulgent 6½-hour Euston–Glasgow schedule than the 6-hour Kings Cross–Edinburgh timing set the same year's Kings Cross–Edinburgh 'Coronation' of the LNER, the LMS decided that its train needed the promotional plug of a record-breaking pre-launch press demonstration run like that of the 'Silver Jubilee'. The only feasible racetrack on the LMS route, the descent from Whitmore to Crewe northbound, was considerably shorter than the LNER's Stoke Bank. So by the time No 6220 Coronation had been pushed marginally above Silver Fox's 1936 mark to 114 mph (184 km/h), Crewe station was just 2 miles (3·2 km) away. Flames streaming from protesting brake blocks, the train hit the first of the crossovers leading to its appointed platform at 57 mph (92 km/h), reeled sickeningly, but somehow stayed erect to halt in the station with no worse damage than contusions to pressmen hurled across their compartments and devastation of the kitchen car's crockery. The LNER ran their press trip with a 'Coronation' the next day. They set out covertly intent on recapturing the record, but A4 No 4489 Dominion of Canada muffed the attempt and managed only 109·5 mph (176·2 km/h) down Stoke Bank.

The Princess Coronation class was built with and without a streamlined shroud (the streamliners, too, were divested of their casing after the war, when the state of the track precluded high speed and accessibility for maintenance was far more important) and it was the unstreamlined No 6234 Duchess of Abercorn which left the type's most distinctive mark in British steam annals. At the start of 1939 Stanier selected No 6234 for modification with a Kylchap double blastpipe and chimney, a fitment later applied to the entire class; and in February that year the change was put to the test by coupling No 6234 to 20 coaches of 610 tons (620 tonnes) gross and setting the Pacific at the hills between Crewe and Glasgow. In a stunning display the Duchess charged the climb from Carnforth to Shap Summit at an average of 56·5 mph (91 km/h), its climactic 4 miles (6·4 km) at 1 in 75 notwithstanding; returning from Glasgow next day Beattock bank, which finishes at 1 in 99, was so powerfully attacked that the huge train made Carlisle in a mere 1½ minutes more than the 50 per cent lighter 'Coronation Scot' streamliner was allowed to that point.

Gresley, too, had at last been persuaded to fit some of his A4s with the Kylchap exhaust and it was with one of these, No 4468 Mallard, that the world steam speed title was wrested from the Germans on 3 July 1938. That summer the LNER was engaged in Sunday trials of a new quick-acting vacuum brake-valve for its streamlined train-sets and decided to exploit them for a new assault on the record – down Stoke Bank, needless to say. Sent storming up the hill out of Grantham to surmount Stoke summit at 74·5 mph (119·9 km/h), Mallard was up to 116 mph (187 km/h) within the first 6 miles (9·7 km) of the descent, then surged into the 120 mph (193 km/h) band for a continuous 2 miles (3·2 km), hitting a peak of 126 mph (203 km/h) before it was reined in.

Until the formation of the unified SNCF in 1938 the energies of the various French railways' traction chiefs were directed chiefly to the rebuilding of their existing front-rank steam power – 4–6–2s and 4–8–2s so far as the express passenger traction was concerned – to the Chapelon formula, some partially, some to the last detail. In every case performance was materially improved, but though the French compounds were still indisputably more thrifty with coal than their simple-expansion counterparts elsewhere, the rising cost of keeping their intricate mechanisms in good order was furrowing a few brows. Under question, too, was the machinery's durability in face of ever more oppressive commercial demands, which by the late 1930s were extending to the operation of 1,000-ton (1,016 tonne) freights at mean speeds of 50 mph (81 km/h) as well as 750-ton (762 tonne) passenger rapides at averages above 60 mph (97 km/h), yet within a 75 mph (121 km/h) ceiling.

On the eve of war some French railway officers were already urging trunk route electrification as the only economical course and plans for the first scheme, from Paris to Lyons, were in fact formulated during the country's German occupation. But though Chapelon's alternative of a new range of super-powered, six-cylinder compounds was rejected (except that a prototype 2–12–0 freight engine was built in 1946, amply fulfilling Chapelon's power prospectus but daunting in its fearsome mechanical complexity) and though post-war procurement was dominated by the importation of the 1,323 classically simple two-cylinder 141R 2–8–2s mentioned earlier, the SNCF did not entirely eschew new high-power steam passenger engine construction. Between 1940 and 1949 the Nord Region was handed a family of eight elegantly streamlined 4–6–4s, three of them three-cylinder simple expansion (Class 232R) and five four-cylinder compound (Class 232S and the unique Class 232U). The solitary No 232U1, not delivered until 1949, was arguably the most sophisticated steam locomotive ever constructed in Europe, embodying a wealth of power-operated devices to simplify a driver's mastery of its management on the road, not to mention a mechanical stoker for the fireman's comfort. The SNCF, though, had long since standardized mechanical firing on its biggest types. To these the final addition, in 1947, was a standard 4–8–2, the 241P, a refined version of the pre-war PLM 4–8–2 class.

The Nord 4–6–4s and two semi-streamlined three-cylinder Class 10 express passenger Pacifics which West Germany's newly-formed Deutsche Bundesbahn had Krupps build in 1957 were born too late for scope to flex their muscles fully. Generally speaking, wherever devastated or war-weary track had been thoroughly rehabilitated, it was to make paths straight for new diesels or for the electrifiers.

No European 4–6–2 or 4–8–2 was ever thrashed like its North American express passenger counterparts in the last decade before their submission to the diesel. The scale, of course, was different. Until the incursion of diesel traction brought with it an advance into weight-saving alloy and stainless steel carbuilding, the ponderous cars of a US 'Limited', all-steel and packed with air-conditioning plant and heavy furniture, could tare 80–85 tons (81–86 tonnes) apiece. Thus it took only a dozen of them to hoist train tonnage into four figures. Yet with that weight on a service such as New York Central's 'Twentieth Century Limited' one of the road's noble breed of 'Hudson' 4–6–4s could sustain an average speed of 70 mph (113 km/h) throughout 100-mile (161 km) or more stretches of the train's route.

In its final Class J3a form of 1938, which was the streamlined refinement of a basic 1927 design styled externally by industrial designer Henry Dreyfuss, the NYC Hudson was a 160·7-ton (163·3 tonne) machine compared with the 105·3 tons (107 tonnes) of an LMS Princess Coronation in Britain; and the 22½ by 29 in (57·2 × 73·7 cm) dimensions of its two cylinders, 275 lb (125 kg) pressure and 5,932 sq ft (551 sq m) of heating surface in its boiler and superheater contrasted with figures of 16½ in by 28 in (41·9 × 71·1 cm), 250 lb (113 kg) and 3,663 sq ft (340 sq m) for the British engine. But if one relates load behind the tender to engine weight,

then the LMS Pacific would need to have run 700-ton (711 tonne) trains from Euston to Crewe at a routine average of 70 mph (113 km/h) to stand comparison with the US 4–6–4s' performance. Inevitably US locomotives' coal consumption per ton-mile was proportionately extravagant.

Some of the toughest handling was meted out to the engines of the Western railroads that traversed the mountain chains inland from the Pacific coast on long and formidable gradients. To lift a 5,000-ton (5,080 tonne) freight up the 31 miles (50 km) in which the Union Pacific transcontinental route rises 1,953 ft (595 m) from Cheyenne, Wyoming, to its 8,013 ft (2,442 m) Sherman Hill summit, for instance, one of the system's gigantic 'Big Boy' 4–6–6–4s would be hammered unremittingly in full forward gear and 65 per cent cut-off for almost two hours. Santa Fe's crossing of the Great Divide, 126 miles (203 km) at 1 in 70 up to a steepest pitch of 1 in 28·5, was more draining still. Yet Santa Fe's classic 6 ft 10 in (208·3 cm) driving-wheel, two-cylinder 4–8–4s, unarguably the North American élite in this format, were set to run unchanged the entire 1,776 miles (2,858 km) from Kansas City to Los Angeles, mountains included – and, moreover, with up to 850 tons (864 tonnes) of train hanging on their gigantic 16-wheel tenders, which alone added 165 tons (168 tonnes) to the oil-burning 4–8–4s' charge. Of course, these phenomenally long runs were not non-stop. All else apart, the crippling US railroad agreements with their unions that prescribed only 100 miles' (161 km) driving as a day's work had to be respected by frequent crew changes, at some of which the engine would be refuelled and even accorded a basic servicing.

The most remarkable speed credited to a US 4–8–4 was notched by a Class J of the Norfolk & Western, a system on which the day-to-day passage of huge coal tonnages over the Appalachian Mountains to East Coast ports counted for much more than passenger revenue. Nevertheless the N&W ran some sprightly passenger services, despite the unhelpful characteristics of its main line. The latter dictated a 5 ft 10 in (177·8 cm) driving wheel diameter for the Class J; and it was that dimension which made the fully attested 110 mph (177 km/h) of one of the type on test with a 15-car, 915-ton (930 tonne) train over straight and level track so remarkable. On an equivalent load 105 mph (169 km/h) was also recorded with a streamlined 'Daylight' 4–8–4 of the Southern Pacific, which in its external styling was one of the most aesthetically pleasing of all US steam giants, and 102·5 mph (165 km/h) with a Union Pacific 4–8–4, both 6 ft 8 in-wheel (203·2 cm) types; but the US

The lighter version of Bulleid's unorthodox Pacific design for the Southern Railway: 'Battle of Britain' class No 21C154 *Lord Beaverbrook* winds a Victoria–Dover boat train through the curves at Chislehurst, Kent, in 1948.

4–8–4 was predominantly the heavy passenger haulier of US steam's ultimate years.

The racehorse of systems in the easier terrain of the Mid-West and East was the 4–6–4; and in that category the stellar performer was the Milwaukee Road's Class F7. The F7s were turned out in 1938 to supersede the streamlined 4–4–2s with which the Milwaukee had four years earlier launched its 'Hiawatha' high-speed service between Chicago and the Twin Cities of Minneapolis and St Paul, a route where it vied keenly with the parallel Chicago & North Western and Burlington systems. The Atlantics were no slouches – on a pre-service demonstration with six cars one held 112·5 mph (181·1 km/h) for 14 consecutive miles (22·5 km) – but immediate acclaim for the 'Hiawatha' soon made much heavier train formations imperative to satisfy demand. Besides, the Milwaukee needed an engine that could return to base from a day 'Hiawatha' duty on a weighty overnight sleeping-car train without fading. So, with the lift of 'Hiawatha' train tonnages from around 400 to 700 (406 to 711 tonnes) in mind, the Milwaukee created the 300 lb (136 kg) boiler pressure, 7 ft (213·4 cm) driving wheel F7.

In the 'Hiawatha' schedules the eastbound morning train was the only one in the world that ever posed steam power a daily start-to-stop timing at an average in excess of 80 mph (129 km/h), with a 58-minute timing for the 78·3 miles (126 km) from Sparta to Portage start to stop that exacted a mean of 81 mph (130 km/h). To observe that and less stringent timings elsewhere, given the existence of one or two quite severe permanent speed restrictions, the 'Hiawathas' had to hit 100 mph (161 km/h) as a daily routine where the infrastructure was conducive. Two illustrations must serve to witness the F7s' command of the job. In 1943 one of them was logged at an average of 100·5 mph (161·7 km/h) for 62 miles (99·8 km) with 780 tons (793 tonnes) in tow, and without exceeding 102·5 mph (165 km/h); and with a lighter, 465–ton (473 tonne) formation another once devoured 148 miles (238 km) of the Minneapolis–Chicago course at 90 mph (145 km) or more, over 58 (93 km) of them at 100–106 mph (161–171 km), so that its average for 62 consecutive miles (99·8 km) was 98·3 mph (158·2 km/h).

Some of the big railroads which made much of their living from coal-hauling were understandably reluctant to join the gathering queue outside the diesel builders' offices. It was one of these, the Pennsylvania, which sponsored the mightiest steam locomotives ever created for a purely passenger role. Right through the 1930s the 'Pennsy' had stuck by its redoubtable K4s Pacifics, conservatively oblivious to other

systems' move up to 4–6–4s, 4–8–2s (which the 'Pennsy' did use, but only for fast freight) and 4–8–4s. But at length, with rising loads and speed compelling costly resort to double-heading of the Pacifics on almost all its main routes, the Pennsylvania backed down and took counsel of the three main builders, Baldwin, ALCO and Lima. The outcome was an eccentric series of duplex drive locomotives – that is, monsters with two sets of driving wheels and cylinders, but with each rigidly fixed to the main frames; the Pennsylvania, idiosyncratic in so many ways, was never enamoured of the articulated layout in which one of the two engines pivoted independently. The first product of the new approach was a gigantic bullet-nosed 6–4–4–6 with a 300 lb (136 kg) pressure boiler, 7 ft (213·4 cm) driving wheels and four 22 by 26 in (55·9 × 66·1 cm) cylinders, which extended just over 140 ft (42·7 m) from front to rear of its 16-wheel tender and which turned the scales (engine alone) at $271\frac{1}{2}$ tons (276 tonnes).

This incredible machine, assembled at the railroad's own Altoona shops in 1939, proved little more than a test-bed for design ideas that eventually took series production form as the shark-nosed Class T1 4–4–4–4 for express passenger haulage and the booster-fitted Class Q2 4–4–6–4 for freight work. The Class Q2 design, incidentally, was reached by way of a prototype 4–6–4–4 in which the rear four-coupled engine had its cylinders facing the tender, a format adopted to permit close grouping of all ten driving wheels so as to reduce the rigid wheelbase to the minimum but one which had the critical disadvantage of limiting firegrate size. As for the T1s, they did not hold the diesel at bay. Certainly they proved capable of rolling 1,000-ton (1,016 tonne) trains

French Railways' post-war mixed traffic type, the Class 141R 2-8-2; in this 1947 scene No 141.R.740 heads an express from the Pyrenees to Lyons.

119

The classic New York Central 'Hudson' 4-6-4 as streamlined to Henry Dreyfuss' designs for the 'Twentieth Century Limited': here No 5448 is bringing a less exalted 15-car train into Chicago in 1939.

at up to 100 mph (161 km/h) on the flat, but they ran up intolerable maintenance bills, not only for themselves but for the civil engineers whose track they tended to ravage, especially at starting, since they were incorrigibly prone to slip when they were getting a grip of their trains.

The 4–6–4 and 4–8–4 had evolved in the late 1920s from a seminal shift in American locomotive design theory. This was largely inspired by a dawning realization that the goal of higher and higher starting tractive effort pursued in the Mallet compound articulated was losing its appeal. The vast, all-purpose freight trains which the Mallets could get moving – the 'drags' – were ceding their higher-rated merchandise to the emergent road transport system because of their abysmally slow pace on the move and the time absorbed in assembling and dispersing them in the marshalling yards. The need of power to sustain good over-the-road speed was coming into sharper focus with each advancing year of the 1920s.

It was Lima, most junior of the big US locomotive builders, which in 1925 pointed the way. Compound expansion was dismissed. The 4–8–2 layout was inverted to 2–8–4 to make room for a stoker-fed firebox with a very spacious grate area that served a chubby 8 ft-diameter (243·8 cm) boiler pressed to the then high value of 240 lb (109 kg), a pair of 28 in by 30 in (71·1 × 76·2 cm) cylinders was matched with 5 ft 9 in (175·3 cm) driving wheels; and a booster was fitted to the trailing bogie for extra starting punch. On test Lima's prototype, known as A-1, immediately demonstrated unprecedented versatility. At one end of the scale it wheeled a 2,296-ton (2,333 tonne) freight of the Boston & Albany over 55 miles (89 km) of that system's arduous route in the Berkshire Hills of Western Massachussetts in half the time normally taken by the B&A's existing traction. At the other extreme it was triumphantly set to

work the Milwaukee Road's 16-car 'Olympian' express unchanged over 2,188 miles (3,521 km) of prairie, Rockies and Cascades Mountains from Chicago to Seattle.

The Boston & Albany promptly bought 55 for its Berkshire Mountains route (hence the type's generic title of 'Berkshire'), the Illinois Central took 50, and soon afterward the Texas & Pacific was a customer for an enlarged 2–10–4 version (hence the 2–10–4's tag of 'Texas'). The supreme expression of the Lima 2–10–4 was Chesapeake & Ohio's order of 1930, the most powerful two-cylinder engines the world ever knew, which with their booster in play could summon up a starting tractive effort of 108,625 lb (49,272 kg). With a grate area of 121·7 sq ft (11·3 sq m), and a 265 lb (120 kg) pressure boiler, the heating surfaces of which aggregated a fifth of an acre (approximately 0·08 of a hectare), each of the 40 C&O T-1 2–10–4s fed their two 29 in by 34 in (73·7 × 86·4 cm) cylinders so adequately that they could roll 12,000-ton (12,193 tonne) coal trains at a much brisker pace than the road's 2–8–8–2 Mallet compounds, which they comprehensively outclasssed even as 'drag' hauliers.

Nevertheless many US railroads remained wedded to the maximum-tonnage, minimum-speed philosophy until the 1930s, when designers grapsed that the Lima principles were as valid for articulated layouts as for rigid-frame designs. The full potential of the simple-expansion articulated was not realized by most of its early adherents, who adopted it for the same high-starting-effort, slow-road-speed role as the Mallet compound articulated had filled. That was true in particular of the Northern Pacific's 'Yellowstone' 2–8–8–4s of 1929, 323-ton (328 tonne) monsters paired with 179-ton (182 tonne) tenders. They had huge boilers pressed as high as 250 lb (113 kg) and an unequalled grate area of 182 sq ft (16·9 sq m), but were rarely run at more than 30 mph (48 km/h). Moreover, they never had a chance to prove their boast of the strongest drawbar horsepower output in steam locomotive history because they were fuelled with very low grade coal.

Right to the eclipse of US steam several railroads were still over-investing in power, seemingly blind to the rationale of allying a free-steaming, high-performance boiler of gargantuan proportions to a well-proportioned simple-expansion mechanism. The stupendous 336-ton (341 tonne) 2–6–6–6s with 5 ft 7 in (170·2 cm) driving wheels and a 260 lb (118 kg) pressure boiler with a combined heating surface of 10,426 sq ft (968·6 sq m) which the C&O and Virginian acquired in the early 1940s, for instance, scarcely ever fully exercised the sustained 8,000 hp output for which they were designed. Such strength was only needed to get the slow-speed coal drags that were their lifetime's employment on the move. Given some aid at starting, less ponderous machines would have done the rest of the job as effectively and more economically.

There were nevertheless some sagacious logical practitioners of simple-expansion articulated theory. Having confounded all received wisdom by successfully operating rigid-frame three-cylinder 4–12–2s at up to 60 mph (97 km/h) in the late 1920s, Union Pacific was naturally one of them. Other roads, such as Norfolk & Western with its 5 ft 10 in-wheel (177·8 cm) Class A 2–6–6–4s, occasionally assigned articulateds to passenger duty, but UP and neighbouring Southern Pacific were unique in rostering them consistently to front-rank passenger work. UP was further distinguished as the only railroad to sanction articulateds' daily operation at up to 60 mph (97 km/h) – and also for its seeming insouciance to articulated drivers' frequent breach of that ceiling. A few of UP's ultimate 1943–4 batch, 65 strong, of its 105 'Challenger' 4–6–6–4s were in fact honoured with the road's two-tone grey passenger steam engine livery. These splendid four-cylinder machines, scaling 283 tons (288 tonnes) – their 14-wheel tenders added 155 tons (158 tonnes) more – with 5 ft 9 in (175·3 cm) driving wheels and boilers pressed at 280 lb (127 kg), were frequently directed to pilot the diesel streamliners over Sherman Hill summit when the new trains' formations escalated to tonnages that would otherwise have reduced the first-generation GM diesel-locomotives to a speed inviting traction motor burn-out.

The biggest and heaviest articulateds were UP's Big Boy 4–8–8–4s. They were, in fact, the most massive steam locomotives ever built. The wheelbase alone of one of these leviathans stretched 72 ft 6 in (22·1 m), while total length over couplers of engine and 14-wheel tender (which could store 30 tons – 31 tonnes – of coal as well as 25,000 gallons – 113,653 litres – of water!) was 132 ft 9⅞ in (approximately 40·5 m), and total weight of both just over 540 tons (549 tonnes). A huge firebox with 150 sq ft (13·9 sq m) of grate area spanned the combined length of the trailing bogie and the two rearmost driving wheels, serving a 300 lb (136 kg) pressure boiler which in conjunction with four 23¾ in by 32 in (60·3 × 81·3 cm) cylinders and 5 ft 8 in (172·7 cm) driving wheels achieved a phenomenal tractive effort of 135,375 lb (61,406 kg). The Big Boys were frequently run in pairs to hump 90–100 freight cars over Sherman Hill and it needed no fewer than 10 of the early Electro-Motive F diesels competently to supplant such a combination. But a Big Boy could just as readily sustain its maximum output at 70 mph (113 km/h).

Whether the spectacle of one making this pace or even more on one of the wartime troop trains to which the 4–8–8–4s were frequently deputed was any less riveting than a pair of them blasting up Sherman Hill on 8,000 tons (8,129 tonnes) of freight is an open question.

The steam locomotive, it has been observed, was a unique piece of machinery in that for a century it defied all attempts to improve its fortuitous combination of simplicity, efficiency and economy. The efforts to enhance that economy by raising its poor thermal efficiency, which ranged from abortive essays with ultra-high-pressure boilers and steam turbine-propelled locomotives to various devices for pre-heating the boiler feed water, persisted but few even passed the test of a prototype. The steam locomotive stood condemned finally, not so much for its performance on the track but above all for the high cost incurred in keeping it on the track. As the second half of this century advanced technology would develop traction, especially electric, with performance characteristics far beyond the practical capability of a steam locomotive. In the immediate post-war world it was the expense of satisfying the steam locomotive's frequent demands for servicing and its limited capacity for continuous work that mainly brought about its supercession.

Maybe that supercession was not conclusive. The traumatic rise in oil costs and the vulnerability of oil supplies on the one hand, the capital cost of electrification on the other, have not merely persuaded some countries with cheap domestic reserves of coal, such as South Africa and Zimbabwe, to rehabilitate the best of their remaining steam power for a further term of life. Notably in the US it has inspired a new school of steam locomotive technology. And at least one of the big US coal-hauling railroads, Burlington Northern, has a keenly interested eye on this school's research and development work.

Articulated as passenger power: one of Union Pacific's 'Challenger' 4-6-6-4s pulls out of Denver with a chartered 16-car special for Cheyenne in 1948.

8

THE RECORD RAIL EFFORT OF THE SECOND WORLD WAR

Civilians brave the live rail in London's south-eastern suburbs to offer fruit to a trainload of British troops evacuated from Dunkirk in 1940: the rolling stock is Great Western.

STEEL WHEEL ROLLING on steel rail achieves the most frictionless movement – short of levitation – yet devised; as a result a train can move more tonnage per unit of traction, per unit of fuel consumed and per staff involved in the transit than any other medium. Of that pre-eminence the Second World War called for a supreme demonstration, above all in the US, with its commitment to supply huge forces to both Europe and the Pacific. In their most exacting year, 1943, US railroads humped 1½ billion tons (1·52 billion tonnes) of freight an average distance of 473 miles (761 km), which adds up to a performance of 737 billion ton-miles. At the same time, with no curbs on civilian travel but petrol rationing and tyre shortages to inhibit use of cars, passenger traffic that year was actually climbing faster than freight tonnage. Extraordinarily, the war was reversing the trend into which the passenger business seemed locked in the 1930s.

Just one astonishing mark of the demand for train travel is the fact that whereas in 1940 the New York Central served just over 850,000 meals in its dining-cars operating out of Chicago, the aggregate on the same services in 1944 was an astronomical 2·38 million.

With the incubus of troop trains, 114,000 of which transported some 43 million US Servicemen and women during the war years and accounted for all but 3 per cent of the armed forces' organized movement, US railroads recorded 910 million passenger journeys in 1944. The average of each trip was 105 miles (169 km), so the passenger-mileage aggregate for the year was a massive 95·5 million (153·7 million km).

At the time the railroads' total operating staff numbered 1,414,000. In that epic year, therefore, each of them could be credited on average with the production of 522,000 ton-miles of freight service and 67,500 passenger-miles (108,628 km) of travel! Never again, probably, will such manpower productivity be attained in transport.

The adaptability of the railroads' operating capacity saved the US more than one serious domestic crisis. For instance, when U-boats frustrated the normal oil supply of Eastern seaboard cities by tanker from the Gulf ports in the south, the railroads, until then negligibly involved in this traffic, somehow rustled up the tank wagons and improvised train working to cope from December 1941 to late 1943, when new pipelines were ready to relieve them. At that juncture trains were shifting some 42 million gallons (190·9 million litres) of oil a day from Gulf and mid-country refineries to the East. For the same reason – U-boat disruption – the railroads had suddenly to absorb 70 per cent of New England's coal supplies which in peacetime had been ferried from Virginian ports by coastal colliers.

Technical advance since the First World War was largely responsible for the railroads' heroic response. Especially valuable was the wartime trebling of trunk route-mileage (to almost 6,500 – 10,461 km) over which operation was governed by Centralized Traffic Control (CTC), whereby a despatcher could oversee up to 400 miles (644 km) of single track and organize the passing-loop meets of opposing trains much more efficiently. But even more influential than improved technology was the determination of railroad manage-

Far left:
Uniforms dominate the platform scene at London's Paddington terminus in May 1942.

ments to co-operate with each other and ward off a Federal takeover as cramping as that of the First World War. They were rewarded by record rates of net income from the flood of traffic, and as a result company after company was able to reduce accumulated debt and avoid the bankruptcy pit that had yawned in front of a good many at the close of the 1930s.

On the other side of the Atlantic the 1940 evacuation of British and Allied troops from Dunkirk confronted British railwaymen with an operating emergency on a scale previously unimaginable. Between 27 May and 4 June they had to improvise 565 special trains, 327 of them from Dover, to lift almost 300,000 men from the English Channel coast ports. The majority of the trains were routed away from London via a cross-country route which entailed their reversal at Redhill, a junction with a none-too-generous layout on the main line from London to the South Coast. At this Surrey crossroads the re-engining of trains and the turning and servicing of locomotives that were displaced summoned up prodigies of operating dexterity, never mind human endurance, throughout that critical week. A measure of the strain was that by the week's end the yard of Redhill's modest locomotive depot was walled in by beetling mountains of ash aggregating around 300 tons (305 tonnes) that had been cleared from locomotive smokeboxes and firegrates during servicing.

This phenomenal operation was planned and executed entirely by railwaymen. Generally speaking, they were always better left to run wartime railways themselves, both at home and behind the battle lines, and whether in uniform

Experimental armour-plating of a Riddles WD 2-8-0 as boiler protection from air strafing; it added almost 8 tons to the weight of the locomotive, which as a result was scarcely ever used.

or out of it. Though the German railway system reacted as efficiently to emergencies, there were severe strains in the relations between the Third Reich's military Directorate of Transportation and its Reichsbahn opposite numbers. Railwaymen denigrated the military officials as interfering staff officers basically ignorant of transport, and the Directorate's structure as rigidly bureaucratic and mistrustful of initiative. They were not best pleased, either, to discover in the later years of the war that wagons labelled as high-priority war supplies not infrequently bore champagne or other luxuries for officers' messes. On the military side, the Directorate's men were often irritated by what they regarded as pettifogging Reichsbahn obstruction of their callow operational schemes.

Almost as surprising as the throughput of tracks immune from enemy harassment was the speed with which railways nearer the front lines rebounded from bomb damage or calculated destruction by retreating armies. The Luftwaffe's November 1940 devastation of Coventry, for instance, left every rail route into and around the city, bar one devious bypass, cut by a total of 122 hits; yet despite the incredible problems even of getting repair trains to the smitten areas the whole network was operational again within a week. The incessant, overwhelming day and night Allied air assault on the rail systems of Belgium and Northern France from March to the Normandy invasion's D-Day in June 1944 failed to halt troop movement by rail; and though it certainly reduced the daily rail movement of supplies from 60–70 to 20 trains, it succeeded only insofar that it forced the Germans to restrict the rail tonnage rigidly to military essentials, and to put up with inevitable delays because under inexorable attack a proportion of the rail network was always unusable.

It was the dearth of transversal main lines and the indifferent capacity of north-south connections, such as there were, which helped to undo the Germans on the Russian front. Their difficulties were exacerbated by the gauge difference, which put a premium on the capture of usable Russian rolling stock, but this the retreating Red Army did their utmost to forestall by destruction or withdrawal of equipment behind their own lines. The German High Command tried vainly to frustrate the Russians by prefacing offensives with air attacks or ground sorties to cut rail lines in the Russian rear, thereby to pen locomotives and vehicles ready for seizure by the following armies; but for the most part the Germans had to re-gauge the railways they overran and import their own locomotives, all too many of which were then found overweight for Russian infrastructure or very vulnerable to Russia's bitter winters. Moscow was saved largely because sufficient fuel could not be railborne to the German armour over supply lines which by then were impossibly over-extended. The Russians, on the other hand, were benefiting from the greater compactness of the rail framework into which they had withdrawn and its unprecedentedly generous stock of locomotives, greatly augmented by machines snatched from the Germans' grasp. Moreover, the Russians were adding as much as 4,500 miles (7,242 km) of new railway to the network still in their hands, including a 600-mile (966 km) north-south route along the Volga from Kazan to Stalingrad.

On the Western Front the Battle of the Bulge, the blunting of the Germans' last desperate lunge through the Ardennes in December 1944, produced an outstanding example of the railway's vital role in the Second World War. To stem the powerful German assault four entire divisions of the US Third Army, including all their support apparatus, were transported laterally across the rear of the front and into position on its south flank within 48 hours – and that despite the nuisance of heavy snow which there were no ploughs to clear, only manual labour. In the heat of that battle shells were on occasion railed through fierce bombing and strafing right up to the artillery positions themselves.

All combatants naturally yoked their locomotive industries to the essential claims of the war effort. In the US, as has been indicated already, the diesel builders were directed to concentrate their production on specific model ranges to obviate wasteful competition. For the same reason some railroads in need of extra steam freight power were bidden to accept fresh batches of designs already proven on other systems.

On both sides of the Atlantic new construction conceived expressly for passenger work was barred for the duration, though in Britain Oliver Bulleid's 'Merchant Navy' Pacific inexplicably eluded the embargo. Granted, the Southern Railway of 1941 sorely needed more high-power traction. But since the design had been shaped in the late 1930s with Continental boat train haulage primarily in mind and considering that after the war these Pacifics were virtually reserved to express passenger duty, the 'mixed traffic' label which the SR management virtuously gave to the engines at their birth was pure public relations window-dressing. It could not have deluded the experienced railway officers who formed Britain's wartime Railway Executive.

The most rigidly conscripted industry was without question Germany's. Perfection of new eight- and ten-coupled types under the Reichsbahn's standardization programme of the 1930s had the Third Reich's war machine better supported with heavy freight power than that of any other European combatant. Nevertheless the Wehrmacht's deep thrusts eastward and westward generated a massive demand for still more traction to serve the railways that had been overrun and that in most cases had had their locomotive stock depredated in the process. The most profuse production run of a single locomotive type in world history was the outcome. The Class 50 2–10–0 design of the Reichsbahn's standard range was revised as the Class 52, the 'Kriegslok', a simplified version that eschewed frills, conserved scarce materials and exploited every conceivable method of man-hour economy in construction. To this was paired a variant with heavier axle-loading, the Class 42, and between 1942 and 1945 around 10,000 of the two types were put together in a score of works in occupied Czechoslovakia, Austria, Belgium and Poland as well as Germany itself. In one month alone, September 1943, the output of Class 52 was 505. US production of spartan Class S160 2–8–0s and so-called 'MacArthur' 2–8–2s, and British manufacture of Stanier's LMS 2–8–0 and later of Riddles' elemental 2–8–0 and 2–10–0 designs for shipment to war zone railways, were nowhere near as intensive.

After the war every European mainland railway it had involved confronted awesome problems of reconstruction. For the Germans they were aggravated by the division of the Third Reich. This split a railway system

As a gesture to the wartime drive for raw material economy the Southern Railway's Bulleid designed his powerful Class Q1 freight 0-6-0 of 1942 without most of the traditional external graces of the British steam locomotive: No C25 heads a train of troops and equipment past Clapham Junction towards Staines in September 1942.

One of the many US War Department 2-8-0s sent to the European war zone heads an LNER Cambridge line freight past Whittlesford in September 1943.

developed on an east-west traffic axis into two independent networks, the newborn Deutsche Bundesbahn (DB) in the west and the residual Deutsche Reichsbahn (DR) in the east, each of which had now to adapt to primarily north-south traffic flows. The great trunk routes of the Third Reich, such as Berlin–Hamburg, were severed by the new frontier between West and East Germany and denuded of most of their traffic. Conversely, north-south routes such as Cologne–Mainz-Frankfurt and Hamburg–Hannover–Stuttgart–Munich in West Germany were to have thrust on them a weight of inter-city passenger and freight business for which their infrastructure was totally inadequate.

Worse still, a high proportion of the German rail system emerged with its main lines reduced to single track. The Germans themselves had begun the process, thinning out less essential routes to salvage material for bomb damage repair, and the occupying powers continued it – especially the Russians, who were quick to

avenge the mutilation of their own railways. The DR in any case started life in a worse state than the DB, because of the more savage devastation of the eastern battle areas. Its miseries multiplied as the Russians sequestered over 5,000 miles (8,047 km) of track – here and there by completely obliterating a route – and dismantled, then shipped to the USSR, the entire electrification apparatus, catenary, supports and sub-stations, of the main lines from Probstzella via Halle to Leipzig, Leipzig to Berlin, Dessau to Leipzig and Halle to Magdeburg. At its birth the DR had just 198 route-miles (319 km) of usable double track, from Berlin to Frankfurt/Oder, Wittenberge via Halle to Erfurt, and Magdeburg to Helmstedt, on the border with West Germany. In the 1980s restoration of double track was still claiming a good deal of the DR's capital resources.

For an impression of conditions on the victors' side, consider the state of the SNCF. When France was liberated, only 11,180 (17,992 km) of the 26,400 route-miles (42,486 km) operated in 1939 were usable and this attenuated system was effectively cut in two by the destruction of all bridges over the Loire river below Roanne. On the SNCF as a whole 2,603 bridges and viaducts had been destroyed, along with a third of all buildings. Of the 17,058 steam locomotives with which the SNCF entered the war, only 10,500 could be unearthed at the Liberation and 7,500 of them were unusable. Half the pre-war wagon stock had disappeared; a quarter of what was left was a write-off; and only 7,800 of the 16,900 passenger coaches left in France were runners, whereas the pre-war fleet of such vehicles had totalled 37,700.

Both in France and in the Low Countries rehabilitation of the railway system was accorded high priority as a key to revival of economic life. With the crucial assistance of Marshall Aid dollars from the US recovery was extraordinarily rapid. As early as May 1946 the SNCF had all but 25,000 route-miles (40,233 km) of its system back in use and by July 1948, following deliveries of massive orders for locomotives (principally the 1,323 Class 141R 2–8–2s referred to in an earlier chapter) and rolling stock placed mostly in the US and Canada, the SNCF had 12,500 steam locomotives, 1,200 electric locomotives, 17,300 passenger coaches and 320,000 freight wagons fully operational. In 1947, astonishingly, it was able to move 20·5 per cent more passengers and 6·2 per cent more freight tonnage than it had in 1938, and under both headings over substantially longer distances on average.

Had the war gone the Third Reich's way to the end, Europe might have been the setting for a phenomenal new railway concept. In the last two pre-war years, inspired to grandiose thinking by Germany's burgeoning network of four-lane *autobahnen*, study groups within the Reichsbahn had already begun sketching ideas for new high-capacity freight railways of 12 ft 2 in (370·8 cm) or even 13 ft 2 in (401·3 cm) gauge. The wider of the two was conceived as high-speed piggyback for standard-gauge vehicles; its huge flatcars would have had floors laid with parallel 4 ft 8½ in-gauge (143·5 cm) tracks, each long enough to carry up to four standard-gauge freight wagons end-to-end.

Then, in 1942, Hitler himself issued direct orders both to his Transport Ministry and to the Reichsbahn to plan a super-broad-gauge trunk railway system, passenger- as well as freight-carrying, to span the whole of the Greater German Reich he aimed to assemble by conquest. As promulgated in a map of 1943, this extraordinary railway was to radiate initially from Berlin to Hamburg, Paris, Vienna, Istanbul, Kiev and Rostov. Later extensions would

stretch it to Brest, Marseilles, Trieste, Rome, the Middle East, Stalingrad, Moscow and Leningrad. The megalomaniac concept was taken as far as fully-fledged designs for track, stations, vehicles and traction, by the Reich's railway manufacturing industry as well as by Reichsbahn and Ministry. The gauge finally selected was 9 ft 10 in (299·7 cm).

Recent research has revealed that over 200,000 drafts and final working drawings were produced for the detail of the proposed passenger coaches alone. These were to have been gigantic double-deckers seating as many as 460 per car in third class, but exploiting their enormous girth to create cruise-liner-like interiors in first class. To judge from full-colour artist's impressions which have survived, America's great transcontinental streamliners would have been made to look cramped by comparison. And in range of accommodation too, for the plans included designs of a sleeping car with its own plush and capacious breakfast room, a car embodying four bathrooms, 20 shower rooms and male and female hairdressing saloons, and a 196-seater cinema car. A luxury dining-car design, oblivious to considerations of non revenue-earning vehicle tonnage, was not double-deck but vaulted to the full possible body height of 14 ft 9 in (450 cm); its windows soared from tabletop height to ceiling and its projected body width of 19 ft 8¼ in (600 cm) allowed installation of three longitudinal rows of four-seater tables with two parallel passageways each of table width, so that its internal appearance was indistinguishable from that of a high-grade restaurant on terra firma.

Freight wagons were envisaged on the same Brobdingnagian scale. Likewise locomotives: details have survived, for example, of a 750-tonne (738 ton), 30-axle diesel-electric four-unit roughed out by Henschel for express passenger haulage, which was to be powered by four MAN 5,500 hp engines for a total output of 22,000 hp; of a three-unit electric freight locomotive on 18 axles with a planned continuous output of 29,500 hp; even of a 1,070-tonne (1,053 ton) twin-unit steam locomotive, in a layout sandwiching a 12-axle tender between two independent 8–8–8s!

The express passenger types, their passenger vehicles and the track were to be fit for operation at up to 250 km/h (155 mph). Even at a quarter that pace, a full-size prototype would have been an awe-inspiring spectacle. But Hitler's imperial dreams had turned sour on both Eastern and Western fronts by the time his super-railway was fully designed. Metal was never cut to realize as much as one vehicle or track length of it.

Cologne cathedral stands
miraculously erect amid the
devastation of the
Hohenzollern rail bridge and
of the rest of the city on the
Rhine's bank.

Top:
Among the 10,000 2-10-0s
produced by the German war
machine was this Class 42.

Above:
Passenger travel on the
devastated German Railways
in 1945, when large numbers
of serviceable passenger
coaches were being handed
over to the Allies as
reparations.

9

ADJUSTMENT TO A NEW TRANSPORT AGE

THE SPREAD AND REFINEMENT of motor transport, spared directly quantifiable payment for the infrastructure and ancillary services it employed, was already raising doubt about the role of railways and the continuing logic of obligations they had inherited from their nineteenth century years of monopoly in the 1930s. Within only a few post-war years those misgivings were intensifying into one of the major and most vexing political issues of the twentieth century's second half so far as Governments west of the Iron Curtain were concerned.

From 1950 onwards the motor manufacturing plants of Europe unleashed a rising flood of motor vehicles exploiting all the economic mass-production techniques and technological advances spawned by the war effort. West Germany, for example, counted only 2·4 million motor vehicles of all kinds in 1950. By 1960 the total had swollen to 8 million, by 1970 to 16·8 million and by 1976 to 22·1 million. Of that 1976 aggregate over 17·7 million were passenger vehicles, either buses or private cars. And at the same time the country's motorway and main road system was substantially expanded to increase the convenience of road passenger or freight transport for door-to-door movement, even over long distances. From 78,300 (126,008 km) in 1950 the aggregate route-mileage of these

thoroughfares had been extended to more than 93,000 (149,665 km) by 1970; and the total went on rising through the following decade.

The concurrent effect on the newborn German Federal Railway's (DB) market share of national passenger and freight movement was traumatic. The volume of that movement, of course, was swelling from year to year. But except in the bulk freight market the railway was incapable of seizing a proper proportion of the growth through its failure to match road transport's flexibility, rapidly advancing quality of service and price. In 1950 the DB commanded a 37·5 per cent share of West Germany's total passenger travel, more than either buses (29·3 per cent) or even private cars (33·1 per cent). Within only ten years the railway's proportion had been more than halved, to 16·6 per cent; a decade more and it was reduced to 7·8 per cent, while by 1976 the DB could claim only 6 per cent. Public road transport had fared less disastrously over the 26 years, finishing them with 11·5 per cent of the total, but the private car share had soared to a massive 81 per cent.

In the freight sector the DB's traffic was less drastically, but still grievously, ended. The railway's share of the country's total movement slumped from 56 per cent to 26·4 per cent between 1950 and 1976, while that of long-distance

The uncompetitive British Rail fast merchandise freight of the mid-century, with its traditional short-wheelbase, low-payload wagons: BR standard Class 9 2-10-0 No 92151 rumbles south through Acocks Green, in the West Midlands, in 1961.

Far left:
The multiple-unit diesel railcar was to be the economic saviour of British Rail's urban and country short-haul passenger services: a three-car set in the then standard BR dmu livery hums out of Tyseley on a Leamington Spa–Birmingham Moor Street service in 1964.

Steam-hauled passenger trains lasted over two post-war decades on some non-electrified routes of the German Federal Railway: this midday departure from Saarbrücken for Frankfurt is headed by post-war mixed traffic Class 23 2-6-2 No 23.047.

road transport rose from 10·1 to 30·5 per cent and the proportion carried by inland water transport declined marginally, despite the barge operators' freedom from all but 10 per cent or so of their true infrastructure maintenance costs. These percentages, however, masked a particularly disturbing aspect of the move into road transport. Whether plying for public hire or privately operated (that is, by companies for exclusive conveyance of their own products), the lorries were creaming away the greater part of the business in consumer goods and other products that offered the most convenient loads and transits and the best financial return. Outside the bulk freight markets to which road transport was not well-suited – the transport of coal, minerals and so on – the railways were left with the dross, which as common carriers they were obliged to accept; and to accept, moreover, at rates controlled by their Governments to prevent the railways pricing themselves out of unwelcome traffics. For that matter, passenger fare levels were also Government-regulated as an instrument of social policy.

These trends had another crucial effect on European railways. The switch of short-haul and small-lot freight to the roads stripped yet more traffic from secondary and rural lines that had begun to feel the pinch before the war. Thus, to cite the DB once more as an example, 90 per cent of its passengers and freight were by the end of the 1970s concentrated on 50 per cent of its network.

On the other side of the Iron Curtain the problems were almost everywhere the reverse. There freedom to opt out of rail transport was strictly circumscribed, either because the State enforced a concentration on its railways of all long-haul and bulk traffic, because road improvement was inadequate, because road vehicle development and production were curbed, or because of all three factors in concert. As a result, the railways were soon stretched to the limit of their operating capacity – and in most cases still are. The USSR's railways were left trailing the rest of industry in the country's first post-war Five-Year Plan of reconstruction, but after Stalin's death the Russians awoke to the calamitous effect continuing capital starvation of the rail system would have on the national economy. In 1956 a mammoth modernization programme was put in hand, with total dieselization or electrification one of its priorities, and 20 years later the comparison between the freight performance of the Russian system, SZD, and West Germany's DB was striking. Whereas that year the DB transported 298 million tonnes (293 million tons) over a network totalling 17,800 route-miles (28,646 km), the SZD shifted more than 12 times as much over a system less than five times as extensive – almost 3·7 *billion* tonnes (approximately 3·6 billion tons) over an aggregate of 86,100 route-miles (138,561 km).

At the end of the 1970s, despite the fact that it had still fully to restore the pre-war track capacity of the railways in its territory, the Reichsbahn (DR) of East Germany was responsible for as much as 65 per cent of its country's freight movement, calculated in ton-mileage. Moreover, it was preparing for its proportion to rise to 73 per cent during the 1980s in the wake of State decisions to trim long-distance road haulage and thereby to restrain oil imports. For years it had been a principle of East German transport policy to entrust all goods travelling more than 50 km (31 miles) to the railway, but the tracks were so

choked that the rule had to be relaxed in the regular conferences between industry and transport authorities, Ministerially chaired, which measured output forecasts against capacity and reallocated traffic as necessary. As hard-pressed as the DR was Poland's national system, PKP, which in the 1970s was funnelling over its busiest main lines two-thirds more freight annually than the DB's were carrying in West Germany, almost twice as much as the chief SNCF routes in France. Consequently the effect on the PKP of Poland's political turmoil in the early 1980s was particularly dire.

In Western Europe the annual debit of secondary lines that had been worrying in the 1930s became a more and more acute anxiety as road transport sapped their traffic. But other factors were steadily worsening the economics of railway working as a whole. Railways were still being run basically as they had been, not merely since the inter-war period but since the days when their only competitors were the barge and the horse. They were still supporting from the same level of resources all the infrastructure, all the apparatus, both mechanical and bureaucratic, and all the staff needed to offer every rural station not merely a passenger service but a delivery service just for single parcels, never mind odd wagonloads of goods.

The overhead costs in fixed plant and staff this kind of traffic incurred would have been gross enough, compared to those involved in doing the same jobs by road, even if inflation had not added its aggravation within a few years of the war's end. The labour-intensive character of traditional railway working was focussed still more sharply by the concern of railwaymen to pace their wages with the attractive rates that

post-war, capital-intensive industry – in motor manufacture, for example – could afford to pay, and with the extra incentive of working conditions that were decidedly more civilised, both environmentally and in shift-timing, than the lot of most railway operating staff.

Britain, inevitably, was the first Western European country to react strongly to the financial deterioration of its railways. Inevitably so, because uniquely in Europe Britain had never statutorily subsidized rail transport, either metropolitan or long-haul, in any way; and except for exercising some control over railway rates and preserving the railways' common carrier status it had never fostered the concept of railways as a public facility on a par with, for instance, the postal service or the police. The 1945 election of a Labour Government with a thumping majority ensured that the Second World War's talk of nationalization, unlike the First's, would be translated into legislation. The Act which created a unified British Railways (BR) from the start of 1948 actually set out to solve the road-rail issues by co-ordinating all public land transport under the aegis of a British Transport Commission. But the latter never had the time to perfect a smooth-running organization within the empire it took over, let alone achieve an effective integration of modes, before the Labour Government was voted out of office in 1951 and a Conservative Government aborted the embryonic national system. Meantime the railways, relegated to the rear of the industrial queue for investment, were slithering into deficit as they struggled to fend off the challenge from the roads with a patched-up, war-weary system.

Not until 1955 was BR at last allowed a large-

The sidings at Alexandra Docks Junction, Cardiff, in the late 1950s are full of the under-used wagons which worried Beeching as Western 'Castle' 4-6-0 No 7014 *Caerhays Castle* on a Cardiff–Bristol stopper passes a 'Hall' 4-6-0 on a coal train.

In the 1950s and 1960s the West German Federal (DB) and East German State (DR) Railways together built well over 1,000 lightweight diesel railbuses: this DB trio was photographed at Cologne.

scale re-equipment. For the most part, sadly, the £1,240 millions Modernization Plan hastily cobbled together that year poured new wine into old bottles. The rural passenger services were to continue, changed only in that their steam trains would be displaced by bus-engined diesel railcars or four-wheel railbuses of the kind Germany had so successfully developed and multiplied. The railcars in themselves, it was sanguinely predicted, would entice travellers back to the trains in numbers enough, allied to the diesels' lower running costs, to make secondary railway operation more economically palatable. It was also thought that the competitive quality of the traditional all-purpose railway freight service would be fully restored if the trains were diesel-powered, universally equipped with continuous brakes for improved speed when they were actually on the move, and sorted in expensively automated marshalling yards. Within 15 years, the British Transport Commission promised and the Government supinely accepted that dazzling new gadgetry alone would have magnetized enough lucrative new business for BR to begin generating the surpluses to pay off the loans needed to execute the plan. Even if the rest of the economic world had stood still for 15 years it was a forlorn hope. But the Government had simultaneously begun to dismantle the controls on road freight transport. Motorways were starting to take shape; and the capacity, convenience and economy of the lorry was being rapidly advanced by both the technology of its manufacturers and the expertise of its operators. Before long, far from getting a better return

from its assets through gains in the high-rated merchandise market, BR was desperately under-pricing to offset the uncompetitive quality of its service and stop more of the better-paying traffic ebbing away to the roads.

If British railways had customarily received the annual State compensation for statutory provision of unprofitable but socially necessary services – for metropolitan commuters, for example – that was taken for granted in mainland Europe, then BR's rising deficits would probably not have provoked the searching probes of its method ordered by the Conservative Government of the early 1960s. (It is worth noting, incidentally, that in the previous decade the Conservatives, despite their concern for free enterprise and the railways' viability, had not flinched from denying BR a fully justified fares rise for purely political reasons!) The outcome of those scrutinies was the appointment of an industrial technocrat with a track record of ruthless rationalization, Dr Richard Beeching, to chair the new British Railways Board established by a further Transport Act of 1962. His remit, unique in Europe, was to make the national rail system fully viable: viable, that is, without aid of public money of any kind. Within six months of the new Board's takeover Beeching issued his Reshaping Report, popularly known ever since as the Beeching Report. In brief, it asserted that in a motor and fast-developing air transport age a railway could only break even if it was reduced to a trunk and metropolitan commuter network concentrating on the bulk flows of passengers and freight.

The corollary of that dogma was the proposed closure of more than 5,000 route-miles (8,047 km) of rural branch and secondary main line and of 2,350 little-used stations; a ruthless scything of local and stopping passenger services; the abandonment of practically all less-than-train-load freight operation, despite the huge sums already laid out on sophisticated new marshalling yards to sort out traffic in wagonloads; and severe contraction of less-than-wagonload freight, or sundries, to a bulk haul between a very limited number of road-served depots in main centers. Moreover, the railway's traditional standby capacity would be drastically curtailed. For example, BR would no longer retain a huge reserve of passenger coaches that barely turned a wheel for three-quarters of each year and were mobilized only to cope with the summer holiday rush. It would also opt out of largely seasonal freight traffic, such as cattle movement.

Beeching's draconian prescription astounded railwaymen on the other side of the English Channel. To this day many of them have not grasped that he was handed a far harder speci-

Since the 1960s oil crisis Spanish National Railways (RENFE) have been one of Europe's most determined electrifiers: at Madrid's Atocha station a Mitsubishi-design Class 269 Bo-Bo on the midday Talgo express to Malaga stands alongside a Class 440 short-haul emu.

fication than they have ever had to satisfy. Apart from a requirement to dispense with any form of operating subsidy, Beeching's BR was expected ultimately to fund its renewals and investment entirely from its own resources: that is, if it had to borrow, it must pay interest until it could eventually repay the loans. Elsewhere in Western Europe direct Government investment in railway infrastructure, varying in degree, was and still is commonplace. Moreover in France and Belgium the railways were drawing from the State an annual infrastructure maintenance grant. For France's SNCF this amounted to over £250 millions at the start of the 1980s. Nowadays regarded as a token equalisation of the terms of competition with road, the infrastructure grant is traceable to pre-nationalization agreements with the individual companies, deals concluded when Belgian and French Governments of the nineteenth century were concerned that ailing railway finances might hobble strategically or socially desirable development of the national rail network. The practice continues in Belgium; but in France, under the new contract between the State and SNCF operative from the start of 1983, the SNCF's grant is subsumed in a new form of global grant – worth almost £900 millions in 1983 – categorized as 'Maintenance of the Railway's Potential.

In Britain, granted, some of BR's remorselessly accumulating debt was eventually written off in capital restructuring, but it was 1968 before yet another Transport Act (this one enacted by a Labour Government) legislated ongoing subsidy of socially necessary passenger services and provided for a State contribution to the total capital cost of approved urban transport improvement schemes. Never before had Britain's railways been assured of any financial support in advance of expenditure; until then the public money absorbed by BR had all been voted post facto, to narrow the widening gap between revenue on one side and rising costs and escalating interest charges and loan repayments on the other. However, by now BR had been freed of common carrier duty and enjoyed a freedom to select and price traffic unique in Europe.

Beeching's response to his commercial remit was perfectly logical. A railway's financial return on its assets hinges on optimum use of its infrastructure, if that has to be self-supporting; in turn that optimum use requires trains to be run at close headway to the maximum extent, which means that the difference in speed between different categories of train must be minimal. It follows that freight trains must be equipped with wagons fit for at least 60 mph (97 km/h) so that they can comfortably share tracks with express passenger trains, and that routes intensively used by such mixed traffic need the very latest signalling systems to keep trains under effective tactical control. The investment money demanded under the last two heads can only be generated and the outlay justified by concentrating the network on routes following the principal commercial axes of the country. And finally, the more expensive and sophisticated the rolling stock, the more critical becomes its productivity;

it must not spend half of its life or more in marshalling yards (besides which, yard processing prolongs transits uncompetitively and is prone to mis-route wagons). Hence the antipathy to working in wagonloads and, in the passenger sector, BR's gradual elimination of through portion operation and dedication to use of fixed terminal-to-terminal train formations. It was an axiom of the Beeching doctrine that the economic unit of rail movement is always the train, not the individual vehicles which form it; and that henceforth BR must, in principle, work in train units, leaving road to take on local freight collection and delivery in the hinterlands of a greatly diminished number of rail terminals.

Beeching did not get his surgery politically approved either in full or at the pace he hoped for, but even so the contraction of BR in the five years from 1963 to 1968 was staggering: total passenger route-mileage cut from 12,915 to 8,471 (20,784–13,632 km), total track mileage from 47,543 to 33,976 (76,511–54,678 km), staff from 476,545 to 296,274, passenger stations from 4,306 to 2,616, freight depots from 5,165 to 912, freight wagons from 862,640 to 437,412 and passenger coaches from 33,821 to 19,544. These were the years, too, of a dieselization far more precipitate than North America's in a desperate, ill-prepared effort to save costs; of 8,767 steam locomotives active at the end of 1963, just three survived at the close of 1968.

But as fast as money was saved the economies were outweighed by a continuing drain of freight revenue and inflation's effect on material and wage costs. The cost of BR to the country was, however, contained; and after the annual rate of investment in railways had been slashed by 35 per cent in 1975 as the country's economy reeled in the wake of the oil crisis, the average British taxpayer was certainly getting a rail service at markedly less expense than his counterpart in any other major Western European country. But Britons were saving in the present to pay later. By the 1980s years of under-investment had either brought BR to the brink of fresh closures through sheer decrepitude, or of an oppressively bulging investment programme to overtake a horrendous backlog of renewals.

While other Western European countries continued to accept rail service as part of the tax-supported social service fabric – and did not, like Britain, tend to veer abruptly from vilification to deification of public industry with a change of Government – all grew increasingly concerned at its rising cost. By 1968, when the Swiss Federal Railways, for so many years the one system that had looked financially impregnable, slid into the red, not one national railway was balancing its books, even when

account was taken of its various grants and subsidies.

There were three key issues to be faced. First, with other forms of transport now capable of performing so many railway jobs just as economically, should so much rail service still be directly or indirectly subsidized as a social benefit? Second, where railways were still used as an instrument of social policy, were they adequately compensated? And third, in sectors where logic now dictated that railways should make their own way as a commercial enterprise – primarily the long haul of passengers and freight – were the terms of competition fair? If for no other reason, the issues must be resolved for the sake of railwaymen's morale. When managements were still fettered by social obligations and tariff controls that circumscribed their ability to bring costs and revenue nearer balance, frustration and depression were an inevitable and mounting reaction to beetle-browed political and press concern at the rising cost of railways. Not one country has yet cut through the thicket of nineteenth century customs and conflict of political and commercial interests to a comprehensive response on all three counts. But most have tinkered with one or other of the issues.

One answer to the problem of equalizing the terms of long-haul competition would be for the State to take over full responsibility for the railway's infrastructure, as it does for a country's main inter-urban roads and – generally – its inland waterways. The French, as mentioned earlier, partially accepted that duty through the medium of an annual grant towards the full cost of railway upkeep. Since the start of the 1960s the idea has been seriously argued both in Britain, West Germany and Sweden, but rejected; the Swedes settled in 1979 for the less politically-charged alternative of a special grant to their railways, the SJ, which meant that a drastic fare reduction could be ordered to make rail passenger travel more competitive with private motoring and the country's fast-developing network of inter-city air services.

In the early 1980s only Switzerland seemed set to tackle the infrastructure cost issue head-on. The Swiss and Austrians are very reliant on their railways as an all-weather standby and also as a means to keep international freight between the North-West, Germany in particular, and South and South-East Europe off their roads. The Swiss have, in fact, pinned over 95 per cent of this transit traffic across their borders to the railways by crippling the use of road transport with deterrent restrictions. So when the Swiss Federal Railways' (SBB) slide into loss was accompanied by warnings that without special aid renewal modernization of the system would falter for lack of cash, the Swiss were naturally perturbed. The Federal Government appointed a prestigious commission to review the whole structure of Swiss transport and the 1978 recommendations of that body, entitled the *Conception Globale Suisse des Transports*, are now being implemented little by little.

The Federal Government moved in 1981 to take over full responsibility for upkeep and new investment in the SBB's infrastructure, based on SBB managerial recommendations. Thereafter the railway would pay a rental for use of the system on a variable rate derived from the year-to-year volume of its traffic. A flexible charge of this kind would go a long way to solve another problem vexing every nationalized railway competing with private enterprise: that whereas a private road haulage company, for instance, could cut or even pass its shareholders' dividends and otherwise trim its commitments in a lean year, the railway was stuck with fixed interest charges on its borrowings and the unvarying cost of its fixed assets and its staff. With the infrastructure a Government charge, and with a new tax levied on the heavy lorries which one country's official study after another has shown pay well below the cost of their wear and tear on roadways, the SBB would be freed of the controls on its pricing and bidden to make its wagon- and train-load freight fully self-supporting. In the freight sector it would be subsidized only to maintain a nationwide less-than-wagon-load freight service, an operation recognized to be inherently loss-making but held to be a national need. However, the Swiss have not conclusively resolved the complex problems of fair payment for socially necessary passenger services. Are they the financial responsibility of central Government or the local authorities which insist that they are essential? And is it possible to ensure that a railway is fully compensated for providing them at less than their full cost without involving central or local Government in the detail of railway management?

When Britain first accepted statutory subsidization of unprofitable passenger trains in its 1968 Transport Act, the Government of the day did assess and quantify grant on a line-by-line basis. But that quickly embroiled the Transport Ministry in a duplication of the railway's own managerial apparatus. Subsequent legislation provided for blanket support of all passenger services under what is termed the Public Service Obligation, the only exclusions being local services in the provincial conurbations which BR operates under contract to the Passenger Transport Executives of each area; these PTEs prescribe the levels of service that

suit their overall public transport plans, and the fares to be charged, then meet BR's account of the difference between full cost and revenue. Decentralization of both planning and financial responsibility for the character of short-haul passenger services is the logical policy. The great flaw of the British system in the 1980s was that it lumped together the commercially viable Inter-City operations and rural services outside the provincial conurbations; thus, while the Government professed pious opposition to further closures, it left BR to work out how to keep decaying rural lines usable when the total of grant, steadily diminishing in real money terms, was not even adequate to sustain more important secondary services.

In 1982 hopes of a more rational approach to BR's financing and also to its acute problems of under-investment were raised when the Government appointed a four-man committee chaired by former Civil Service mandarin Sir David Serpell to investigate the requirements for an efficient and more financially gratifying rail operation by the end of the century. But the eventual Serpell Report, published early in 1983, was a bitter disappointment. Sketchily researched and bedevilled by the blatant anti-rail bias of the committee's most imperious member, the report glibly rejected most of BR's complaints of under-investment and almost throughout took the negative line that network and service contraction was the most effective path to improved efficiency. Attitudes to rail transport, urban or inter-urban, in the rest of Europe were competely ignored. Not the least depressing feature of the report was the patent absurdity of some of its conclusions, resulting from the callow character of its research and the latter's misuse of computer models.

The Austrians and the Swedes have sensibly treated the commercial and social services of

The Cannes–Ranguin branch service is one of those now operated by French Railways for a local authority under contract: the diesel railcar twin-set standing at Cannes is in the authority's livery but is basically of standard modern SNCF diesel railcar design.

The 3 ft 6 in-gauge network of Japanese National Railways has become the free-enterprise world's most financially embarrassed national system: a Class ED76 electric locomotive heads the 'Sakura' express on Kyushu island.

their national railways, the OBB and SJ, as separate sectors for budgetary purposes. In Austria central Government financed basic secondary passenger services and the uneconomic levels at which their fares were pegged, but provincial governments were free to conclude supplementary agreements with the OBB, at their own expense, for higher standards of service in their own areas.

Even in France, with its tradition of firm control from Paris (until the Socialist Presidential triumph of 1981, that is), regional authorities were given new licence to decide for themselves how they would spend that part of the national budget allocated to local transport. As a result some not only contracted for improved train services at the expense of bus operations, but invested in the rolling stock to furnish them – in the case of the authority presiding over Northern France from the Channel ports to Lille, to the extent of almost 200 new passenger vehicles.

To revert to the Swiss, Berne attempted in 1981 to offload from the Federal budget to the country's Cantonal Governments and their ratepayers half the cost of the SBB's local passenger services, but was politically thwarted. The move was prompted partly by the theory of the national transport plan, mentioned earlier, that all transport users should pay directly or indirectly a fairer share of the true cost of the services they employed, partly by the need to remunerate the railways fully for operating the local trains if the SBB was to be restored to a sensible financial footing. The sum involved under this last point underlined how far short, even in Switzerland, compensation had been falling of full restitution for obligations to run stopping trains and charge many of their passengers ludicrously uneconomic fares. Suddenly the sum for the SBB's support from the Government was to jump from about Sfr 270 millions to Sfr 459 millions.

The national railway systems with the biggest

problems of adjustment to the new competitive transport environment were West Germany's DB and Japanese National Railways (JNR). Throughout most of the years of the German economic miracle, when the country was luxuriating in an astronomical trade surplus, the nation lived quite happily with a formidable expenditure on railways. Its magnitude was attributable chiefly to the need to redevelop a route system at odds with the new country's commercial axes; to generally underpriced long-haul services because of the strength of *autobahn* and air competition; to massive development of the most enviable metropolitan rail systems in Europe (on which, furthermore, the DB was grossly under-compensated for obligatorily low fares); to prodigal rail service of practically every rural station and depot inherited from the previous century; and not least to over-staffing, which was difficult to cure because of the established civil servant status of more than half the total operating staff at ground level. None of this gave the average German taxpayer any pause at all. But it added up to a very dispiriting job framework for the DB's management, forced to diffuse its effort so widely instead of concentrating cash and expertise on clear-cut viability objectives in the long-haul traffic sectors.

The powerful self-interest of the provincial or Land administrations foiled a mid-1960s plan concerted by the DB and the Federal Government to shut a peripheral fifth of the railway system and contract it to the core carrying most of the traffic, though the elements of the plan designed to stimulate more use of that core by a savage new tax on heavy long-haul lorries and some curbs on their operation were salvaged. It was not until the German economy turned sour at the end of the 1970s that the bill for railways, by then a cumulative £3·5 billions a year under all sections of grant, subsidy and compensation, became an acute political anxiety. Even then it stirred little public unease. The average German

still took low-cost, generous rail service as a God-given citizen's right. 'If we raised local passenger fares 15 or 20 per cent to cover more of the costs,' a DB director in Bremen said to me in the summer of 1981, 'we'd have mass demonstrations in the main square tomorrow morning.' By 1981, however, Bonn was steeling itself to curtail the £750 million a year of Federal taxpayers' money which was being laid out purely to support local passenger train services. A merger of the national post-bus network with the German Federal Railway was ordered, with the objective of enforcing bus substitutions of hopelessly loss-making rural passenger services. Where local governments insisted on retention of the trains, they would be obliged to shoulder more of the support costs.

Even so, all political parties agreed in principle that the evolution of attractive, conveniently integrated urban public transport systems must continue unchecked (the capital costs of this were in part financed by a percentage of the country's petrol tax). They were virtually unanimous, too, that heavy investment in the DB's trunk system must not be severely curtailed. Further reduction of the mammoth railway bill could only come through enhancing the DB's competitiveness by construction of new high-speed bypasses of speed-constricting bottlenecks, by building new automated yards, and by maximizing the potential of electronics to accelerate decision and save labour in all the routines that interlock to secure a precisely controlled railway operation.

This determination to press on with re-orientation of the DB's half of the old Reichsbahn to modern West German need, almost regardless of cost, was fuelled by an important new factor – the oil problem (another influence was environmental concern, particularly keen in West Germany). The worry was not just the never-ending rise in the cost of oil to the national trade balance, but also the now quantifiable duration of world supplies and not least their

vulnerability to sudden severance through political crisis. That had wonderfully concentrated the political mind where railways were concerned in many other countries besides Germany. For instance, after complacent decades of under investment in its national railway system, RENFE, Spain took only a year to consider the implication of the 1973 oil crisis for a Spanish economy 70 per cent reliant on imported oil for its energy. As early as 1974 the Government ordered extension of electrification of the remainder of RENFE's trunk network; and at the start of the 1980s further conversion was approved as part of a £7,240 million 10-year plan covering also widespread track improvements and big purchases of traction and rolling stock to increase operating capacity and efficiency. Every other Western European country, with the significant exceptions of oil-rich Britain and Norway, was taking a similar line, though by no means all were prepared to invest as lavishly as the Spanish. In the Third World the revival of enthusiasm for rail transport was dramatic.

The financial mess into which an unfocussed West German policy of the first post-war decade allowed the DB to sink is a mud-patch to a quagmire set against the Japanese National Railways' plight on the 3 ft 6 in (106·7 cm) gauge which constitutes the bulk of its system. A 3 ft 6 in gauge national railway certainly can be made to run profitably. It does in South Africa, but only because SAR's dominant trunk traffic is long-distance movement of minerals in great bulk. Japan's post-war industrial growth has virtually exhausted its indigenous mineral resources and the substitute imports can be brought by sea almost to the doorstep of the industry that crowds the country's teeming industrial belts. The closely-spaced, massively populated cities in those belts generate a big rail passenger demand which for the first three post-war decades was politically spared payment of anything like the true cost of its travel; but on

The Montreux–Oberland–Bernois Railway (MOB) is one of Switzerland's numerous private railways, subsidized by both Federal and local Cantonal Governments as a social necessity – although many, like the MOB, are also tourist attractions: uniquely on European narrow gauge the MOB now runs dome observation cars in its Montreux–Gstaad–Zweisimmen–Lenk 'Panoramic Express', approaching Château d'Oex in 1981.

the other hand, the cities knit into a tight market where a 3 ft 6 in-gauge railway has little chance of competing with road for high-rated merchandise. In 1981 JNR's share of Japan's total freight market was a beggarly 12 per cent. In the rest of the country JNR not only had to run a rural system untrimmed since the war but also a mounting number of new lines, almost all of them created purely for political ends, which were irretrievable loss-makers from the moment they were drafted. As a result 40 per cent of JNR's 3 ft 6 in gauge produced just 4 per cent of total income. Add to all these problems an excessive staff's implacable resistance to productivity measures but annual achievement of wage increases far outstripping any permitted rise in JNR's uneconomic charges, so that wages pre-empted 70 per cent of the railway's budget, and the inability of any part of the 3 ft 6 in-gauge system, bar one Tokyo suburban line, to cover its costs was understandable.

Much less intelligible was the lack of any corporate political will to tackle JNR's problems until they had become almost intractable. In 1978 JNR was at last freed of the most rigid price controls endured by any railway in the free industrialized world; but otherwise its finances ran on out of control, further distorted by the charade of fresh loans to keep up with the interest on cash already borrowed, until by the end of the 1970s JNR's accumulated loss had soared past £15 billions. At last, at the close of 1980, political parties and unions seemed to agree that the farce must be brought to a stop. In the spring of 1980 the Diet passed a law which on the one hand wrote off some of the mountain of debt, but on the other required substantial contraction of JNR's 3 ft 6 in-gauge operation by 1985: reduction of route-length operated by some 1,800 miles (2,897 km) or 13·5 per cent; closure of 715 of a total of 5,185 passenger stations, 800 of 1,358 freight depots and 93 of 193 marshalling yards; matching cuts in traction and rolling stock; and not least sacrifice of 95,000 staff.

Even then, ability to achieve the rural line closure programme in full was in doubt. Law is law, but some impassioned local opponents of the shut-downs were soon finding artful ways to confound the legislators' intent. For example, at least one local authority started dishing out cut-price season tickets to boost peak-hour travel on its neighbourhood railway and inflate daily passenger journeys above the number the Transport Ministry had set as the floor below which a line was a closure candidate.

More drastic measures yet were propounded in 1982. A Japanese Government think-tank, holding that any industry of JNR's labour force size and spread was incapable of efficient central management, advocated nothing less than the break-up of the system into half-a-dozen or more regional railways. Responsibility for them should at first be thrust on the appropriate regional authorities, it was suggested, but in time private enterprise might be persuaded to take over one or more of them. Later in the year the Japanese Diet passed a law setting a target date of mid-1987 for JNR's dismantling and subsequently a five-man Reconstruction Management Council was set up to plan the execution.

In the one remaining country of exclusively private enterprise main-line railroading, the USA, one might expect adjustment to the post-war transport environment to have been comparatively simple. The companies would simply contract their assets and their offer to the demands of the traffic they could carry at a respectable financial margin. But not so. The railroads were still common carriers; and most of the regulatory apparatus constructed in the nineteenth century to prevent them exercising selectivity or otherwise exploiting their captive markets of those days was still operative. Without such constraints the US long-haul passenger train would have come to the brink of death even faster than it did. The final war years' travel boom rolled over into the first months of peace and encouraged many railroads to invest heavily in a fresh generation of luxury streamliners; but before long these were running into intolerable losses as on the one hand passengers decamped to the expanding airline and highway systems, and on the other the trains' prodigal staffing expense was worse swollen by inflation. No withdrawal, however, was possible without the approval of the appropriate regulatory authority. That was not always prompt, but even so the pace of 'train-off' petitioning was so hectic that by 1968 US railroads were operating no more than 500 or so long-haul passenger trains a day, compared with 15,000 at the start of the war.

At that the country took fright. President Nixon's administration was prepared to let market forces decide the fate of remaining trains, but a majority of Congress was not. So, in April 1971, a public corporation now known as Amtrak, part-capitalized with Federal money and with the shortfall on its operating costs Federally guaranteed, was set up to operate a slender, politically approved national network of inter-city passenger trains. Of Amtrak, more in Chapter 11.

Their rate-making regulated and their commercial freedom circumscribed in other ways as well – for instance, they were debarred from striking specially price-negotiated long-term

deals with individual customers or from developing a door-to-door intermodal service with their own road vehicles – many railroads found it no more easy to make good money out of freight business. (It has to be admitted, though, that reactionary refusal to rethink time-worn operating methods and feather-bedded labour practices were culpable for some of the inefficiency.) As early as 1955 not a single Class 1 railroad in the US was earning enough to cover the interest on its capital as well as its direct costs. Two decades later the average annual return on a Class 1 railroad's assets was hovering around an unappetising 1·5 per cent. Some big railroads pursued a better deal for their shareholders by diversifying into property management, oil or manufacturing industry. Union Pacific, for instance, is today a multi-faceted corporation in which the railroad is only one of several major companies. The supreme UP board only allocates a fair share of the corporation's investment resources to ongoing railroad development because the UP rail system is by common consent one of the country's most astutely run, extracting a well-above-average return from its inherently lucrative transcontinental bulk freight.

The greatest change post-war conditions have brought about in the US railroad scene, however, is the disappearance of many historic railroad identities through mergers to realize the economies of scale. Here again the process would probably have been much more rapid but for the enforced submission of merger proposals to regulatory scrutiny. That scrutiny could be incredibly laborious. As much as a dozen years were spent picking over the proposals in the case of an abortive Union Pacific-Rock Island alliance, to cite the more egregious case.

In 1945 there were 137 different railroads in the US Class 1 category, for which the qualification then was a gross income in excess of $1 million. They were a heterogeneous collection, ranging from inter-urban and big city systems acting as a bridge between trunk railroads to dedicated coal hauliers and transcontinentals. Within 30 years mergers had not only pared the total by almost three-quarters, depersonalizing in the process such historic concerns as the Baltimore & Ohio, the Burlington and the Great Northern, but had steadily erased the old functional and geographical distinctions. The Class 1 railroads of the 1970s had their traffic specialities, but they were all-purpose systems to a far greater extent than in the 1930s and 1940s.

The unlikeliest and one of the biggest mergers combined the arch-rivals of the North-East, the New York Central and Pennsylvania, in a marriage consummated after protracted legal disputation at the start of 1968. Both were driven to this once unthinkable union by a critical financial state. More and more of their vast and largely overlapping networks had become excess capacity as the effects of road and air competition were aggravated by a westward drift of the heavy industry which was their freight lifeblood, besides which both were saddled with more heavily loss-making commuter passenger traffic than the rest of the Class 1 companies put together.

Rationalization of the ramified Penn-Central empire would have been a long job for an archangelic genius, but the logic of the merger was nullified right from the start by persistence of the old inter-company jealousies at every level from the boardroom downward, by mismanagement and even by chicanery. In 1970 a suspicious Wall Street slammed its doors in Penn-Central's face. After that, unsure of a cash flow adequate even to cover its wage bill the company had to declare insolvency. The bankruptcy of one of the country's largest industrial conglomorates was shocking enough, but it soon fused the financial apparatus of a number of Penn-Central's neighbouring railroads as well. The total collapse of railroading in the North-Eastern States had become a serious risk. That galvanized Congress. The realization dawned that the crisis in the North-East could spread unless railroads were given more freedom to work out their own commercial destinies; and unless, in the short term, some patently ailing concerns were financially aided to make good the failure of their rates to generate the cash for adequate maintenance and renewals. The proportion of Class 1 main-line track in bad order and subject to severe speed restriction was rising alarmingly.

The so-called '3-R' and '4-R' Acts were the outcome – the Regional Rail Re-organization Act of 1973 and the Rail Revitalization and Regulatory Reform Act of 1976. Between them they established, under the aegis of a Federal Railroad Administration, a new corporation, Conrail, to run and rationalize the freight network of Penn-Central and its five bankrupt neighbours; they created a Federal fund to assist asset renewal in deserving cases; and they set course for de-regulation of the railroads commercially and for a more liberal Inter-State Commerce Commission treatment of mergers.

In the declining years of the Pennsylvania one of its classic GG-1 electric locomotives heads a train at Lancaster, Pa, in 1951.

Pennsylvania GG-1 electric in new guise, wearing Conrail livery shortly before its withdrawal.

Conrail was not an instant panacea for North-Eastern problems, not entirely for want of the right method. Effective union lobbying had its founding statute loaded with ludicrously generous wage and job protection clauses; its network rationalization schemes had to negotiate the objections of local interests; the physical assets it took over from the bankrupt companies were mostly in a deplorable state; its traffic was depressed by the recession; and it was still saddled with much of the Penn-Central commuter operation. By the time President Reagan took over the White House in January 1981 Conrail had swallowed up more than $3 billions of Federal money in deficit relief and renewals and was still uncertain of the viability its creators had confidently envisaged. The new men decided enough was enough and prepared to dismantle the quasi-Government railroad before their four-year term was over, selling off as much of the system as other railroads were prepared to buy and discarding the rest.

Although Congress frustrated the Reagan Administration's ambition of a fire sale, it enacted a Northeast Rail Services Act of 1981 which gave Conrail only until mid-1983 to prove ultimate profitability potential and thereby fend off dismantling. That at least encouraged hope of keeping Conrail intact, even if in private ownership. The 1981 Act also rescinded the very indulgent labour protection provisions which had been written into Conrail's founding legislation, to safeguard the jobs of staff caught in the bankruptcies of its constituent railroads; ordered Conrail to sell off all its lines in Connecticut and Rhode Island and in part of Massachusetts; and relieved it of all its commuter train-operating responsibilities from the start of 1983. The five

local Transport Authorities for whom Conrail ran the commuter trains would either have to take on the full financial and administrative responsibility themselves, or else negotiate for a take-over by an Amtrak offshoot founded under the same 1981 Act, the Northeast Commuter Services Corporation (NECSC). In the event all five decided to take on the job themselves, killing off NECSC at birth.

The rationalization clauses of the 1981 Act added momentum to the striking recovery Conrail was starting to achieve by its own management effort. Its freight service now reliable and competitive after an intensive rehabilitation of the decrepit traction, track and rolling stock it inherited, Conrail at last scored an operating surplus in the second half of 1981 and sustained it in the first half of 1982, despite recession-eroded traffics – and in contrast, for example, to Southern Pacific's collapse from a $60 million surplus in 1981 to a $15·4 million operating deficit in the first six months of 1982. It looks certain to pass intact into private ownership.

Meanwhile, merger applications were getting quicker attention from the ICC. The results of a 1970 alliance of the Great Northern, Burlington, Northern Pacific and Pacific Coast railroads into a 26,398-mile (42,482 km) system, the Burlington Northern, which stretched from the Great Lakes and the Ohio river to the Pacific Coast, with a foothold in 19 States, had added a stimulus; it was demonstrating very impressively the benefit to the customer as well as to the railroad's balance-sheet of concentrating previously parallel flows of traffic on a single route, and of creating longer through routes that eliminated interchange delays at former railroad frontiers. Thus it took little more than a

couple of years for the addition of the Frisco Railroad to the Burlington Northern combine to pass all regulatory scrutiny, in the spring of 1980.

Before 1980 was out three massive new mergers had been tabled. Union Pacific sought to combine with Missouri Pacific and Western Pacific as the Pacific Rail System; the Chessie and Family Lines, each already agglomerations of companies that were once household names, wished to create a system provisionally titled CSX that would run from the Great Lakes south to New Orleans and Miami, and command almost a third of all US railroad coal traffic; and Norfolk & Western and Southern aimed to unite as NWS in the area between the Mid-West and the Gulf of Mexico. By 1982 CSX and NWS had passed ICC muster and become fact, and soon afterwards the ICC gave the tripartite Pacific Rail System its approval.

Few believed that this was the end of the merger road. By 1982, in fact, a new corporate grouping of the Delaware & Hudson, Boston & Maine and Maine Central was shaping, and Canadian-owned Grand Trunk was seeking to add the Milwaukee to its empire of lines on the US side of the 49th Parallel. Expert betting was that by the end of the century ten Class 1 companies or groups at most would command the country's trunk freight movement by rail. In 1982 the total stood at 39 individual systems (including Amtrak), but of these no fewer than 26 were either already absorbed by or seeking absorption in nine corporations.

Moves to relax the constraints on US railroads' pricing were halting at first, but in the late 1970s the Carter administration made the de-regulation of all public transport a priority objective. Last to be cleared were the railroad proposals, which nearly foundered on skilful, determined lobbying from coal-mining and coal-consuming public utility interests in particular.

In October 1980, nevertheless, the epochal Staggers Rail Act was passed. That freed almost two-thirds of all rates from the power of the Inter-State Commerce Commission to set maxima, and in markets where rail was the dominant medium assured the railroads a reasonable pricing margin above direct costs. In addition the companies now had reasonable scope to raise their prices in line with inflation of their costs. And they were now authorized to negotiate special-price long-term contracts with major customers. Most importantly, inter-modal activity was completely de-regulated.

Though 1980 also saw bankruptcies strike in the Mid-West, with the collapse of the Rock Island and Milwaukee Railroads (the former had been tottering for decades), it looked as though the corner had been turned. By mid-1981 several companies were reporting encouraging first-results of the new order. And these, coupled with the improving efficiency derived from advancing technology and an increase in coal traffic generated chiefly by export demand, were curving the average financial return on US railroading back past 5 per cent until the country's economy buckled under the severe recession of 1982. That sliced away almost 15 per cent of the railroads' tonnage and drove the average return back down below 3 per cent. But whereas such figures in the 1960s would have had the business analysts forecasting new railroad bankruptcies, in the 1980s the newly market-oriented and more efficient US railroad business was acclaimed a potential growth industry even by President Reagan.

Amtrak begins to acquire its own new equipment: the cars of the New York–Chicago 'Broadway Limited' have not yet been renewed, but the locomotives are new EMD Class SPD40F diesels.

10
THE FIGHT FOR FREIGHT

A FEW MILES SOUTH-EAST of Hamburg, close to the divergence of the main lines south to Bremen and Hannover, one of the most spectacular rail installations in the world fills the landscape. No less than 190 miles (306 km) of track are concentrated in serried ranks within little more than 690 acres (283 hectares), but of the means to control movement over them and 1,014 sets of points interconnecting there is scarcely a sign. For that matter any human movement is hard to spot among the thousand or so wagons banked up on the parallel tracks and looking from above like the trimly ordered stock of a model manufacturer. This is the DB's Maschen yard, the biggest in Europe and almost certainly the most highly automated anywhere. Arranged to sort north-south and south-north traffic in two similarly-shaped and parallel layouts, it can process freight trains at a combined rate for both halves of up to 700 wagons an hour.

In each half the sorting is planned and directed entirely by interconnected computer systems. One, which is integrated with the DB's system-wide apparatus that continuously monitors all wagon movement and produces instant management and accounting data, is the source of advance information on incoming trains. Their make-up is transmitted from a total of 13 terminals at reporting points on the main lines leading to Hamburg from the north and south, and from 25 depots originating traffic in the great port and industrial area of Hamburg itself. The operations control computer compares such in-coming data with its memory banks of information on the yard layout and daily train plan, then prepares a marshalling programme for each train; this a co-ordinating computer makes sure is ready and available to the hump control computer at the moment when the train concerned has materialized in Maschen's reception sidings and is ready for sorting.

The designers of Maschen yard and its electronics had to provide for wagons to be sorted according to a total of more than 3,500 possible transits, taking north-south and south-north traffic as a whole. That and the high planned throughput determined the remarkable aggregate of 16 reception roads and 48 sorting or classification sidings in the north-south yard and 18 reception roads and 64 sorting sidings on the south-north side.

The north-south yard is the more compact because it is mostly forming trunk trains to concentration yards elsewhere in Germany and abroad, whereas the south-north is disassembling trunk trains for distribution to the many individual depots in Hamburg and its hinterland. Maschen marshalls not only the empties and full wagons catering for the 27 million tonnes (26·6 million tons) of freight the railway claims annually from the port of Hamburg, but also 7 million tonnes (6·9 million tons) to and from East Germany via Büchen and the heavy Scandinavian exchanges via Flensburg and Puttgarden, plus substantial business with the ports north of Hamburg. It needs manual labour,

The German Federal Railways' Maschen marshalling yard near Hamburg is Europe's biggest and most highly automated.

Far left:
Swiss Federal Railways' marshalling yard at Zurich Limmattal, with hump in foreground.

Hump operator's console at Hamburg Maschen yard: the VDU reproduces the shunting orders for an incoming train which the equipment will execute automatically.

question. If all proceeds smoothly the men on the operating floor of the yard control tower have only to watch the operation unfolding, either physically on the ground outside their panoramic windows commanding the 'throat' between hump and classification sidings, or electronically in continuously updated displays on full-colour VDU screens at their elbow.

Marshalling yard efficiency is critically dependent not only on the speed of humping but also on the behaviour of cuts from the moment they leave the hump crest until they come to rest. If they roll too fast they may cannon into wagons already occupying their destination siding, risking damage to contents as well as to vehicles. If they roll too slowly, on the other hand, they may come to a stand well short of earlier occupants, perhaps so close to the hump end of the siding as to block further admissions; that will bring humping to a stop until a locomotive has been called up to push the offending cut further down. Ideally humping of a train should end with the cuts on each classification track nicely buffered up to each other and ready for coupling into a fresh train without need of any further movement at all. And that is what happens at Maschen. The first essential is to brake each wagon or cut rolling down the 1 in 16 slope of the hump to an exact 1·25 m/sec (1·4 yd/sec), the desirable speed of contact between moving and stationary vehicles, by the time it enters its siding. Two successive sets of track-mounted retarders do that job. The first is a metal jaw type that applies a graduated pressure to passing wheels, the second a novel apparatus that lifts passing wagons briefly off the rails on elastic rubber beams which squeeze the wheels as the wagon weight distorts their cross-section, thereby exerting a braking force proportional to the axle-load thrust upon them.

Wagon weights vary empty, let alone loaded, besides which discrepancies in running characteristics are countless even within a single wagon type. Consequently attainment of precise target speed at a classification siding's entrance demands a braking readjustment for each cut. Hence the array in the yard's throat of electronic devices, from railhead contacts and weight gauges to radar beams, which in addition to checking headway between shunted cuts to ensure safe resetting of the throat points are measuring each cut's acceleration, and hence its 'rollability', as well as its tonnage. Their readings automatically dictate the necessary degree of braking to the retarder controls.

Speed control does not end at the rubber-beam retarders. Immediately beyond them, and automatically activated when a cut passes over the retarders, is a device that protrudes a roller-

of course, to prepare an arrived train for sorting by uncoupling its wagons into singletons or 'cuts' of two or more for the sidings prescribed them by the operations control computer's programme (daunted by the huge capital cost, European railways have deferred indefinitely their post-war decision to follow the North American and Russian example and standardize automatic couplers). But once the cuts have been isolated the only manual control normally in play thereafter is that of the driver on the diesel locomotive propelling the train from its arrival track to the crest of the hump, from which a sequence of turnouts debouch the cuts into their appointed classification sidings.

Even the driver's work, though, is simplified by the locomotive's fitment with an automatic control that holds its speed rigidly to the precise low figure necessary for accurate functioning of the array of electronic devices directing the rest of the operation. Locomotives maneuvering sorted wagons between the main classification area and a subsidiary yard in the south-north section, one might add, are unmanned; they are radio-controlled by ground staff.

Point-setting and re-setting between the passages cuts rolling down from the hump is ordered entirely by the hump control computer, based on its reading of the marshalling programme which has been submitted to it by the operations control computer for the train in

A French Railways fast merchandise freight (*Régime Acceléré* or RA), headed by a class CC6500 electronic Co-Co.

tipped ram just above rail level to push the cut on by its wheel-rims at a steady 1·25 m/sec. At the head of the siding is yet another automatic mule. This comes into action every time its controlling sensors have counted the passage of 13 axles, whereupon it, too, applies wheel-rim pressure to move the wagons on, yet again at a meticulous 1·25 m/sec, until all the wagons on that track are perfectly buffered up. At that the mule automatically retreats to the head of the siding ready to reactivate after the next total of 13 axles. When a classification siding has gathered in a full train, of course, a print-out of its make-up is instantly available for onward transmission to the recipient yard or depot, since the operations control computer has been continuously updating its record of the wagons' distribution during humping.

The total cost of Maschen was a formidable £175 millions, including the expense of a comprehensive modernization of signalling in the surrounding railway area. How can the DB justify such an outlay on a single project? Or for that matter its expenditure on a comparable scale in the automation – not always at the same high level of sophistication – of key yards at Munich and elsewhere?

The answer starts with the determination of every major railway in the world to stay in the fight for less-than-trainload freight. In every case their Governments want it that way too. Only Britain stood by unconcerned when BR, pres-

sured to break even on its freight working, set firm course for an exclusively trainload system, as described earlier. But BR soon realized that it could not afford to dispense with wagonload traffic's contribution to total infrastructure costs. Now it is striving to win business for a limited network between main traffic centers which it has brand named Speedlink. Holland's Netherlands Railways, worse placed than BR to compete with road because of the small size of the country and the tight grouping of its principal cities, also tried to discard all wagonload business but was balked by its Government. For the rest of the world's railways wagonload freight has always ranked as vital business. Even in so small a country as Switzerland the Swiss Federal Railways was in 1981 providing it to some 3,000 customers through its own depots or private sidings. For France's SNCF, serving 10,500 clients through private sidings, wagonload traffic represented almost 50 per cent of its gross annual tonnage. The DB's proportion was even higher, at 60 per cent, much of it passing through over 11,000 private sidings. In every country, though, state-owned as well as private railways were under pressure to keep wagonload operating costs and income in balance. That put an even higher premium on concentration of marshalling work, to curb both labour and operating costs and also the idle, unproductive time of wagons. Still more importantly, swift, utterly reliable sorting of wagonload traffic –

Typical of today's special purpose wagon design is this German Federal (DB) sliding roof transporter for steel coil.

and the minimum of it during each transit – was vital to the achievement of a quality of consignor-to-consignee movement competitive with to-day's road transport.

Thus Maschen and similarly automated yards are the nuclei of the DB's strategic freight plan for the century's last quarter. Most European railways are working to the same scheme in principle, if not so expensively in terms of automation investment and not in identical detail. With its capacity to sort up to 4,500 north-south wagons or 120 trains daily, and 6,500 south-north wagons or 150 trains in the same time, Maschen has absorbed the activity of five former yards dispersed around the Hamburg area. As a result outbound wagonloads go from their local assembly point straight to Maschen for gathering into a trunk train. Before Maschen they might have to be 'tripped' from one yard to another, perhaps even to a third, before they made an appropriate trunk train connection. The time spent in getting a wagon away on the long-haul is cut even further short by the fact that Maschen's electronics are designed to halve the hours a less ambitiously equipped yard would take to sort the same volume of traffic.

A further important gain accrues from reduc-tion of a system's marshalling yards to a small number of high-capacity installations serving a far-ranging network of local wagonload assembly and dispersal points. Much more of each wagonload transit is covered at sustained speeds of 50 or 60 mph (81 or 97 km/h) in the long-distance fast freight lines which interlink the main marshalling yards, to the benefit of

rolling stock productivity as well as customer satisfaction. As for the latter, by meticulous planning of feeder services between local as-sembly points and the main yards and by the tightest feasible timing of its overnight inter-yard long-haul freights, the DB had by 1981 gained the assurance to offer a maximum 36-hour transit for merchandise wagonloads be-tween almost any pair of significant towns or cities on its network, even ones as far-spaced as Hamburg and Munich. It could confidently publish and issue a timetable listing, with load-ing deadlines and times of unloading availability at destination, 30 or 40 such connections for each of 100 or so traffic centers from Schleswig-Holstein in the north to Bavaria in the far south.

Speed and reliability are not the only influen-tial factors in the quest for high-rated merchand-ise. Another is convenience, a heading which, amongst other things, covers ease of loading and discharge. No longer can railways in the industrialized countries economically bulk their wagon fleet with just two standard wagon types, the traditional box car and the half-sided open wagon; they must offer the same wide range of purpose-built carriers as their road transport rivals. The second half of this century has seen a great diversity of rail wagon development. Bogie vans built to the maximum length and cross-section the loading-gauge allows, and fitted with sliding doors that open up half a bodyside, not only make forklift loading of palleted goods simplicity itself but offer individually a payload capacity fully competitive with a road juggernaut's. Sliding-roof wagons to facilitate overhead loading have become a European commonplace. And for chemicals, grain and powdered products like china clay which demand specially protective vessels designers have created a whole catalogue of custom-built vehicles with inbuilt devices for rapid loading and discharge. Much of this development has been privately financed, since its scope would have been beyond the resources of many railways. Britain's BR, in particular, has had to leave special-purpose wagon-building very largely to private industry. Both in Europe and in North America private wagon-building, leasing and hiring has been one of the outstanding growth sectors of the railway industry since the Second World War.

Where road scores above all on convenience is in ability to work door-to-door. Using orthodox wagons, a railway is on level terms where it is hauling from one private siding to another. Every railway management is keen to market more private sidings, as figures cited earlier for some European railways testify. Thus a very high proportion of major railroads' freight tonnage nowadays is siding-to-siding or at least makes it departure from or delivery to a private siding.

A private siding is an extra, expensive capital investment for the client; furthermore, it is not worth the railway's attention if it has to be shunted for just a wagon or two per week. Few railways are prepared to contribute to the capital cost unless the business a siding promises is regular and substantial. Though some local authorities may be ready to foot the bill for rail connections in the creation of new industrial estates, Britain is the only Western European country in which Government money is on offer, to the extent of 60 per cent of the price, to encourage new private sidings. But in Britain the economic criteria prescribed for service of a private siding, whether privately financed in toto or not, are by far the Continent's highest: hence BR caters for no more than a fifth the number of private terminals directly connected to either West Germany's DB or France's SNCF.

The obvious alternative to throughout rail transport is an inter-modal arrangement that cedes local collection and delivery to road, leaving the railway with just the trunk hauls over which the freight can be bulked in economical trainloads. After the Second World War US railroads were the first to embrace a successful new inter-modal technique – piggyback, the transport of road trailers on rail flatcars. Two factors peculiar to North America outweighed an inherent economic flaw of the piggyback concept and fostered a striking growth of US services from the late 1950s onwards. One was

Gantry crane transfer of a piggyback road trailer in Union Pacific TOFC operation.

the generosity of the North American loading gauge, within which any standard box trailer employed in US road haulage could be accommodated on a rail flatcar of orthodox floor height; the other was the great length of several high-volume US merchandise corridors – over 2,000 miles (3,219 km) between the Great Lakes and California, for example, and 1,000 miles (1,609 km) or so even between New York and Chicago. The comparatively low per-mile cost of trainload working over such distances left a fairly comfortable margin not only to absorb the considerable cost of terminal equipment to top-lift trailers on and off flatcars, but also to offset the dead-weight penalty of the piggyback principle: the fact that while it is on rail the payload is encumbered with the excess tonnage of two carrying chassis. Of some 22 million freight-car loadings recorded by US Class 1 railroads in total during 1980, around 1·6 million were TOFC – Trailer On Flat Car, the official North American acronym for piggyback. But the traffic was almost entirely rail-hauled for a 1,000 miles or more. Below that level piggyback has so far made negligible impact on the US merchandise freight market.

Its saleability over shorter distances, nevertheless, has been fully attested by two services inaugurated in the late 1970s with the stimulus of start-up money from a Federal administration by then eager to promote research and experiment in more fuel-efficient freight systems. One is a shuttle with fixed flatcar train-sets over the 410 miles (660 km) of the Milwaukee between Chicago and the Twin Cities of Minneapolis and

St Paul, the other a similar exercise by the Illinois Central Gulf over the 298 miles (480 km) between Chicago and St Louis. Both have attracted a healthy tonnage on every run in a multi-journey daily schedule. Both, moreover, have been blessed from the start with an unprecedented relaxation of union train-crewing rules to help make them competitive as far as price is concerned; ICG's 'Slingshot' TOFCs, for instance, were exempted from the otherwise mandatory two crew changes on the Chicago–St Louis run and were also licensed to dispense with half the customary total of crew. Yet neither service has yielded its sponsor much profit because the train-haul distance is too short for bulk rail economy to offset the fixed cost elements of the technique.

However, those overheads are being trimmed. The mouth-watering size of the market which persistently soaring oil prices is likely to make more amenable to the piggyback concept – and also the boost the latter has had from deregulation under the Staggers Rail Act – has induced a number of US private industries as well

Above:
Sante Fe lightweight 'Tenpack' unit awaits loading of TOFC trailers for Chicago at Hobart Yard, Los Angeles.

Top:
Illinois Central Gulf's 'Slingshot' piggyback shuttle between Chicago and St Louis.

150

as the railroads themselves to invest heavily in the research and development of more fuel-efficient inter-modal equipment. Another spur is the railroads' own vulnerability to the pressures applied by OPEC. The cost of their diesel locomotive fuel, an almost inconsequential 4 cents a gallon in 1945, jumped to 26·6 cents in the wake of the 1973 oil crisis, but has since surged relentlessly to well over 80 cents a gallon. The effect of that on railroad accounts is exemplified by Union Pacific, which reckons that whereas fuel pre-empted 3 cents of every revenue dollar in 1970, by 1980 it was collaring 14 cents.

The first-fruits of the new inter-modal research and development were unveiled as the 1970s faded. The majority of the new concepts sought in different ways to eliminate substantial dead weight by lightening the rail car – for example, through articulation of adjoining cars over a single bogie – and to obtain a more aerodynamic outline for a loaded piggyback train by designing for a closer packing and lower positioning of the road trailers. The gains which were possible were demonstrated by Santa Fe's 'Ten-Pack', an articulated set of 10 units reduced to little more than skeletal center sills with lateral aprons to support road trailer wheels, and 35 per cent lighter than an equivalent rake of orthodox piggyback flatcars. Operated in trains of 10 sets apiece, with a payload capacity of 100 road trailers, the 'Ten-Pack' has saved Santa Fe about 5,500 gallons (25,004 litres) of diesel oil on the regular TOFC block train haul from Los Angeles to Chicago and back, totalling 4,400 miles (7,081 km) for the round trip.

Potentially the most promising concept was the Roadrailer, because it eliminated the extra chassis almost entirely and dispensed with extravagant road-rail trans-shipment gear. Its excess dead weight – and cost – compared to a road trailer pure and simple was virtually confined to interchangeable rail and road rear axle assemblies, each with its own statutory braking gear and other essential safeguards. For grouped rail haul as a train each Roadrailer locked securely, coupling and brake controls included, into the rear of its neighbour, of which the rear axle was competent to bear the combined load. The Roadrailer was devised by Chesapeake & Ohio engineers in the 1960s but excited scant interest then, partly because in its first incarnation it lacked the payload capacity of the average road trailer, partly because the incentives to break with well-tried, universally practiced inter-modal systems were lacking. In 1980 the weight-saving and flexibility of the Roadrailer were much more appealing; and moreover it had been reborn, under the sponsorship of a major international wagon-building and leasing combine, Tiger, with

a cubic capacity comparable to a standard road trailer's though with less payload tonnage potential on the road because of the higher weight of its amphibian rear axle assembly.

Nine months of trial on four different railroads with a prototype Roadrailer train had shown by mid-1981, not only that on a 1,000-mile (1,609 km) trunk haul at an average speed of 50–55 mph (81–89 km/h) a Roadrailer train of up to 75 trailers was 19 per cent cheaper to run than a conventional TOFC train, but also that it gave the freight a smoother ride. Keen interest from several railroads, notably Burlington Northern, in testing a Roadrailer train exhaustively, was, however, slow to translate into firm commitment. The first regular commercial use came in 1983, when freight forwarders Inter-Rail Express pioneered a tri-weekly 30-hour Roadrailer train service for fresh produce between Florida and the heart of New York, and the Roadrailer company itself opened up a general merchandise operation between Buffalo and New York.

In Europe the piggyback idea was slower to

A RoadRailer transfer point needs no cranage, only a road surface around the rail tracks: for road movement the rail wheel assembly at the rear has been retracted, the twin road-axle assembly lowered.

151

take hold for the obvious reasons of less inviting trunk-haul distances and a more inhibiting loading-gauge (a totally prohibitive one in Britain). Since the 1973 oil crisis, nevertheless, it has become the European mainland's fastest growing rail freight traffic in year-on-year percentage terms, spurred chiefly by West Germany.

One reason for the German's piggyback enthusiasm is that the DB's key main lines have a slightly more ample loading gauge than the so-called Berne gauge norm of Continental European railways generally. In contrast France's SNCF can only piggyback with wagons built to 'pouch' road trailer wheels well below normal wagon-floor level, so as to keep the loaded trailer's roof within an acceptable height; that complicates trans-shipment, predicates special fittings on the road trailer in the case of one variety of French piggyback wagon, and discourages international piggybacking into or out of France – deterrents which in sum have circumscribed the SNCF growth of this inter-modal business.

Loading gauge permissiveness has been no means the DB's only inducement to pursue piggyback freight. With the threefold objective of energy conservation, environmental protection and rolling back the DB's deficit, the Bonn Government in 1978 set the DB a goal of tripled inter-modal traffic by 1985, which it supported with a £250 millions grant towards investment in inter-modal terminals and equipment and loss-leader rates that would bring in new business; it then made the plan even more feasible by freeing all road vehicles dedicated to piggyback movement of the swingeing axle tax clapped on heavy lorries and trailers in the 1960s. At the same time weekend movement of heavy lorries was prohibited on German main roads. By the start of the 1980s the DB was on target with piggyback carryings striding past a total of 20,000 lorries or complete tractor-and-trailer rigs a year to a likely 100,000 by the end of the 1980s.

Besides interconnecting 20 terminals within West Germany, in some cases with complete piggyback trains, the DB's piggyback operation was the center of an expanding international traffic between the Low Countries (and their roll-on/roll-off sea ferry ports) and Central and South-East Europe. Two factors were fuelling the growth of the international business. One was Swiss and Austrian determination, backed by deterrent limits on vehicle size and use in one case, severe border taxes in the other, to prevent use of their roads as a foreign lorry corridor; additionally, the Swiss Federal Railways enlarged their transalpine Gotthard route tunnels specifically to simplify piggyback operation. The second influence has been the development by both Austrian and German manufacturers of rail transporters with wheels so tiny that the resultantly low-slung floor will keep virtually any standard covered lorry in European use within the loading-gauge all the way from the Low Countries' coastline to Northern Italy. The latest German version has four-axle bogies with wheels of only 368 mm diameter (1 ft $2\frac{1}{2}$ in). Within West Germany it can take road vehicles of up to 4 m (13·1 ft) roof height above road level. Moreover, an ingenious design of retractable bufferbeam-and-drawgear assembly allows a train of the cars to be turned into a continuous roll-on/roll-off platform for simple loading or discharge of complete tractor-and-trailer rigs. Lorry drivers travel in a couchette which is attached to the train once it has been loaded.

The container is a much older inter-modal freight medium than piggyback, but it did not

DR Class 47 No 47198 heads a Stratford (London) – Southampton Freightliner on the Western Region between Twyford and Reading.

become such a universally important tool until some US shipping lines pioneered use of the 8 by 8 ft (244 × 244 cm) cross-section, high-capacity box for a whole gamut of international traffics at the start of the 1960s. This ISO or international standard container remains primarily an ideal means of door-to-door transport for seaborne merchandise, because the number to be offloaded from or loaded on to a ship generates continuous work for high-cost transfer equipment. To justify the heavy expense of trans-shipment gear for purely domestic container transits, a railway may have to be very selective in its terminal siting; as a result, it is likely to leave a good many potential customers beyond the range within which it makes economic sense to road-haul containers to make connection with a container train.

The first European railway to glimpse the significance of the shipping lines' move into containers, Britain's BR, learned the domestic lesson the hard way. One tenet of the Beeching theory was that most of the wagonload merchandise it was unprofitable to carry the old way and a great deal of new domestic business besides could be coaxed into a limited network of high-speed, fixed-formation container trains, the Freightliners. The trains must shuttle intact between terminals restricted to the focal points of the country's biggest traffic flows; there could be no local rail collection or delivery of containers. Only that way would the high productivity be extracted from train-sets and terminal apparatus that was essential to vindicate their cost. But the expected growth of domestic container traffic was never secured. That was partly because the original Freightliner prospectus under-estimated operating costs but more specifically because the terminals' disadvantageous road distance from many putative users at the start of the system in 1966 was aggravated as many firms deserted the cities for new green-

153

fields sites. The salvation of BR's Freightliner volume became the inland movement of sea-borne containers, which by 1980 accounted for over 40 per cent of the annual tonnage – a ratio never remotely envisaged at Freightliners' birth.

Of Europe's principal container ports, Bremen and Bremerhaven (created in the 1970s further down the Weser estuary than Bremen to suit the growing size of container ships) provide particularly impressive testimony to the growing dependence of deep-sea shipping on the modernized railway for the inland legs of their transits. Together the two harbours handle over 400,000 containers a year, 90 per cent of them through Bremerhaven, and of this aggregate just over a half reaches or leaves the docks on rail; where the inland transit is more than 100 miles (161 km) the DB commands as much as 75 per cent of the traffic. The greater part moves in dedicated container trains that guarantee incoming seaborne containers which have been train-loaded by 17.00 hours availability for terminal collection as far away as Munich by 08.00 next morning, or at Basel no later than noon.

The national railways of Japan, Spain and South Africa are the only major systems to adopt the British Freightliner model of a strictly exclusive container train network. The rest have insisted that container service must be included in their general wagonload freight offer, either to railway-owned depots or to private sidings. That has had the advantage of stimulating research in low-cost, mobile trans-shipment devices; of these the most promising is a German loco-motive-and-crane hybrid that can both lift loaded containers across itself and, with its gantries cleverly retracted, haul a string of container wagons between a main container train center and a nearby industrial estate.

The reverse of the coin, however, is a risk of tarnishing the inter-modal image through the protraction of wagonload container transits by intermediate processing in marshalling yards. This has undeniably undermined North American railroads' inter-modal sales effort, in the piggyback as well as the container sector, and of late the effort to concentrate US inter-modal traffic in dedicated trains has intensified. Santa Fe's Chicago–Los Angeles 'Ten-Pack' operation mentioned earlier is an example.

In Western Europe a number of dedicated container trains are operated for Intercontainer, the multi-railway agency entrusted with all marketing of international rail container transits (between 1975 and 1980 its annual business leapt from 332,100 to 640,500 containers), but within their own borders the railways have mostly passed container traffic through their general fast freight train system. By 1981, though,

the DB was steadily channelling deep-sea containers especially into a so-called 'Green Network' of dedicated inter-modal trains inter-linking its 60 or so container and piggyback terminals countrywide.

It would be wrong to give an impression that the container age's influence on the modern railway's drive for a bigger share of the inland merchandise market has been insignificant. With containers, for instance, the railway has become an increasingly useful pipeline between the interdependent plants of big manufacturers that have rationalized their production, allocating each factory in the group its own part of the process. Ironically it is the motor industry with which the railway has become most conspicuously integrated in this way – on a Continent-wide basis in the case of Ford's European plants. And at the end of the assembly line the railway has become the economical, damage-free means of ferrying new cars by the trainload from factory to distribution railheads in the most distant market areas. On average every other new American auto reaches the sales room after a rail haul (three out of every five in the case of the particularly rail-oriented Ford company) and the Class 1 railroads dispose of no fewer than 36,000 special-purpose carriers to shift them; many of these are tri-levels thanks to the indulgence of the US loading-gauge, but European railways have to be content with bi-levels.

The strength of the railway as a freight haulier, however, remains its competence in high-tonnage movement, above all in bulk minerals. Since the Second World War that faculty has been considerably sharpened by technological advances in wagon and track construction that have lifted tolerable axle-loads beyond 20 to 25 (20·3 to 25·4) and even 30 tons (30·5 tonnes) on some specialist mineral railways, and by the evolution of traction at ease with trainloads grossing 10,000 tons (10,161 tonnes) and more, even over undulating routes.

Experts from the world's power generating industries are forecasting that global coal consumption will double during the 1980s and rise a further 50 per cent on that total in the 1990s, but in the late 1970s resurgent demand was already driving railways in the coal-rich countries to screw their coal-hauling productivity a notch or two higher and in some cases to invest in extra operating capacity to meet the challenge. Except where inland waterways allowed the operation of massive barge lash-ups – the 30-barge trains of the Lower Mississippi in the US were an extreme example, but in Europe the 10,000-tons (10,161 tonnes) capacity trains of the Rhine, paying little for their use of the

river, were vigorous enough opposition – the
coal train was still the most efficient means of
inland movement. The distances and flow volume
justifying the capital cost and operation of new
coal slurry pipelines were held by most experts to
fall within narrow limits. The consensus of those
experts was, moreover, that the real cost of
moving coal by rail had been reduced thanks to
the railway's refinement of unit coal train
technology.

It is primarily for this reason that Britain's
latest baseload electricity generating stations
are coal-fired where they are non-nuclear. In the
1960s, a decade before OPEC unsheathed its
pricing weapons, coal was chosen because of the
low pit-to-power-station transport price BR
was offering through a new 'merry-go-round', or
MGR technique. This was basically full-size
exploitation of the toy railway's simplicity.
Fixed train-sets of high-capacity bottom-door

wagons would shuttle continuously between
input and discharge points. Not only would the
trains never be uncoupled: ideally they would
never change locomotives in a day's work. At
the pithead MGR trains would be backed intact
beneath the overhead loading plant. At the
power station they would take a circular layout
from which they would emerge facing the track
back to the collieries. In the middle of the
layout the loop tracks would bridge bunkers
into which the MGR train would disgorge its
full load without stopping, the bottom doors of
its hopper wagons opened and closed in succession by automatic devices, and the train's
locomotive held rigidly to 0·5 mph (0·81 km/h)
during the discharge process by a supplementary
low-speed control (remote control of the locomotive during the operation by the discharge
plant's ground staff has since been perfected: if
it is adopted, that would add the modest

155

A Canadian Pacific freight leaves the Connaught Tunnel in the Rockies; a new 8.9 mile (14.3 km) tunnel is now to be bored at a lower level to ease gradients and make more operating capacity for increasing freight traffic.

economy of relieving the train crew for a meal or other break during unloading).

The greater part of BR's coal tonnage is now handled the MGR way, not only to power stations but, for example, to suitably equipped ports for export. And the technique has been extended in principle if not identical detail to other bulk commodities, such as aggregates borne in trainloads from country quarries to railheads serving construction industry in the big conurbations, and imported ore ferried from docks to steelworks. This last is conveyed in trains of 100 tons (102 tonnes) gross bogie wagons with rotatable couplers, so that each wagon can be tipped individually to discharge its load without having to be uncoupled from its trainload neighbours. Individually, workings of this kind attain operating ratios as strikingly low as 20 per cent.

The 2,250 tons' (2,286 tonnes) gross weight of BR's heaviest, 45 two-axle hopper wagon MGR coal trains pales against the weight of some unit mineral trains regularly operated on the European mainland, where track layouts and signalling arrangements permit longer train forma-

tions. In West Germany the DB has in daily circulation between Hamburg's Hansaport and a big steelworks south of Hannover trains of 40 six-wheel bogie ore hoppers with a 3,600-tons (3,658 tonnes) payload capacity and a gross weight of over 4,800 tons (4,877 tonnes). Trains almost as heavy feed Saarland plants with ore from the Rhine port of Duisburg. With ore in particular unit train-working efficiency is proving a valuable complement to the move into gargantuan deep-sea carriers; the cheapness of sending Brazilian ore over the Atlantic in a 270,000-ton (274,347 tonne) ship, for instance, has handed the Netherlands Railway rail hauls as far even as Poland because Rotterdam's Maasvlakte is as yet the only North or North-West European port capable of berthing the deep-sea behemoths.

North American railroads supply still more impressive testimony to the long-haul economy of rail as a bulk mineral conveyor. Over 7 million tons (7·1 million tonnes) a year of coal mined in New Mexico, for instance, is shipped out in Santa Fe unit coal trains ranging in size from 65 to 105 bogie wagons each of 90–100 tons' (91·5–102 tonnes) gross laden weight. With that calibre of performance it pays to feed an electricity generating plant as far away as the neighbourhood of St Louis, more than 1,350 miles (2,173 km) distant, with railborne New Mexico coal. Numerous other unit train coal circuits of more than 1,000 miles (1,609 km) each way could be cited; and they are going to rise considerably in number as world demand for steam coal swells the flow from the western coalfields of Wyoming, Montana and Kentucky to the ports. Rail coal movement in the US was already rising at such a pace in the ebbing 1970s – in 1980 the railroads' export tonnage soared as much as 60 per cent above the 1979 figure – that Burlington Northern was spending over $320 millions on expanding operating capacity, including the construction of a brand-new 116-mile (187 km) short-cut in its route from the Wyoming and southern Montana coalfields to the power plants of Colorado and Texas; this was the longest stretch of new main line added to the US railroad map since 1931.

A much more daunting enlargement exercise is being forced on Canadian Pacific by unrelenting demand on its mountainous 625-mile (1,006 km) transcontinental route from Calgary to the Pacific coast at Vancouver. Prime cause is world demand for Canada's rich resources in raw materials such as potash, for its grain, but above all Japanese hunger for coal mined on the eastern slopes of the Selkirk mountains, all of which has inflated the route's tonnage already by 160 per cent since 1960. Originally single-track throughout, with passing loops, this CP route clambers up to a 5,339 ft (1,627 m) summit at the Continental Divide amid the 11,000 ft (3,353 m) peaks of the Rocky Mountain ranges, yet it deals in trains of 10,000 tons (10,161 tonnes) gross or even more. But the steepness of the grades compel mobilization of assistant locomotives for the climb, which even then humbles the gigantic loads to a snail's pace. The limitations that imposes on operating capacity are increased by the need to clear the single track periodically simply to return the assistant locomotives to the foot of the hill.

If the gradients confronting loaded trains making for the Roberts Bank coal port near Vancouver were no fiercer than 1 in 100, five 3,000 hp diesels would suffice to power a 12,500-ton (12,701 tonne) train the whole way from the pithead to the docks. CP has already achieved that over a good deal of the route by expensive construction of some 20 miles (32 km) of additional, more easily graded bypass in very difficult environment where the original line's slopes were the most unfriendly to westbound traffic. There remains the long climb, 1 in 38 at its steepest, up Beaver Hill to the Connaught Tunnel under Rogers Pass. To lift a 12,500-ton train up that – and at no more than 20 mph (32 km/h) – demands the punch of a dozen 3,000 hp diesels, some in front, some at the rear and some inserted mid-train to reduce wagon coupling stress. The mid-train units are remotely-controlled 'slaves', on which a receiver reacts appropriately to the commands of a radio transmitter linked to the manned controls of the lead locomotive group. To overcome this hurdle CP is about to bore a new 8·9-mile (14·3 km) tunnel through Mount MacDonald below and on easier grades than the 64-years-old Connaught Tunnel. That done, 12,500-ton trains will need no helper at any point; the line will be able to

pass up to 19 more massive trains each way every 24 hours; and its annual gross tonnage throughput should be improved by as much as 50 per cent.

The Japanese appetite for minerals has helped to spark perhaps the most remarkable unit train development of all, because it has materialized not on standard gauge but on the 3 ft 6 in (106·7 cm) narrow gauge of South African Railways. Here, thanks to impressive advances in track and vehicle running gear technology, trains just as heavy as those of North America have become a commonplace on two routes. Specifically to cater for coal exports SAR laid an essentially new railway from Ermelo, east of Johannesburg and the Transvaal coalfield, to Richards Bay port in Natal in the 1970s through a fusion of new construction, upgrading of some existing track and electrification at 25kV 50Hz ac – SAR's first high-voltage ac project. By 1980 the Richards Bay line was moving 14 loaded trains daily, seven days a week, each of 84 bogie wagons grossing around 4,500 tons (4,573 tonnes). But test loads of up to 184 wagons – the train was over 1·5 miles (2·4 km) long – have been successfully run. With a commitment to increase the line's tonnage throughput almost 50 per cent by 1985 SAR was busy at the start of the decade strengthening the track and easing gradients in preparation for standardization of 200-wagon trainloads by the contract date. Far greater trainload tonnages are already daily practice on a 534-mile (859 km) railway completed in 1977 to transport export ore from Sishen, west of Johannesburg, to the deep-water port of Saldanha Bay, north-west of Cape Town. On this line, electrified at the unusual value of 50kV 50Hz ac, trios of British-built 5,070 hp locomotives customarily haul trains of up to 200 four-axle wagons grossing a phenomenal 20,000 tons (20,322 tonnes).

A diesel hauled ore train on South Africa's Sishen-Saldanha ore line before its 50kV ac electrification.

157

11

THE 'INTER-CITY' RESHAPING OF THE EXPRESS TRAIN

MOST WESTERN EUROPEAN railway managements took at least the first 15 post-war years to
appreciate a new sophistication in the travel
market. The higher wages of the new industrial
society, holidays with pay, the steadily cheapen-
ing cost of motoring in real terms, better roads
on which to exploit it, and an improving
quality of life in general had greatly enlarged
the passenger travel market traffic potential; but
at the same time these factors had freshly
segmented the market and made it more
discriminating in depth. For a decade and
more the majority of railways complacently ran
the bulk of their passenger trains to the same
broad timetable pattern as they had in 1939. The
preoccupation of their passenger managers and
the focus of most commercial initiative was
protection of premium-fare traffic from airlines
equipped with the first generation of aeroplanes
benefiting from wartime technology. Other
market sectors were left an easy prey to fast-
refining road transport, public as well as private.

Thus the newborn BR expanded its network
of all-Pullman trains, revived the summer
London Kings Cross–Edinburgh non-stop,
selected a train or two on each trunk route
radiating from London for acceleration to
cultivate the business market, but otherwise
left the 'Big Four's' pre-1939 timetables basically
unaltered until the early 1950s. The Italian
State Railways (FS), glumly certain that it would
take them the whole of the 1950s at least to
recuperate from wartime devastation and restore
their electric train speed standards of 1939,
gilded their Milan–Rome route in 1953 with
sumptuously furnished, air-conditioned electric

multiple-units, the 'Settebello' trains, which
were exclusively first-class and expensively
surcharged as well.

In France the Paris–Lyons 1·5kV dc electrification begun in 1946 had a remoulded passenger service as its principal stimulus. The
electrification gained Europe its first post-war
passenger services timed start-to-stop in the
70–75 mph (113–121 km/h) range by the 1952–3
winter, but here again the beneficiaries were
supplementary-fare payers in selected business
peak *rapides*, or in the day's exclusive first-class-
only service between Paris and the Riviera, the
'Mistral'. By 1959 the 'Mistral's' clientele were
cosseted with the Continent's first post-war
schedule at an average speed in excess of 80 mph
(129 km/h), the product of the train's booking
over the 195·3 miles (314·3 km) from Paris to
Dijon in 146 minutes.

For the 1957 launch of the Trans-Europ Express scheme French Railways' rolling stock contribution was its standard type RGP diesel train-set; one arrives at Paris Gare du Nord in 1958 on the 'Parsifal' service from Dortmund.

Power car of German Federal Diesel-hydraulic TEE train-set of the late 1950s.

On the Continental mainland the epitome of the immediate post-war policy was the 'Trans-Europ Express', launched in 1957. At that juncture creation of the European Economic Community was still a year off, but earlier pointers to closer trade relationships such as the 1952 establishment of the European Coal and Steel Community inspired the Netherlands Railways' (NS) contemporary president, F. Q. den Hollander, to enthuse six of his neighbours with his TEE idea.

Again the business traveller was the target. If he was to be kept out of the air, the railways must give him special treatment in an updated version of Wagons-Lits' pre-war Pullman trains. The ordinary international day train, lumbered with accommodation and stops for a wide mix of traffic and slowed by protracted halts for through-coach exchange or frontier routines, was a non-starter in the international business sector now that comfortable turbo-prop airliners were smoothly border-hopping on a spreading network of intra-European routes. The 10 services linking over 70 centers of European commerce which inaugurated the TEE network conformed to certain agreed standards – first class-only, three-a-side, fully air-conditioned accommodation with full restaurant service; traction capable of at least 140 km/h (87 mph); a common level of supplementary fare; and provision for Customs and other border formalities to be conducted on the move, obviating tedious frontier station halts. But the purity of den Hollander's original vision, which pictured a supra-national body, independently financed, managing a fleet of standard train-sets timed on all TEE routes at the same average speed, was never realized.

Like so many proposals for logical – and economical – standardization of practice or equipment amongst European railways, it was seriously adulterated by reluctance of individual railway administrations or their Government paymasters to surrender sovereignty over design and commercial policy, or to risk loss of manufacturing business for the railway supply industry in their own countries. Another frustration was the disinclination of the three train catering companies operating within the network, the Wagons-Lits internationally, the Deutsche Schlafwagen und Speisewagen (DSG) in West Germany and Switzerland's domestic concern, to provide a homogeneous restaurant car service at a standard tariff.

So the TEEs began and have remained ever since a mixture of equipment. At the start the Dutch, Swiss, Italians and Germans did at least commission special designs of diesel multiple-unit as their contributions to the TEE rolling-stock pool – not that the Italian units, contemptuously tagged 'the Lorries' by their German partners, were worthy of the concept's ideals. The French, on the other hand, simply adapted to TEE service the RGP diesel multiple-unit introduced for some of their internal intercity services in 1954, setting a precedent that later became general practice. The bulk of TEE services today are furnished by locomotive-hauled cars of types that also cater for some domestic inter-city services in their countries of origin. This blurring of distinction has helped to bring about a further depreciation of the original TEE concept, though an equally if not more

influential factor has been the acceleration of many internal services to average speeds well ahead of the TEE norm. Starting with the 'Mistral' in 1965, a number of purely domestic first class-only trains in France, West Germany and Italy have been granted TEE status. Some of the French and Italian examples do not bother with even a vestige of the originally standardized TEE red-and-cream external livery. That, however, had already been deprived of exclusivity when the DB appropriated it for the first-class cars of its new internal Inter-City service of the 1960s, which at first was indistinguishable in quality or equipment from DB-furnished TEEs except that it was confined to the West German system.

All the original TEE equipment of the late 1950s is now superseded. Diesel traction was outmoded as TEE routes were brought under catenary from end to end and multi-current electric traction technology made light of operating the same power unit under Western Europe's two dc and two ac current systems in the course of a single journey. The reversals necessary at several TEE network stations that are dead-end termini and which inclined the participant railways to adopt a double-ended multiple-unit format in 1957 are still obligatory, but all international and most domestic TEEs are nowadays locomotive-hauled. Managements consider an occasional locomotive change much less of a handicap than the inflexibility of a fixed-format train-set, which is for all practical purposes incapable of adjustment to fluctuating traffic demands and vulnerable to total immobilization by a defect on one of its vehicles.

The Paris-Brussels-Amsterdam service is the only major international TEE service surviving unscathed in the 1980s: its train-sets include a bar.

By the start of the 1980s the international TEE was a dying breed; slowly maybe, but certainly nevertheless. No TEE route is a well-aligned racetrack from end to end. Thus the ability of the Milan–Paris 'Cisalpin' to sustain 100 mph (161 km/h) for miles on end once it has gained the SNCF main line at Dijon cannot offset the restricted pace it has to observe until it gets that far, especially in its sinuous passage of the Jura mountains on the Franco-Swiss border. So its end-to-end average is not better than 63 mph (101 km/h). That is poor pace against a jetliner, which can get a businessman from Milan to Paris between the end of a working day and dinner, whereas the 'Cisalpin' leaves at 14.48 and does not gain the French capital until 22.59. Over inter-capital distances as short as the 195 miles (314 km) between Paris and Brussels, where favourable track geometry permits a transit time of less than $2\frac{1}{2}$ hours at an average speed above 80 mph (129 km/h), the TEE's comfort and high-class but pricey cuisine keeps it a very valid business travel option; here a market fortified by shuttling EEC bureaucrats still fully justifies a service of no less than six TEEs each way daily. The same goes for national TEEs running at peak business hours over prime routes in their own country where high speed is possible over considerably longer distances. Outstanding in this category are French Railways' 'Aquitaine' and 'L'Etendard', which comfortably link Paris and Bordeaux each way be-tween breakfast and mid-morning or in an evening, each eating up the 360 miles (579 km) between the cities in just over 4 hours, inclusive of three intermediate stops, at an end-to-end average speed of close on 89 mph (143 km/h). But in the spring of 1983 Europe's timetables showed only 23 surviving TEE workings each day, compared to almost 100 on offer in the 1960s' prime of the concept.

The North American luxury train has long since surrendered to the airlines. In fact, skidding into losses, even on the direct costs of running passenger trains, that deteriorated abruptly from nil to around £250 millions (in the money values of the period) between 1953 and 1957, US railroads extricated themselves so precipitatedly from all kinds of passenger service that within a decade total victory by cars, coaches and planes was on the cards. At the end of the 1960s only 500 or so main-line daily passenger trains were left in the length and breadth of the country. Many railroads had already rid themselves of all passenger operation. Some years earlier, however, a sufficiently weighty fraction of US opinion had volubly protested the threatening dominance of the country's score or so of densely-populated inter-city corridors by close-packed road transport and aircraft to prod Washington into action. Another spur was the triumphant inauguration in 1964 of Japan's first high-speed Shinkansen ('New Railway') between Tokyo and Osaka, discussed more fully

A Class 6500 Co-Co heads French Railways' Paris-Bordeaux 'Aquitaine', formed exclusively of 'Grand Confort' first-class-only stock.

in Chapter 16. This convincingly proved not only the public appeal of an inter-city railway fully exploiting the latest technology but also the viability of investment in it.

The first product of this anxiety to revive the US passenger train was the 1965 High Speed Ground Transportation Act of the Johnson Administration. It accepted the principle of Federal aid for judicious inter-city rail experiment, if in decidedly modest terms at that stage. A year later the Act gestated a Federally-sponsored project to assess public reaction to a refurbished rail service in the North-East Corridor, from Boston south to New York and over the Pennsylvania's electrified main line on to Washington. Execution of this so-called demonstration project was rather botched. First of all, direction was entrusted to an unwieldy committee of Washington bureaucrats, railroad men and consulting engineers, a guarantee of infighting and buck-passing. Next, oblivious to local industry's innocence of any recent experience in high-speed electric traction, this body not only placed its orders unhesitatingly with US builders but handed them a staggering specification: an electric multiple-unit for the New York–Washington sector capable of acceleration from rest to 150 mph (241 km/h) in three minutes on level track.

The outcome was the 'Metroliner', powered on every axle by a motor with a 300 hp continuous rating but with a one-hour reserve of

340 hp more, so that each 75-tonne (73·8 ton) car packed a short-term punch of over 2,500 hp. This was ludicrous over-design for a track which the committee sanguinely expected would need little more than titivation to accept 125 mph (201 km/h) operation, and which soon had the Metroliners ill at ease above 110 mph (177 km/h). Worse, the Metroliners were immediately racked by equipment failures because of the amount of innovation their traction suppliers had had to risk without bench-testing's essential complement of foolproofing in road tests.

A Metroliner car, mechanically refurbished and in Amtrak livery.

Amtrak has refurbished the cars it inherited from US railroads, which it now terms its 'Heritage Fleet'; they predominate in this train of the late 1970s.

New bi-level 'Superliner' cars
have now re-equipped many
of Amtrak's long-haul
services; this is a 'Superliner'
upper level family bedroom.

Even partial implementation of the planned service was impracticable until 1969 and a reasonable approximation of the original prospectus was deferred for two years more. Nevertheless when it did materialize a Metroliner timing of just under three hours for the 226·1-mile (363·9 km) New York–Washington run, incidentally featuring some sprints between intermediate stops scheduled at average speeds as high as 95·4 mph (153·5 km/h), enticed enough trade away from the airline shuttles and highway coaches to build up a healthy 70–75 per cent load factor on the trains.

Tolerable Metroliner reliability was secured just in time to hand at least one commercially viable inter-city passenger operation to the Federally-aided corporation, Amtrak, which Congress coerced a grudging Nixon Administration to create in 1971 in order to salvage a skeletal network of main-line services. Whether the objective was a holding operation to mollify the ecologist lobbies or determined reincarnation of a dying business, on the other hand, was far from clear at the start.

Amtrak's founding Act guaranteed it backing for only two years and its start-up funding was scarcely munificent. Its inaugural network, prescribed by Washington, was limited to 21 routes operating a beggarly total of 184 daily trains; and to furnish them, the Metroliners apart, Amtrak was totally dependent on a heritage of the railroads' elderly streamliner diesels (plus 40 Pennsylvania GG1 electric locomotives) and their by now decaying passenger cars. Furthermore, Amtrak had to operate its trains with the hired crews and over the tracks of railroads which in a number of cases were quite antipathetic to a revival of passenger service: it was so much easier to run freight trains without them.

Despite these discouragements Amtrak demonstrated within two years that there was detectable US demand for continued rail passenger service, even if it came from a fraction of the national market in total. Granted, prospects of viability outside the busy North-East Corridor and on the Florida vacation route from the Eastern seaboard were negligible, but from 1973 onwards Congress was sufficiently encouraged to legislate Amtrak indefinite life, some scope to exercise its own commercial judgement in network expansion, and a rapidly rising scale both of capital investment grants and operating subsidies. Now it could buy new cars, first for its shorter-haul day services, then handsome new bi-level 'Superliners' including sleepers and cafe-lounges for its long-haul routes. It could also purchase new diesel and electric locomotives, though here, unfortunately, it bought a series of troubles because in the interests of economy it ordered some adaptations of existing freight types which for one reason or another proved ill-suited to fast passenger work.

As Amtrak re-equipped Canada was heading down the same path as its neighbours. At the instigation of a Government suspicious that freight shippers were being penalized with inflated rates to prop up loss-making passenger

train. In these sectors the perceived costs of using the now all but universally-owned family car, its instant availability and its door-to-door convenience were making an anachronism of the train, with its inflexible pricing, its fussy, incomprehensible timetabling and its institutional format. It was BR which first appreciated that one of its own antecedents, the Southern Railway of the 1930s, had pointed the way to effective challenge of the private car's convenience. In its main-line electrifications of the 1930s – granted, with the considerable benefit of routes well below 100 miles (161 km) in length – the SR had exploited the productivity potential of electric traction to install a day-long, precisely repetitive timetable. One had only to register that trains going one way left one's station at *x* minutes past the hour, the other way at *y* minutes past, to have the timetable on instant recall. Connections at junctions en route were just as immaculately timetabled. An additional convenience was the frequency of service: at worst it was hourly, at best half-hourly. The SR could afford that because it insisted on standard multiple-unit train-sets, quickly reversed at termini, so that the intensive timetable was operated with a comparatively restricted fleet and the marginal cost of the extra journeys was low – especially if the additional trips were off-peak, when traction current costs were reduced.

In 1951 BR's Eastern Region valiantly adapted these regular-interval precepts to a steam-worked service between London Liverpool Street and Norwich, employing the nationalized system's new standard two-cylinder 'Britannia' Pacifics, and with marked commercial success. This exercise emphasized the strictly patterned, standard train-set operation's relevance to another crucial competitive requirement of the new transport age: increased end-to-end speed to combat the quicker motoring made possible by road improvements. The longer the distance for which a more intensive, regular-interval timetable was drafted, the faster the trains must go to fit in one or more complete out-and-home trips of traction and coaching stock in the day.

One corollary of this drive for productivity was that trains could not be held up for detachment or attachment of through coaches. Sectional working had to be replaced by connections between through trains and local services, but the deterrent of a train-change in mid-journey was generally mitigated by substantially faster overall times to destination, if not always by ease of interchange.

With the aid of new 3,300 hp, 105 mph (169 km/h) 'Deltic' diesel-electrics delivered at the outset of the 1960s the East Coast Regions of BR next built up by stages a dramatically accelerated

Britain's only electric multiple-unit all-Pullman train, the 'Brighton Belle' of the Southern, approaches Clapham Junction on its way into London in 1969.

British Rail Class 55 3,300hp 'Deltic' diesel No 55017 leaves Newcastle Central with the 08.00 Kings Cross-Edinburgh in 1977, overtaking a Class 40 making for Heaton yard with the empty cars of a Liverpool-Newcastle train.

and greatly intensified service between London Kings Cross, Yorkshire's West Riding, the North-East and Scotland. At nationalization in 1948 this route offered only seven weekday trains from London to Newcastle, just three of which – one a Pullman – continued to Edinburgh, and the best time on offer between Kings Cross and Newcastle, 268.3 miles (431.8 km), was a lethargic 5 hours 20 minutes. By 1963 the daily London–Newcastle tally was 12 trains, all bar one leaving London precisely on the hour, half of which carried on to Edinburgh. The fastest schedule to Newcastle was down to 4 hours, but much more significantly the average London–Newcastle transit time of the entire service was no more than 4½ hours: in other words, one could walk in to Kings Cross and expect a common standard of speed and comfort to Newcastle at

Opposite top:
In the new national passenger operator's livery, a trio of inherited GM type F diesel units head a transcontinental train through the Rockies in the VIA Rail era.

Opposite bottom:
In its final years Canadian Pacific's transcontinental 'Canadian', including dome cars, crosses the Stoney Creek bridge in British Columbia.

See a friend this weekend

There are many rail travel bargains – ask for them.

⪢ Inter-City makes the going easy
(and the coming back)

any hour of the day. Ten years later nine London–Newcastle trains each way were averaging only a fraction over $3\frac{3}{4}$ hours in each direction. By then product appeal had been burnished still more through BR's decision to extend air-conditioning to second-class in all new coaching stock being built. BR was the first European system to conclude that the considerable cost and weight penalties of this equipment must be accepted in second- as well as first-class cars because the mass market was beginning to take air-conditioning for granted in public places such as stores, cinemas and restaurants.

The bottom line of this development was that the speed and convenient frequency of the Deltic service attracted sufficient new business on the one hand, and its productive use of assets kept the extra running costs sufficiently in check on the other, for the East Coast Route to cash in a bigger 1965 contribution to fixed system costs than any other BR trunk passenger operation. More powerful testimony still to the competitive strength of a regular-interval timetable of standard speed was forthcoming the next year when BR inaugurated 25kV ac electric service between London Euston and the North-West, promoted it for the first time in European rail history with the full armoury of TV commercial and other contemporary advertising techniques, and sold it with a similar marketing deployment of cheap off-peak fares as that used by Canadian National. This was the operation

for which advertising agents conceived the 'Inter-City' brand-name. Once some excessive generosity in the initial BR fare scheme had been corrected, it succeeded where CN's had failed because of the much more intensive exploitation of assets on every route covered by the British fare-cutting. Especially with electric traction the long-run margin for down-pricing without prejudicing coverage of direct costs with something to spare was greater. From this point on the art of BR passenger management would lie in discerning markets capable of penetration by suitably pitched fare offers at periods when full-fare traffic was low, and at the same time of avoiding any abstraction of more-or-less captive full-fare business. Or put another way, BR pioneered rail service marketing in the modern sense of the word.

To be fair, BR was the only European railway capable of such front-running, because it was unique in the price-fixing freedom which post-war Transport Acts had progressively bestowed on it (this went for freight as well as passenger business, and here, too, marketing became the mainspring of BR's commercial effort). By the 1980s, however, almost every other Western European country had adopted the British model. Maximum fare levels were still ordained by Governments, but below the ceiling railway administrations were given elbow-room to maneuver and prompted to make marketing commercial management's right arm.

Most Continental railways have also followed BR into a framework of standard-speed, regular-interval passenger service. In a number of cases they have appropriated the 'Inter-City' brand-name as well, in certain instances without translation even into the national tongue; West Germany's DB has gone as far as registering among the country's industrial trade-marks the 'IC' contraction it uses in logo form. Like 'Trans-Europ Express', however, the term 'Inter-City' has lately become ill-defined because the International Union of Railways, apparently bereft of original thought, has also borrowed the term to categorize the two-class trains which have taken the place of TEEs on a number of international routes.

The most perfectly developed nationwide regular-interval passenger service is the Netherlands Railways' (NS), which is understandable because the country's small size makes organization of self-contained patterning easier. Outside the morning and evening peaks, when supplementary trains are run, the working even of big city stations such as Amsterdam, Rotterdam and Utrecht is rigidly cyclic from hour to hour, with a standard sequence of trains into and out of each platform that is interrupted only by

Well-designed, easy-to-understand passenger information displays and devices make Netherlands Railways' regular-interval services simple to use.

passage of international services. These, naturally, are hard to dovetail into a national fixed-interval pattern because their paths are dictated by the needs of all the countries they traverse – another reason, incidentally, for disaffection with the long-haul TEE. As each European administration dedicates more effort to intensifying and quickening internal inter-city operation it becomes progressively harder to accept, at an hour which suits the neighbours, trains that must be accorded immediate track space if they are to maintain acceptable TEE end-to-end speed standards.

The greater part of the Netherlands rail passenger service is furnished by electric multiple-units. This format not only secures the rapid terminal turnrounds predicated by frequencies that even on some inter-city routes are half-hourly, but facilitates the multiplicity of connections by which the NS train service interlinks almost any pair of rail-served Dutch towns at fixed intervals the whole day long. On many lines units from different routes converge on a key junction station to combine as one train for the rest of their journey, reversing the process in the opposite direction. Main stations are mostly laid out for this style of working, with their platform lines bisected by crossovers to and from a through line so that the individual units of a multiple train can arrive or depart in any order. Scharfenburg automatic couplers that securely engage all control and brake lines between units on contact make swift work of train assembly or dispersal.

In one respect the most remarkable of

Europe's new fixed-interval services is the 'Inter-City' operation of West Germany's DB, because it preserves almost identical intermediate station calling times in each sequence even though it covers routes as long as 508 miles (818 km) from Hamburg to Munich. And this despite the DB's vastly greater volume of freight than the Dutch system's and its inability to confine as much of the freight operation to the night hours as the NS can, because of the smaller size of the Dutch network. Furthermore the West German capital, Bonn, is not a national hub like London or Paris that radiates the country's principal commercial axes. The DB's trunk passenger service has to treat equally a web of routes interconnecting the cities of the country's north and south, such as Hamburg and Munich, with a quadrilateral of cities in the center between the Rhine-Ruhr territory and the Main, and the cities within this latter core with each other.

The DB took note of BR's 'Inter-City' achievement and launched its own version, identically titled, at the start of the 1970s. At first, as hinted earlier in this chapter, DB 'Inter-City' was specifically designed to defend the premium travel business from Lufthansa and the *autobahnen*. The two-hourly interval trains on each route were supplementary-fare, first class-only domestic replicas of DB-furnished TEEs, employing the same types of air-conditioned stock in TEE red-and-cream livery. A unique hallmark of the DB 'Inter-City' trains for many years was their standard offer on-train of both secretarial and telephone service. French and Italian Railways had also installed these

Right:
Train secretary in a German
Federal TEE in the 1970s.

Coin-operated passenger
telephone kiosks are now
standard in almost all
German Federal IC trains
and are also available in the
Austrian Federal
'Transalpine', seen here.

'Rheingold', the first train to be equipped with what remains the DB's standard pattern of TEE and 'Inter-City' stock.

By 1980, however, the DB had limited the secretarial service to TEEs and a few 'Inter-City' trains with substantial executive trade because of its declining patronage, and in 1982 this frill was dropped altogether. On the other hand the telephone, now developed to the stage of a simple coin-in-the-slot kiosk from which any national or international number can be dialled via a radio link, has been standardized throughout the now greatly expanded 'Inter-City' system. One commonly hears 'Inter-City' conductors summoning passengers by name over the train's public address to take an incoming call, since it is just as easy to phone an 'Inter-City' traveller en route: in fact DB publicizes the individual telephone numbers of each 'Inter-City' train in the timetable. So far only the Austrian Federal Railways (OBB) has been prompted by the DB's enthusiasm to take a fresh look at train telephone service. And they, too, have been encouraged by market response to their first essays, on business services between Vienna, Salzburg and Innsbruck where the train apparatus can tap transmissions along the parallel *autobahn*'s radio-telephone system, to

facilities on some of their exclusive trains in the immediate post-war years, but abandoned them as a costly frill that attracted little use when the equipment fell due for renewal. The DB, however, had set marketing store by both facilities ever since their initial application in 1962 to the

plan extension to other routes.

The expansion of the DB 'Inter-City' service just mentioned ensued from the DB's belated appreciation in the 1970s that its passenger policy was mis-directed. On the one hand underpriced, but on the other still incapable of attracting consistently high load factors because airlines and *autobahnen* skimmed over and through the central ranges of hills where what had been pre-1939 the Reichsbahn's secondary routes severely cramped latter-day DB speed, the first-class 'Inter-City' network was losing money. At the same time road transport, public as well as private, was draining away the DB's second-class traffic, because the rest of the passenger timetable had undergone no major re-cast since its post-war institution. It lacked any discernible pattern; and encumbered by frequent stops, its D-trains averaged barely 50 mph (81 km/h) from starting-point to destination. The exclusive 'Inter-City' exercise had cherished a business sector that constituted no more than 15 per cent of the DB passenger business in toto; meanwhile, from 1960 onwards the DB's share of the national long-distance travel market as a whole had been slumping from 20 to 8·5 per cent. So the DB embarked on the most complex remoulding of a trunk passenger service Europe has ever seen. Unlike BR's, this one embraced the whole national trunk network in a single redraft which entailed widespread, intricate re-timing and in some cases re-routeing of freight traffic to create space for an intensified passenger service as well as the reshaping of countless local connections into and out of the new 'Inter-City' timetable. The product, unveiled countrywide in the 1979 summer, was a daily programme of 152 dual-class 'Inter-City' trains that offered a perfectly patterned service between any pair of the country's 33 major towns and cities once in every weekday hour, either by through journey or by simple cross-platform interchange between 'Inter-City' trains during their smartly-timed meets at key stations in the network. A number of TEEs were sacrificed to accommodate the extra 'Inter-City' workings; others were preserved as extra business market capacity in the morning and evening peaks.

Overnight the average DB second-class passenger had his inter-city journey time cut by a quarter and in short order the descending graph-line of second-class traffic was sharply reversed. This German experience stressed afresh the critical value of speed and regular-interval convenience in strengthening the railway's share of the mass travel market, since the DB's new second-class business was not deterred either by the modest surcharge imposed on their use of 'Inter-City' trains, or by the DB's initial dearth

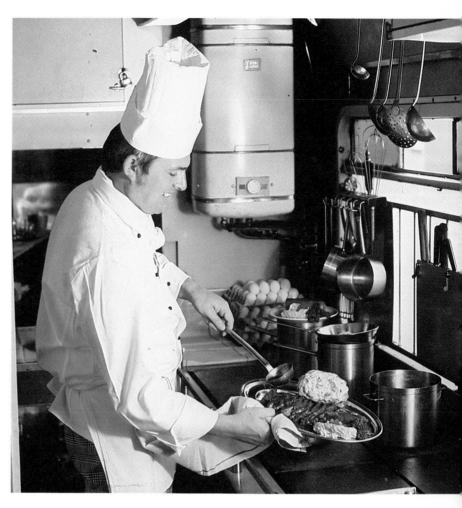

of air-conditioned second-class vehicles. The same type of second-class stock served both 'IC' and D-train services. It needed French experience, to be described next, as well as British to change the DB's obstinate conviction that air-conditioning was justified only as a first-class perk; consequently the dual-class DB 'Inter-City' service was begun with availability of a new design of air-conditioned second-class saloon limited to a prototype batch of 40 cars, though a series production order for 400 soon followed.

Through its DSG subsidiary the DB lavishes its 'Inter-City' network with Europe's most generous train catering. Full meal service, DB passenger managers insist, must be offered on every train. In most cases it is furnished by kitchen-restaurant cars that purvey an extraordinarily compendious à la carte menu, with a choice of up to ten hot entrées, from start to finish of the train's itinerary. The turnover from such continuous service improves on the potential of table d'hote catering within fixed meal hours, but the only other European railway prepared to face the cost of stocking cars for wide-ranging à la carte service as a justifiable marketing overhead is the Austrian Federal. The DB accepts a far heavier revenue shortfall on

The DSG-run restaurant cars of German Federal Railways' IC trains serve an extensive *à la carte* menu throughout their journeys.

Service aboard a DSG 'Quick-Pick' cafeteria car on the German Federal Railways.

the expenses of its train catering than any other European system apart from Italian Railways.

These days the capital cost of a fully-equipped new kitchen-restaurant car is around £500,000. Well before it had reached that level, in 1962, the Wagons-Lits company saw no hope of generating a margin on train meals to fund renewal of its restaurant car fleet and persuaded all the railways from which it had a catering concession to take responsibility for the vehicles off its hands. Today the company merely provisions, staffs and serves on the cars it operates. Except in Austria, the charge for upkeep and renewal of the Wagons-Lits sleepers has also been passed to the railways in a 1971 agreement which additionally transferred the marketing of both Wagons-Lits and German DSG sleeper services to a consortium of the principal Continental European railways, with the exclusion of Norway and Sweden.

Along with material expense the cost of staffing catering cars has risen alarmingly, aggravated by the frequent need on long runs to lodge crews overnight. And at the same time there has been some flux in eating habits, partly the result of dietary obsessions, partly because of the higher cost of conventional meals even on terra firma, and not least as the outcome of growing addiction to pre-packed junk foods. These factors in concert have persuaded a number of European managements to curtail traditional restaurant car service and to cater for the bulk of their express train service with self-service cafeteria or buffet cars exploiting the latest in pre-prepared meal science and microwave oven technology. As the DB persuasively demonstrates in the 'Quick-Pick' cafeterias it operates on a few 'Inter-City' as well as many D-trains, the latest self-service method and equipment allows dishes that stand reasonable comparison with freshly-prepared meals to be served at a considerably higher turnover rate than in an orthodox diner, and with a substantially smaller crew.

In France traditional restaurant car service was already confined to international and domestic TEEs by the start of the 1980s. All other inter-city trains had been converted to 'Gril-Express' cafeteria or buffet-bar catering, supplemented in some cases by tray-meal service for first-class passengers from galleys in their part of the train, in the course of a transformation of French Railways' (SNCF) trunk passenger working during the 1970s. As in West Germany, the motivation was research that awoke management to the size of a popular

market it had inertly let take to the car as the only conceivable medium for optional journeys because so much of its effort was devoted to courting the business market with exceptionally fast, supplementary-fare *rapides* in the peak hours. Despite the emphatic trend to regular-interval working in every neighbouring country bar Italy, the SNCF has sensed no case in France for deviation from the country's historic pattern of concentrated departure from Paris and main provincial centers in breakfast-time, midday and early evening 'flights', with a comparatively sparse offer of trains in mid-morning and mid-afternoon. (This pattern of working, incidentally, simplifies the mixing of freight and express passenger traffic on the same route very considerably by cleaving a substantial gap between each 'flight' of expresses through which slower-moving trains can be passed in operational comfort.) Enough, in the French view, to invest a huge sum in the re-equipment of all inter-city services with an elegant new breed of rolling stock, with only modest revision of the time-table and acceleration wherever feasible. Since 1979 the SNCF has been able to apply a considerable range of market-priced fares to the new-look service.

The new standard 'Corail' stock, as it is

called partly to mark its predominantly grey livery, is a masterpiece of the contemporary rail coach designer's art. Air-conditioned in both classes, its saloon layout adroitly masks the fact

that the ratio of passenger seats to dead weight
has been kept economically high because of the
thoughtful attention applied to the fine detail of
furnishing and aids to passenger convenience
and comfort, and not least the expertise of the
decor. Since mid-century most European railways have taken a degree of advice from high-
ranking firms in the industrial design field
instead of entrusting external styling and interior
appointment to the usually hidebound concep-
tions of their mechanical engineering depart-
ments. The SNCF, however, is the only one to
have committed its industrial design entirely to
the professionals. The benefit is patent in all new
French passenger equipment of the last two
decades, the Corail cars above all. They are a
sharp lesson to some of their European neighbours, BR included, that the economies of a
high payload/tare ratio and easy-to-maintain
plastic surfaces inside the vehicle are attainable
without reproducing the rolling equivalent of a
third-rate hamburger saloon.

Besides interior appeal, a more mass-market-
oriented train catering service, rising speed and
marketing ploys, it is the vastly improved ride
quality of Corail and the latest stock of other
European railways that has contributed most to
restoration of rail's competitiveness. This is the
product of several factors.

The extension to practically every trunk route

of continuously welded rail has eliminated the
wheels' rhythmic battering of rail joints, while
the other extraneous noises of travel have been
excluded both by the insulation essential for
effective air-conditioning and by scientific sound-
proofing of sensitive areas of the bodywork.
Most important of all, the inexorable commercial
demand for higher speed has driven railways to
undertake their first scientifically-based research
into the interaction of wheel and rail, as much to
minimize wear and tear in intensive operation at
100 mph (161 km/h) or more, as to eradicate un-
pleasant reaction of vehicles to slight imperfections in their running gear or in the track. The
outcome has been a new sophistication in the
design of bogies, in the marriage of metal-spring
and air suspension systems, and in the carefully
calculated match of running gear to super-
structure design, which has added serenity of
ride, over junctions as well as plain track, to the
quietness achieved by modern sound-proofing.
The new science has benefited freight stock, too,
enabling 100 ton (102 tonne) glw bogie wagons
imposing a 25-ton (25·4 tonne) axleload on the
track to be run without detriment at 60 mph (97
km/h) or even more. On BR it has evolved a
rigid two-axle vehicle proved a smooth-rider at
up to 100 mph; from this the British system has
developed a new bus-bodied diesel multiple-
unit, its Class 141, that is a feasible successor to

its big fleet of life-expired bogie sets and almost
a third of the capital cost of their replacement
by a new diesel-electric bogie railcar set, the
Class 210.

Improved quality has also helped to keep
about a million travellers a year riding the 265
sleeping cars forming the 'Trans-Euro-Nacht'
(TEN) pool operated by the consortium of
Western European railways mentioned earlier,
despite the ease and speed of daytime air
connection between the cities served by the TEN
routes. Despite, too, most sleeper trains' deprivation of a restaurant car, because of the now
unacceptably high cost of working a diner crew
overnight for the service of only two meals,
maybe just breakfast: for that one has to be
content on the majority of TEN routes with
a pre-packaged tray from the attendant's
pantry, though the coffee comes fresh and hot.
Dominance of today's TEN fleet by the so-
called 'Universal' type of sleeper, in which each
compartment is easily arranged for one-, two-
or in some cases three-berth use, has brought
about a marked improvement in asset productivity, because a car is so simply adjusted to
seasonal or even day-to-day fluctuations in
demand between one class and another. Thus,
while the total of TEN customers has changed
little since 1970, they are currently being
accommodated in 20 per cent fewer sleeping

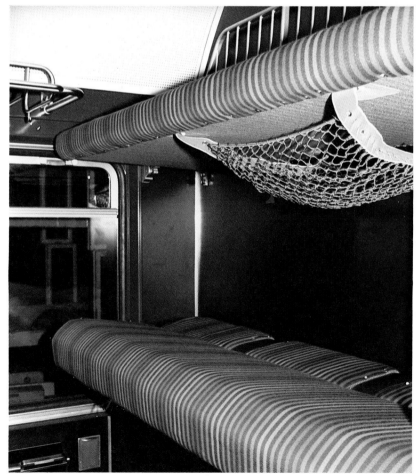

175

cars, each of which, aided by more intensive work allocation, is 40 per cent more productive than the norm of a decade ago.

At the same time the overnight Continental European train's mass-market validity as an option to eight hours or more of family saloon motoring has been fortified by refinement of the couchette car. As recently as the mid-1970s the best one could say for a second-class couchette compartment was it made room for six occupants to lie full length without tangling limbs. The tier of berths which were unfolded from the walls or converted from the daytime bench seats were plank-like as beds, their single rugs primitive as

blankets and in the topmost berth gave skimpy protection from open window draughts that had to be tolerated for minimum ventilation if the compartment was full. Decor was institutionally severe and the provision of washrooms per car generally inadequate. The latest couchette cars, however, are air-conditioned and much more attractively furnished. Berths are better sprung (the SNCF at least now treats its couchette passengers to sheets); and some railways have begun to accept a maximum of four occupants per second-class compartment. Evidence of these developments' remoulding of the overnight travel market mix is the SNCF's

A de luxe suite on Australia's transcontinental 'Indian-Pacific'.

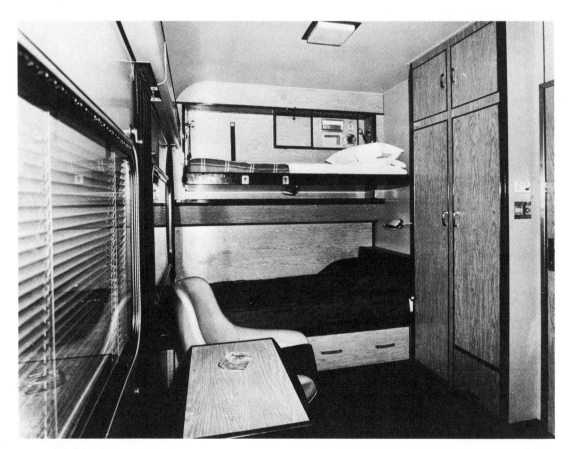

The first 'Indian-Pacific' Express leaves Perth, Western Australia, on its eastward trip across the continent on 30 August 1974.

installation of new trains formed exclusively of sleepers and couchette cars on routes that have never previously warranted a night service devoid of orthodox day cars, such as Paris to the Pyrenees and from Lyons across country to Nantes. Even more significantly, the legendary Paris–Riviera 'Train Bleu' is no longer a single all-sleeper train but two, each a mix of sleepers and couchettes, that share service of the Côte d'Azur resorts.

Thus has the 'democratization' of Europe's inter-city railway network all but completed the extinction of the luxury train concept on both sides of the Atlantic. In the 1980s only one Pullman service survives, on BR's Euston–Manchester route. That cliché of inter-war railway publicity machines, the 'hotel on wheels', is today applicable only to South Africa's 'Blue Train' and the 'Indian-Pacific' that transits Australia from east to west, with their offer of palatial suites for premium fare-payers. But these are both national showpieces run regardless of cost to entice the tourist trade, or for political ends, not trains required to pay their way in the everyday travel market.

The lounge of South African Railways 'Blue Train'.

The 'Blue Train' at Lawley, headed by a pair of Class GE electric Bo-Bos.

12

ELECTRONICS REVOLUTIONIZE RAILWAY OPERATION

IN 1981 THE ENGINEERS OF BRITISH RAIL Scottish Region's signalling department and their equipment suppliers were rounding off a five-year project that epitomizes the remarkable changes electronics have brought to railway operation in the past quarter-century. Completion of the job would concentrate railway working throughout the south-east of Scotland under the control of one center, at the heart of the network in Edinburgh. At any one time the operating floor of the Edinburgh signalling center will have on duty just five signalmen, a traffic supervisor, a broadcaster of train announcements and someone managing the remote control of platform train indicators at stations in the area overseen by the center. Yet this small group will be responsible for signalling of traffic over 236 miles (380 km) of route ranging from the Anglo-Scottish border just short of Berwick-on-Tweed in the east, to Falkirk in the west, and over the Forth Bridge to Cupar, Fife, on the way to Dundee and Aberdeen, with the crossroads of Edinburgh, its Waverley station and its yards,

depots and dock branches in the center. That area embraces altogether 508 miles (818 km) of single track under signals, of which there will be 540. The number of points operable from the Edinburgh center will be 450, and the total of routes through them that can be selected by the Edinburgh signalmen will be around 1,200.

Before the staged commissioning of the new Edinburgh signalling center began in the late 1970s its domain needed no fewer than 66 signalboxes for traffic control. Two of them were models of early power signalling technology and commanded operations at Edinburgh Waverley station; the rest were old-style boxes with mechanical, manually-operated lever frames. With provision for work-shift reliefs to cover round-the-clock manning, these 66 boxes employed 300 signalmen, whereas the staff establishment for the new center is 20 signalmen, five supervisors and five train announcers. Despite this rigorous manpower economy, through traffic in south-east Scotland will move more smoothly than it has done under the old order, because of

Far left:
A modern signalling centre on French Railways at Versailles Chantiers: in the background the signalmen sit at route-setting consoles in front of a panoramic illuminated track diagram, in the background traffic controllers face diagrammatic displays of the timetable.

Below:
Before colour-light signalling Britain's railways indicated junctions by a mass of semaphore signals, one set for each route, as on this gantry at the southern approach to Rugby Station, LMR.

Control room of an early
CTC installation on New
Zealand Railways.

the new center's continuous, detailed overview
of trains' progress throughout the territory and
its resultant ability to pre-plan effectual impro-
visations the moment scheduled operation be-
trays a hint of going astray.

The operating console of the Edinburgh
center is a panoramic diagram of the entire
layout under its control that is draped hemi-
spherically across two walls of the operating
floor, and studded with illuminated displays and
push-buttons. Each push-button sets a defined
route: that is, it combines activation of points as
necessary with clearance of relevant signals,
provided, of course, that the interlocking has
first proved the route free of interference and
safe to set. In addition the signals will not clear
for the new route until the apparatus has
automatically detected the positive re-setting of
any points involved. A line of white lights will
instantaneously indicate on the layout diagram
the track-circuited sections through which the
new route has been set and markers at the sites
of their protecting signals will change from red
to green. Elsewhere on the layout diagram the
progress of the train for which the route has been
prepared will be verifiable from the advance of a
line of red lights that shows up in each succeeding track-circuited section occupied by the
oncoming movement. Not only that, but the

train will be specifically identified by its four-
character alpha-numerical designation in the
railway working timetable. This, too, will
automatically move with it on the layout display,
lit up in small windows alongside each track-
circuited section through which the train passes
and extinguished after it has gone.

Without electronics and their faculty for
extreme miniaturization of control devices,
without microprocessors and without computers
such concentration of traffic direction and the
data for its efficient exercise would be impossible.
Take for instance the transmission of commands
from the panel to signals and points and the
return from the ground apparatus to the console
of proof that they have been obeyed, which is
registered by illumination of the relevant panel
indications. In the Edinburgh scheme the actual
functioning of the points and signals is activated
by two dozen remote relay interlockings, which
are in effect unmanned, remotely-controlled
signalboxes, strategically sited throughout the
Edinburgh center's territory. Each of these
remote relay interlockings takes its instructions
from the Edinburgh console and acknowledges
correct compliance over a mere pair of wires.

The very first essays in electrical remote control
of signals and points throughout a considerable
mileage of route also needed just two wires.

They were the pioneering American installations of Centralized Traffic Control (CTC) in the 1920s, which brought 100 miles (161 km) or more of single-track main line in the sparsely populated Middle West and West under the supervision of a single operator, so that he could organize the meets of opposing trains in passing loops more efficiently. But in those days the only medium for selection of a specific address for a command from the operating console was a variant of the contemporary automatic telephone dialling system. The operator flicked the panel switch, for, say, point No 23 on his layout and the apparatus would automatically send out over one of the two wires the code for point No 23; the latter would reverse in response, then return a similarly coded acknowledgement over the second wire. The limitations of this method were first, that only one command could be issued at a time; and second, that it took up to five seconds or even more to complete each sequence of transmission, function of apparatus addressed and receipt of response at the operating console. This was of no consequence in CTC's early application to US or rural Swedish single lines rarely occupied by more than two or three trains simultaneously, and those unlikely to be fast-moving. But in five seconds a 100 mph (161 km/h) express of today will have covered almost 250 yards (229 m), besides which the volume of train movement in an area like Edinburgh would overwhelm the capacity of so ponderous a transmission system.

In the electronic age transistors have accelerated the speed of transmission more than a hundredfold. Not only that, but a single wire can convey a considerable number of commands or responses simultaneously, either by use of a variety of frequencies, each with its own complex of codes – the Frequency Division Multiple (FDM) system – or by what is known as the Time Division Multiplex (TDM) method. In TDM a high-speed electronic scanning device at the console end of the wire and another at the remote interlocking end, each precisely synchronized with the other, simultaneously check each console control against its addressee several times a second for lack of correspondence. In other words, as soon as the remote interlocking scanner detects an altered state in one of the console controls, signifying a re-set route, it will activate the appropriate ground apparatus through the remote interlocking; and as soon as the latter has changed state the console scanner will observe and automatically adjust the operating panel display to conform.

This electronic capacity for ultra-rapid transmission of commands and responses has simplified a valuable feature of modern traffic control

in busy areas, reversible signalling. Each running line can be safely signalled for two-way working, so that a peak flow in one direction can pre-empt extra tracks when traffic in the opposite direction is sparse, or fast trains can overtake slower.

Computers have become a key component of modern traffic control technology, as will be described shortly, but it may already have been inferred from the term 'route relay interlocking' that BR's signal engineers are among the majority who for some time hesitated to apply direct computer control to route-setting. 'Fail-safe' is still worldwide the signal engineer's credo and for that reason most have persisted with relays for ultimate actuation of points and signals. In Japan, Italy and Scandinavia, however, some engineers have now begun the plunge into computerized interlocking. In 1982 the most ambitious venture of this type was the Swedish State Railways' (SJ) at Göteborg, where one signalling center controls the junction of five routes and access to a couple of marshalling yards, six public freight depots, a comprehensively rail-served port area and a number of private sidings outside it. The Swedes claim to have eliminated all the risks of a defect in computer programming by resort to parallel systems which double-check each other. All the probes of interlocking states necessary to verify that a route is safe to set are simultaneously conducted by two computer programming systems, each of which is arranged to examine the data and the addressee apparatus involved in a different way. Their outputs are then

Operator's desk in the control centre of Swedish State Railways' computer-based interlocking at Göteborg: routes are set on an alpha-numerical keyboard and displayed on VDUs.

compared in fail-safe relay apparatus and proved devoid of discrepancy before the commands to set the route are transmitted to the relevant points and signals.

Electronics have greatly extended the scope of track circuitry's functions. Its essential purpose remains, of course, that of detecting a train's occupation of a circuited section of track – or, in the area of a modern electronic signalling console such as Edinburgh's, an independently-circuited route-setting – and locking signals to a safe distance behind it, additionally preventing the clearance of any conflicting routes. On suitable stretches of plain line the track circuitry can be made to operate signalling automatically, clearing signals as soon as a specified number of sections in rear of a train have been detected as empty. Nowadays the track circuitry also activates the automatic signal console train description displays mentioned earlier. On a route controlled exclusively by signal centers of the Edinburgh kind – BR's 401-mile (645 km) line from London Euston to Glasgow Central, for instance – a signalman has only to dial or key in a train's four-character description to the number of the track circuit berth from which it starts its journey and that description will automatically travel with it the whole way. As the train passes from one circuited section to another, so its description will step forward from one illuminated aperture on the illuminated signal center diagram to the next, finally jumping from the last aperture on the despatching panel's display to the first one on the layout diagram of the next center down the line as the train crosses the border from one control area to another. Given

this continuous recording of each moving train's location, it is obviously a comparatively simple matter in terms of today's electronic technology to tap the train describers for accurate activation of the travelling public's train information indicators on station platforms. The train describers are also being exploited to generate a growing amount of real-time traffic data for management.

The most recent BR signalling centers process the train description data through computers. As a result the operating floor's traffic supervisor does not have to peer the whole length and depth of the signalmen's wall display to discover the whereabouts of a specific train engaging his attention. Nor for that matter need similarly exercised station managers or other key staff on the ground bother the signal center with telephone calls. They can be provided with terminals to interrogate the computers direct, then call up on their own VDU screens a display pinpointing the location of the train at issue.

Some railways now reject the huge one-piece combination of illuminated layout diagram and geographically-sited route-setting buttons as too unwieldy, seeing that component miniaturization and electronics can centralize control of 200 miles (322 km) or more of route. In the computerized SJ center at Göteborg mentioned earlier, for instance, each signalman sits at a desk fitted with a typewriter-like keyboard and a pair of VDUs. One VDU reproduces in colour the whole area of the layout for which he is responsible, the setting of its routes, its occupation by trains and so on. On the other, through a panel of buttons, he can summon from

Interior of British Rail's West Hampstead signal-box controlling 270 track-miles between London's St Pancras – Moorgate and Sharnbrook, Bedfordshire. In the foreground are traffic controllers, at rear the signalmen in front of the illuminated layout display.

the computer a close-up – also in colour – of the state of a specific sector of his charge or other kinds of real-time data on individual train movement. And with the 'typewriter' he selects by their code number the routes he wants to set.

When a distinctive description can be made to move electronically through a signalling system in step with the progress of the train to which it refers, the logical next step is to exploit the code to set the train's route automatically. This is achieved by reserving one or more characters in the code to denote route. At interlockings arranged for automatic route-setting, devices read the codes of approaching trains as these are processed through the train describer system, identify the route-indicating character and adjust the route appropriately.

West Germany's DB was the European front-runner in automatic route-setting in 1957, in the first of its post-war electronic signalling concentration projects at Frankfurt. The rail network here was invitingly shaped for the innovation. Its hub is the huge main station and its neighbouring freight depot, but both are dead-end termini. A considerable volume of through traffic, predominantly freight, bypasses this terminal complex on orbital lines inter-sected by several simple junctions which drain off trains bound for the termini. These junctions were not difficult to equip for automatic route-setting on the principles just described, since at each of them the apparatus had to distinguish between only two basic routeings. The benefit of automatic operation was its relief of the traffic regulators' and signalmen's workload, enabling them to focus their expertise on the

formidable job of weaving many conflicting streams of passenger trains into and out of the main station's score of platforms – where, of course, every conventional locomotive-hauled train (push-pulls excepted, in other words) complicated their tactical work by reversing and demanding a fresh locomotive.

The scope for automatic route-setting on main-line railways is inevitably restricted because of the intricacy of their traffic flows. The multiplicity of routeings into and out of a junction like Crewe and its platforms, for instance, would of itself defeat contrivance of an economical processing apparatus, but to be fully effective the latter must also be capable of discriminating judgement when trains scheduled to make crucial connections start running out of course.

Consequently automatic route-setting has been generally confined to railways where lay-outs are simple and trains of common charac-teristics run to a clear-cut, consistently-repeated pattern over short distances that limit vulner-ability to serious delay. That, of course, is the conurbation Metro in a nutshell. It is on the latest of the world's Metros, as described in Chapter 14, that automatic route-setting has integrated with other electronic innovations to bring the completely automated passenger rail-way not merely into view but to practical reality.

Nevertheless, the new technology does have more to offer the traffic regulator on the mixed-traffic main-line railway. In its Glasgow Central signalling center, for example, BR has been evaluating what it terms a Junction Optimisation

At Swiss Federal Railways' Oerliken signalling centre, controlling a complex and very busy sector on the Zurich outskirts, route-setting is normally automatic, controlled by computers working from the timetable; operators intervene only when a train is running out of timetabled path.

183

Modern signal centre architecture at Frankfurt am Main, German Federal Railways.

Technique, wherein a computer apparatus surveys the progress of approaching traffic as it is recorded by the train describer system and the occupation of the terminal station's platforms, compares the moment-to-moment state of play with the area's timetable and track layout stored in its memory bank, then advises the traffic supervisor and his signalmen of the order of priority in which they should accept incoming trains for optimal employment of the station's capacity and most effective realization of the timetable's prescriptions. The JOT system does not impose the computer's will, but valuably produces instant data to assist the signalmen's decision-making.

A similar principle informs the elaborate computer-based traffic regulation aids in the control centers of the DB's S-Bahn networks in Munich and Stuttgart. These S-Bahnen converge suburban passenger routes from all quarters of each conurbation on a single subterannean passage of the city center. In that tunnel the

timetabled headway between trains is naturally close. The risks of disrupted operation are consequently great because on the city outskirts a number of the S-Bahn routes have to share trackage with longer-haul passenger and freight traffic, which may delay their advance downtown and bring them to the city-center tunnel-mouth behind time. Computers are therefore arranged in each center to supply the S-Bahn traffic regulators with continuously updated predictions of the time at which each incoming S-Bahn train will reach the critical junctions where their routes are channelled into the cross-town tunnel.

Incessantly and automatically interrogating every interlocking in the S-Bahn network and the train describers, the computers not only check each train's running against its schedule but from its section-to-section times estimate its average speed. From the latter data they forecast the likely moments at which each train will enter sections ahead and ultimately reach the system's crucial intersections. Needless to say, these forward projections are constantly undergoing split-second adjustments to reflect each train's actual progress. The findings are reproduced on an array of colour VDUs fronting the regulators in the traffic center. One set of VDUs shows each regulator the traffic and route-set state of the area he supervises, in the same fashion as the route-setting console of a mainline signalling center but with the refinement in this case that each train description displayed is suffixed both with its schedule time at the interlocking it is traversing and also the amount, if any, by which it is running late or ahead of time. The second battery of VDUs extrapolates the estimates of the trains' speed to predict graphically, in time-mileage co-ordinates, their forward path to the city center in relation to the progress of other traffic. Thus the traffic regulators are forewarned where junction conflicts may occur and the timetable disintegrate unless they take preventive action in good time.

When the mammoth Parisian scheme for interlinking the east-west limited-stop, deep-level RER express underground railways of the city and its northern and southern French Railways suburban networks beneath the capital's heart is finished late in the 1980s, the network's underground core between Gare de Lyons and Châtelet may become the busiest double-track in the world. In the morning and evening peaks up to 120 trains an hour could be converging on it from different routes. Under pressure of that intensity traffic regulators need a further degree of computer assistance to bring the trains up to the bottleneck in good order.

Here, therefore, the driver of a train detected

as falling behind time will automatically be transmitted an injunction to adjust his speed to a figure computed to restore him to schedule by the time he reaches the threshold of the mid-town section. Should the computer judge the train to be irredeemably off course it will instantaneously plan a retimed path that will keep it clear of the central area until the latter has track space into which it can be squeezed without delaying the rest of the service. However, at the start of 1983 the French were beginning to question whether even with computers operation at 60-second train headways was feasible, and to conclude that the planned intensity of service would be impracticable without laying in additional tracks.

Still more sophisticated is the computerized control system of the Keio Teito Railway which serves one sector of the Tokyo conurbation and operates a very intensive service on a line that debouches into four branches in the suburbs. Unless the traffic regulators intervene the computers will execute all route-setting automatically in accordance with the train plan stored in their memory. As soon as they detect that the working is not going to plan the computers will come up with a remedial course of action. This involves them in a maze of split-second calculations, for besides catering for four routes the Keio Teito also runs a mix of all-stations and limited-stop trains. The computers must, therefore, ponder whether to revise priorities, vary points at which faster trains overtake slower, or maybe to go as far as turning round a train or two short of timetabled destination to get operation back on course.

Only if the traffic regulators decide to take over or if the emergency becomes really complicated to unravel will the computers surrender the initative. Normally, having convinced themselves of the optimal improvisation, they proceed to execute it automatically.

Obviously, it takes only the means of conveying orders from central computer complexes of this kind to trains' driving controls to slot the last component of a fully automated railway into place. The framework is in fact complete on several Metros in Europe, in the US and in the Far East; but even with the safeguard of closed-circuit TV for supervision of passenger movement on and off trains from the control center only one Metro administration, that of Lille in France, with its new VAL line scheduled to open commercially in 1983, has so far had the courage to dispense with train attendants altogether. Helsinki, in Finland, is preparing to follow suit. Elsewhere automation is fully in command only from the moment the train attendant closes doors and presses a start button at the conclusion of one station stop until the train is brought to rest and the doors reopened at the next.

Though West Germany's DB is developing the microwave broadcast of coded commands to traction units, the customary method of transmission at present is by passage through the rails or through a separate track-mounted cable of low-frequency current impulses picked up by receivers on the traction units. Besides its applications to fully automatic Metro train driving, this system is a vital element of modern high-speed railway practice. Railway manage-

Control room of the Amsterdam Metro, of which the signalling is completely automated.

ments differ whether 100 mph (161 km/h) or further into the three-figure speed range is the ceiling at which intermittent lineside signalling is inadequate for a driver's peace of mind, but so far no one has dared to indulge sustained running at more than 125 mph (201 km/h) without provision of means to reproduce a continuous display of signal aspects on the driver's desk and associate with it an over-riding control of speed should the display's commands be flouted.

On France's new 160 mph (258 km/h) Paris–Lyons LGV*, to discuss one example, automatic train and speed control works this way. The simplicity of the LGV as a railway, with its exclusive traffic of standard passenger train-sets and bare minimum of intermediate stations and junctions – just two of each from its start and finish on the previous Paris–Lyons main line – keeps the range of necessary commands low. Some systems demand such a profusion of data to be transmitted both ways – instructions to the train and responses or advice of location from train to control center – that it takes the expense of a separate wired system to accommodate them. The running rails are adequate channels for the dozen or so coded instructions that suffice for TGV train control. The only lineside signals on LGV open line are fixed markers at the start of each track-circuited block section. In normal working a headway of three block sections has to be maintained between trains. On the open

*French Railways nowadays describe their 160 mph railways as *Lignes Grandes Vitesses*, the trains which travel them as *Trains Grandes Vitesses* (TGV).

line the signalling which preserves it is actuated automatically by making a train's occupation of a section determine the code of the current passing through successive rail or block sections in its rear. As soon as a following LGV train gets within unacceptable distance of its predecessor a display on its driver's desk will change as an altered code is picked up by an inductive coil beneath the cab and translated.

An indication authorizing the driver to proceed at maximum line speed of 160 mph (258 km/h) will change to one warning him that at the next section entrance marker he may get a deceleration signal. If the train is in fact checked, his cab display, reacting to new codes picked up by the receiver in succeeding sections, will now alter to show him both the maximum speed he must observe in the section in which he is running and also the limit to which he must have decelerated by the next section entrance marker. The maxima are prescribed in set figures – either 220 km/h (137 mph), 160 km/h (99 mph) or 80 km/h (50 mph) – and there is obviously a last step of ordering a halt at the next section entrance marker. A TGV train can be braked to a stand from its top 160 mph pace within three sections, so the 80 km/h code does not come into play when it is stopped quickly.

In the equivalent automatic speed control and continuous cab signalling system of West Germany's DB, microprocessors in the traction unit equipment calculate a braking curve that will most efficiently respond to the deceleration commands within the section's length and reproduce it on the driver's display. This is not a feature of the LGV system, but in view of the

French line's incessant and often abrupt changes of gradient, created for reasons that are described in Chapter 16, TGV power cars are fitted with an electronic device which automatically senses profile variations and adjusts input to the traction motors as necessary to hold the maximum speed set by the driver on his controller.

With the elimination of the lineside signalbox, either by fully automatic signalling of the character just outlined or by concentration of human control in electronic centers which are often totally out of sight of the traffic they manage, lookouts from which some potentially dangerous defects on passing trains might be spotted have gone. Here again electronics have in some instances taken over. Lineside infra-red detectors, for example, read the temperature of passing vehicles' axleboxes and automatically warn signal centers if they sense an incipient hot box; the most sophisticated versions also count the axleboxes of each passing train, so that they can precisely pinpoint the delinquent axlebox. Other lineside apparatus can identify dragging brake apparatus which may cause trouble. At the same time, the spread of radio communication between train crews and ground-based control centers has helped compensate for the reduction of signal boxes.

This chapter has concentrated on the revolution electronics have wrought in train and traffic control. Other chapters outline their benefits to traction, to freight train sorting and to elements of Metro railway operation not discussed above. It would be wrong to conclude without reference to the impact of computers and microprocessing on almost all branches of

railway administration: from establishment of computerized all-line seat and sleeper berth reservation apparatus to systems, such as BR's TOPS, which keep a real-time check on the availability, state of repair and deployment of all traction and vehicles.

BR has been progressively bringing all the elements involved in the planning, execution and appraisal of its train service under the supervision of interconnected computer systems. The 'Carousel' system with which BR organizes the 'merry-go-round' coal feed of eight electricity generating stations and a steel works in the North Midlands-South Yorkshire region is a microcosm of the method that is gradually being applied to the whole British rail system.

For a number of technical reasons the National Coal Board varies the source of power station coal. Close on 100 different pits are called upon to supply the generating plants in the Carousel scheme and those to be brought into play and the tonnages they will supply to the respective power stations during any working week are not advised to BR until a few days before that week's start. Yet through TOPS a train working plan to cover the week's programme with optimal use of traction, wagon and train crew resources is produced, printed and distributed to all depots involved before the end of the preceding week's work, so that everyone involved knows his duty for the following Monday before he goes off for the weekend.

In brief, the process consists of setting TOPS to consider the tonnages to be moved, their sources and destinations, against a library of fixed data in its memory banks. Some of the

Above:
Cab of a French 270 km/h TGV, with driver in radio telephonic contact with control centre; above his controller wheel are the displays on which signal aspects and speed commands are automatically illuminated.

data is geographical, such as details of the collieries involved, their pithead layout capacity, the times they are open for work, how long they take to load a train, and so on; similar information on the receiving power stations; and characteristics of the routes between pitheads and power stations, including such detail as the normal opening and closing times of signalboxes en route. Resource data covers the 72 locomotives allocated to the scheme, the 6,000 hopper wagons, and the 450 trainmen who are based on 12 different depots, together with, in the case of the last-mentioned, details of their conditions of work which effect the planning – for instance, agreements concerning locomotive single-manning (the computer will naturally seek to maximize the opportunities for single-manning within the rules extant at the time). Other data held by TOPS is operational: train running times for the types of locomotive involved with specific hopper-train loads over each section of route in the scheme, recognized routeings for all known and possible pithead-power station flows, the depots accepted as furnishing locomotives and crews for each route, etc. Apart from the fact that to draft a train and

traincrew plan for such large-scale working within so short a time would be extremely difficult without the aid of computers, the Carousel scheme has achieved a remarkable economy in the resources needed to move the million or so tonnes of coal a week involved in the exercise.

In the longer term BR sees train service planning, supervision and real-time control concentrated in centers which integrate the management and signalling functions. On the passenger side, automatic revenue collection equipment would be plugged into the centers, generating information on demand for services. The monitoring functions of TOPS would be supplemented by automatic means to register continuously the individual locations of all locomotives, fixed train-sets and individual wagons (this can be done by fitting each item with its individually coded transponder, which is read by ground devices wherever it moves). And much more besides, for because of its strictly disciplined working over its own fixed roadway the railway is of all means of transport by far the most suited to productive exploitation of the still advancing technology of electronics.

Above:
The headquarters of British Rails' Total Operations Processing System (TOPS) which continuously monitors all wagon distribution and freight train performance.

Left:
Every local TOPS terminal receives information from and reports to the central TOPS computer on wagon movements into and out of its territory.

13

THE AGE OF HIGH-VOLTAGE
AC ELECTRIFICATION

LOUIS ARMAND, the Chairman of French Railways and also of the International Union of Railways (UIC), was the outstanding European railway technocrat of the immediate post-war years. His prescience was not confined to technological possibility, as witness this passage from his writings in 1957.

'We must give thought', Armand warned at a time when no one had dreamed of forging an oil-price weapon, let alone wielding it, 'to the position in which we would find ourselves if in fifteen years' time there were to be a shortage of imported coal and oil. It would be disastrous. Not only would our Sunday outings be in jeopardy, but indeed all the activities of our working week too.' Incredibly, with his 'fifteen years' Armand was no more than a year out so far as oil was concerned. The Arab-Israeli war flared in 1973; and at a stroke the world was brought face to face, not only with the real value of oil but also with the finite character of oil resources, and the vulnerability of countries without them to industrial fuel starvation in a political crisis.

Suddenly national transport policy had to take account of a critical new dimension. In the developed world transport was on average absorbing 20 per cent of all energy consumed; but as much as 95 per cent of transport's energy was derived from oil, because of the massive post-war growth of road transport.

However, the energy-efficient supremacy of the railway was becoming more clear-cut by the year. Statistics compiled by the OECD for countries of the European Economic Community in 1979 showed that although rail was carrying 21 per cent of the member nations' surface freight and covering 8 per cent of all passenger journeys, it was responsible for no more than 6·5 per cent of all energy consumption in the transport sector of the EEC's economy. That was largely because more than two-thirds of the train-miles performed in EEC railways were by then electrically-powered, to a large extent, moreover, with current generated in non-oil burning plants. And because the post-war advances in technology and the resultant gains in efficiency had been more rapid and more substantial in electric traction than in any other form of rail power.

The first breakthrough was French Railways' perfection of high-voltage ac electrification with single-phase current straight from the national grid at the industrial frequency. The Germans had been experimenting with this technique since 1936 on their 34-mile (55 km) Höllental Railway in the Black Forest. That fell into the French Occupation Zone in 1945, whereupon industrious French railway engineers took up where the Germans had left off.

The prizes for success were a sizeable reduction in electrification's capital cost and more power per tonne of traction unit weight. Under the first head, economy began with the obvious saving of a feed straight from the national supply system. But since the power derived from electricity is a multiple of its voltage and current, traction running off a 25kV supply would absorb less current per ton-mile worked; thus a lighter conductor wire could be used and consequently a less ponderous support structure, for a great saving in expensive copper and steelwork. The higher the voltage, moreover, the further current can be transmitted without becoming inefficient, so fewer sub-stations would be needed. As for the traction itself, the ability with an ac supply to control the speed and torque of each motor independently, obviating the risk of a sympathetic slip of all powered axles, promised superior starting adhesion and hence more assured acceleration with heavy tonnage or quicker attainment of top speed in passenger service.

In the mid-1940s, with electronic science still in its infancy, there was no practical alternative to the well-proven dc traction motor. That posed the problem of rectifying the ac to dc as well as transforming it down to a manageable value of around 1kV before it reached the motors. Until then the unacceptable addition to a locomotive's weight and mass of bulky mechanical converters – and their high cost – had been a barrier to ac electrification progress. In their first locomotive essays for the new system the French did employ ac motors and

French Railways' first post-war high-power express locomotive design, the big-wheel, 144-tonne, 4,810 hp Type 2D2-9100.

Opposite:
A Swiss Federal Class Ac 6/6 Co-Co begins a rapid gain of height in the Gotthard route's southern side series of spiral tunnels with a freight of Italian-built cars for North-West Europe.

191

were plagued by difficulty.

Fortunately their anxieties were soon relieved by the evolution of effective non-mechanical rectifiers, first of the mercury-arc type, then semi-conductor, using media such as germanium and silicon. Within a decade the fast-moving electrical industry was turning out transformer and rectifier packages slim enough to fit snugly under the frames of a commuter multiple-unit and leave almost its entire body free for passenger accommodation. Electric traction had taken a stride ahead as auspicious as Stephenson's *Rocket* compared to previous steam locomotive endeavour.

The SNCF opened its high-voltage ac electrification account in 1950, while the Paris–Lyons 1·5kV dc scheme was still on the way to completion two years later. The test-bed was a secondary line on the threshold of the French Alps, from Aix-les-Bains via Annecy to La Roche-sur-Foron, deliberately chosen as a trial of the new method's economy. In view of postwar Europe's insufficiency of coal, the French Government was badgering the SNCF to electrify rapidly, over secondary as well as trunk routes. But the SNCF's economists had so far resisted the pressure, well aware that only the key main lines' heavy traffic generated enough revenue to amortize the huge capital cost of 1·5kV dc electrification.

The results of the first project, then of a second limited scheme in the heavily freight-occupied network of the industrial north-east between Valenciennes and Thionville, confirmed the economic and performance promise of the 25kV ac 50Hz system. From 1957 onwards the SNCF was feverishly stringing up catenary the breadth of Northern France, knitting the Valenciennes–Thionville wires into a tracery that stretched from Paris to Amiens and Lille, to the Belgian border at Aulnoye en route to Brussels, to Metz, Strasbourg and Basle, and not long afterward from Paris to Rouen and Le Havre.

The economy was not so breathtaking that it paid to rip up existing 1·5kV and substitute high-voltage ac. Before long, moreover, the traction industry could offer multi-voltage locomotives which, for a negligible sacrifice of power or weight penalty, could operate under any of Europe's four main-line current systems, two dc and two ac, with equal facility. Today a Paris–Amsterdam express can be hauled throughout by one of the SNCF's or SNCB's four-voltage classes despite the variation of current supply en route from 25kV ac to 3kV dc then 1·5kV dc. At first the SNCF persisted with 1·5kV dc for electrification extensions in the southern half of the country below Paris, but 25kV ac was adopted between Marseilles and the Italian Riviera border and is now being spread into Brittany.

The bottom line of SNCF ac electrification balance-sheets and the prowess of the early French ac locomotives persuaded several countries to change method, in several cases to the lucrative benefit of French industry. Soviet Railways, previously wedded to 3kV dc, opened a gigantic high-voltage ac programme with conversion of the whole 3,375-mile (5,431 km) western section of the Trans-Siberian Railway from Moscow to Lake Baikal. In 1956 Britain's BR switched to ac for all the electrification optimistically scheduled in its 1955 Modernization Plan except for new schemes within the Southern Region's firmly established dc thirdrail preserve. China's railways were one of the first to espouse the new method for a first step in electrification; and in the under-developed world especially the economy of ac now made electrification economically tenable for countries where traffic levels had been inadequate to sustain the cost of a dc system. Portugal is an example.

By the close of the 1950s the power obtainable per tonne of electric locomotive weight had been halved. Pre-war development had made a good deal of headway in the weight reduction of electrical gear, especially traction motors, the power/weight ratio of which had been improved by about two-thirds between 1920 and 1945. As a result electric locomotives need no longer be as cumbersome as their steam predecessors, with groups of idle wheels to spread the load of bulky electrical apparatus and provide guidance for large, rigidly frame-mounted driving wheels. Motors had been slimmed to a size capable of bogie or even axle-mounting, though at first for only limited power: the 1941 1·5kV Bo–Bo manufactured for the Manchester–Sheffield 1·5kV dc electrification of Britain's LNER, the subsequent BR Class 76, for instance, offered only 1,868 hp from its 88 tonnes' (86·6 tons) total weight.

Three years later, in 1944, Switzerland's BLS Railway commissioned Swiss manufacturers SLM and Brown Boveri to produce a locomotive that could sustain maximum line speed continuously with 350-tonne (345 ton) expresses on the sinuous 1 in 40 grades of its transalpine Lötschberg route. But the machine had to ride the curves comfortably and not exceed a 20-tonne (19·7 ton) axle-loading. The Swiss firms' response was the trend-setting, all-adhesion Ae4/4 Bo–Bo: a 4,000 hp unit with each axle separately powered through a flexible drive by its own bogie-mounted 1,000 hp motor – an unprecedented output in such a configuration – and of only 80 tonnes' (78·7 tons) all-up weight

through extensive resort to light alloys in its all-welded bodywork and the industry's latest compression of electrical component mass.

A comparison with the SNCF 2D2-9100 class, unveiled six years later, highlights the daring of the Swiss design. The 2D2-9100, a refinement of pre-war French classes, was that country's last main-line type in the classic mould, with driving wheels of almost 5 ft 9 in (175·3 cm) that were rigidly frame-mounted and powered by motors within the chassis. Conceived to haul 850-tonne (837 ton) expresses at a sustained 87 mph (140 km/h) over the newly electrified Paris–Lyons route, the 2D2-9100's 4,810 hp continuous rating was more generous than the BLS Ae4/4's. But it scaled a great deal more: 144 tonnes (142 tons), compared with 80 tonnes.

Two years after the 2D2-9100's debut the French adopted the all-adhesion principle. Following the 1952 acquisition of five Bo–Bo prototypes, of which No BB-9004 was a participant in the 205·6 mph (330·9 km/h) feats of 1955 (see Chapter 16), the SNCF set the style of its latter-day electric traction production in 1957 with simultaneous 25kV ac and 1·5kV dc variants of the same mass-production design, in this case the BB16000 and BB9200. Both were Bo–Bos of more than 5,000 hp, but for total weights of only 77·8 and 84 tonnes (76·6 and 82·7 tons) respectively.

Nowadays all-adhesion is a standard prescription for electric locomotive design, normally employing two bogies, but sometimes three to spread the weight and enhance the adhesion of units assigned to chronically curved or sharply graded routes. The Italian State Railways (FS), for instance, operate three classes of Bo–Bo–Bo in which the center bogie articulates two short bodies (some of the earliest of these types, the E636, have frame-suspended motors); Japanese National Railways operate several non-articulated Bo–Bo–Bo classes on their 3 ft 6 in-gauge (106·7 cm) network; Spain's RENFE has Japanese-designed machine of the same layout and the world's most powerful single-unit electric locomotive is a Bo–Bo–Bo, the 9,700 hp Class Re6/6 which is the Swiss Federal's heavy transalpine haulier, capable of sustaining 50 mph (81 km/h) up the Gotthard route's 12 miles (19·3 km) of 1 in 38½–40 with 800 tonnes (787 tons) in tow.

The Re6/6 is geared for a high tractive effort and a maximum speed no higher than 87 mph (140 km/h), the ceiling throughout Switzerland's winding main line apart from a curve-free stretch of the Rhone Valley route from Lausanne to Brig. But these days some equally striking but short-term power output is obtainable from high-speed all-adhesion types. The 100 mph (161 km/h) 84-tonne (82·7 ton) Class 1044 Bo–Bo of the Austrian Federal, for instance, is credited with a one-hour rating of 7,075 hp; and the 116-tonne (114 ton) Class 103 Co–Co of the German Federal, the 125 mph (201 km/h) mount of that system's Inter-City trains, can be similarly

193

The design which was the trend-setter for modern electric locomotive design: a BLS Type Ae4/4 Bo-Bo on the Lötschberg transalpine route with a Basle-Berne-Brig express of air-conditioned cars.

The first French railways all-adhesion high-power designs were the 1.5kV dc BB9200 and 25 kV ac BB16000 types of 5,200-5,500 hp; No BB16043, in its original livery, enters Paris Gare du Nord with an express of Corail stock.

Austrian Railways' thyristor-controlled 7240 hp Class 1044 Bo-Bo.

Italian State Railways thyristor-controlled 6840 hp Class E633 Bo-Bo-Bo heads an international express between Milan and Chiasso, on the Swiss border.

One of French Railways mixed traffic types: a dual voltage (1.5 kV dc and 25 kV ac) 3500 hp Type BB 25500 makes light of a heavy tonnage of privately-owned mineral hoppers.

exerted to a brief effort of as much as 10,425 hp.

A hallmark of French electric locomotive practice since 1958 has been a device that varies an individual locomotive's relation of top speed and tractive effort at the operator's will. Having discovered adhesion benefit in coupling powered axles by interconnecting gears, the French then realized they might just as well save weight by powering all axles of a bogie with a single motor. That suggested – and made relatively simple – the insertion in the motor's drive of double-reduction gearing which, when the machine was at rest, could be switched to reduce maximum speed and raise tractive effort proportionately. The outcome has been locomotives of striking mixed traffic versatility, though not all electrified railways have been persuaded of the mono-motor bogie's resilience in intensive operation.

Typically expressive of the monomotor-bogie locomotive's economy in SNCF employment was several years' coverage of all the newly-electrified Paris–Le Havre line's trunk passenger and freight traffic by a single class. This, the 3,940 hp BB-17000, could be fielded with its gearing set either for 93 mph (150 km/h) top speed and a maximum 45,000 lb (20,412 kg) tractive effort or for 56 mph (90 km/h) top speed with a lift of its peak effort to 73,850 lb (33,498 kg). Such easy adaptability to the contrasting parameters of daytime *rapide* and nocturnal freight haulage obviously curtailed the size of fleet needed to operate the route.

From 1950 onwards electric traction's productivity steadily advanced as on the one hand operators mastered work diagramming that optimized the electric unit's unparalleled availability for continuous work without servicing attention, and on the other, design benefited from the rushing stream of new technology,

especially in electronics. Between 1950 and 1965 the SNCF, for example, cut from 27 hours to $14\frac{1}{2}$ the *average* time per 1,000 miles (1,609 km) which its entire electric locomotive and multiple-unit stock had to sacrifice to examination and maintenance routines; by the mid-1960s the norm for its latest types, however, had been pared to only 6 hours. The average mileage run between general overhauls had been hoisted from 100,000 to 385,000 miles (160,930 to 619,581 km), while for the latest express passenger classes the mean was stabilizing at no less than 750,000 miles (1,206,975 km). The number of locomotives required for a newly converted route's traffic, computing the latter in terms of tonne-mileage, had been almost halved. And the total of depots required to service the SNCF's electric traction fleet was rapidly contracting, not only because of the units' mobility and scant need of attention but also through satisfaction of every traffic specification with a restricted range of locomotives. Within that range, moreover, the highest possible degree of component standardization had been made a cardinal policy aim, thereby rationalizing the deployment of spares.

Yet another plus of high-voltage ac electrification at the industrial frequency was that it helped to balance demand on the national grid. Urban rush-hour traffic, granted, aggravated peak appetite for current, but much of an electrified railway's heavy haulage, above all its heavy night-time freight, fell conveniently in the troughs of industrial and domestic demand.

In the past decade commuter multiple-unit current consumption in particular has been significantly curbed by one of electronics' outstanding contributions to traction science: solid-state thyristor control of traction motors

in what is known as chopper circuitry. By the 1980s thyristor control has become almost a standard feature of new electric traction design.

Pre-electronics, control was generally electro-pneumatic. The necessarily gradual application of full voltage was by stepped dis-connection of resistances and re-connection of motors in series and parallel. The thyristor, functioning as a rapid-action, split-second switch in which the 'on' and 'off' periods of each cycle can be fractionally varied, could secure smooth, stepless control without need of resistances. Besides eliminating most wear-prone parts and greatly improving adhesion, that also saved current.

Another virtue of thyristor control is its simplification of rheostatic or dynamic braking, the system which spares wear and tear of a train's disc or shoe brakes by switching the traction motors into generators that oppose momentum. The current thus produced is absorbed by resistance in rheostatic braking, but in regenerative braking it can be fed back into the conductor. The regenerative arrangement is only feasible, however, in operations where frequent braking is balanced by simultaneous demand for high power. An obvious main-line example is Switzerland's Gotthard route, where the current regenerated by trains braking on the long, steep descent from the Gotthard Tunnel is readily absorbed by those making the climb, but there is wide scope for the technique in urban passenger systems where a proportion of trains is always accelerating away from stops and avid for extra power.

The next phase of electronics-led development is sure to be replacement of the dc motor by the three-phase ac motor, with its appeal of smaller size and weight, simplicity, minimum of wearing parts, and remarkable adaptability to a wide range of operating demands. The historic deterrents to use of ac motors, especially the bulk of the apparatus to mutate a single-phase current supply to a three-phase motor feed, have been eliminated by electronics, though as yet the voltage control systems are dauntingly intricate and costly. A cost of about £1 million has been quoted for each of the five 7,500 hp, 84-tonne (82·7 ton) ac-motored Class 120 Bo–Bos which West Germany's DB commissioned at the start of 1980 for an exhaustive evaluation of the three-phase ac motor locomotive's reliability and efficiency. If the 120 passes muster it must herald a new age of electric traction versatility, since it has been billed as equally suited to Inter-City haulage (one has been tested already at up to 143·5 mph–230·9 km), 1,500-tonne (1,476 ton) fast freight work and heavy 5,000-tonne (4,921 ton) mineral train traction, the last in multiple-unit pairs. This prospectus has already persuaded the Norwegian State Railway to invest in three-phase ac electric locomotives and other railways are keeping a very watchful eye on the DB's Class 120 quintet.

The scope for technological reduction of the real cost of running an electric railway is by no means exhausted. Achievement to date, however, has already revised the traffic criteria justifying investment in catenary. One Government after another, recoiling from the oil crisis, has readily endorsed extension of electrification to secondary lines that would not have qualified for it economically in the 1960s, or else authorized main-line electrification for the first time.

In Europe, Spain is expanding its electrified mileage by over 150 per cent compared with its pre-oil crisis total and aims to have 59 per cent of its route-mileage under wires by 1992. From a total of 9 miles (14·5 km) converted in 1976,

Spanish National Railways (RENFE) 6170 hp Class 250 Co-Co with monomotor bogies nad dual gearing.

the SNCF has an annual electrification programme of some 180 miles (290 km) a year. Secondary route gaps in the catenary are being steadily closed in Austria, Belgium and West Germany, and Denmark is embarking on its first main-line electrification. Behind the Iron Curtain eagerness to electrify is desperate, but has to be subordinated to available resources – except in the USSR, the globe's most frenetic electrifier, at a current rate of around 500–600 miles (805–966 km) a year. By the end of 1981 the total of Soviet Railways route-mileage under wires had already scaled 28,000 (45,060 km), constituting 31·4 per cent of the whole system, and some end-to-end stretches of continuous electrification had reached spectacular lengths: 4,391 miles (7,066 km) for instance, from Orsha in the west through Moscow, Kuibyshev and Novosibirsk to Karymskaya in the east, and 2,840 miles (4,570 km) from the Finnish border at Luzhaika through Moscow, Kharkov, Rostov-on-Don, Tbilisi and Yerevan to Zod.

At the start of the 1980s South African Railways were embarked on an electrification pro-

gramme covering some 1,700 track-miles (2,736 km), to curb oil consumption. It was also budgeting for purchase of as many as 440 new electric locomotives, including 155 more of its trusty 3,350 hp Class 6E1 Bo–Bo, to lift that type's total beyond 1,000 and make it the most prolific electric locomotive class in the world. By the mid-1980s SAR aims to have 80 per cent of its traffic, measured in tonne-km, electrically powered.

SAR is another system which has moved over to high-voltage ac despite earlier dc electrification, at 3kV. Apart from the ac system's lower first cost, the latest SAR ac Class 7E3 locomotives are proving as much as 60 per cent cheaper to deploy on multiple-unit freight haulage up the country's trunk route gradients, sometimes as stiff as 1 in 66, than the dc 6E1s.

The South African electricity generating authority prices its current quite stiffly, so much so that SAR paused for reappraisal after launching its first high-voltage ac electrification on the Transvaal-Richards Bay coal line in the 1970s. The problem was how to achieve the even

Spanish National Railways (RENFE) 6,170 hp Class 250 Co-Co with monomotor bogies and dual gearing.

demand for current possible on a typical European double-track main line, where there is a daylong each-way flow of passenger trains, all of more-or-less common weight and appetite for power, and during the night a steady stream of freight as the passenger movement falls off.

South African main lines in the open country are frequently single-track. To make the most of their limited operating capacity – and of electric traction's economy – each freight train needs to be packed with as much tonnage as possible. But if a single-line section is lengthy and its train-working pattern is a repeated cycle of a massive freight travelling one way, then a long pause until the section is clear for a massive freight travelling the other way, the current supply will have to be extravagantly geared for a peak demand that is exerted very infrequently. To resolve this difficulty – hitherto one of the main deterrents to electrification in North America. SAR had to plan for closer spacing of passing loops and also to work out a scale of optimal maximum speeds in relation to load and changing route characteristics, so as to come as close

as they could to a constant level of current demand, before they could confidently resume electrification as a totally economic proposition.

Elsewhere in the African continent Zimbabwe has launched its first electrification and other states have it in mind. Further east, India seeks to electrify at a rate of over 300 miles (483 km) a year; and China, with only 2 per cent of its rail traffic electrically powered in 1980, is striving to make electric traction the dominant force of its rail system by the century's end. With all its heavily-trafficked routes already energized, Japanese National Railways has started wiring some 3,000 miles (4,828 km) of secondary line. For the same reason Australia's Federal Government has moved for electrification of Australia's busiest trunk route, from Sydney to Melbourne, and the State Governments of Queensland and Western Australia have enshrined rail electrification in their transport policy; New Zealand, too, has lately joined the electrifiers. And Argentina, Brazil and Mexico are leading South American railways into a new electrified age.

199

Even in the seemingly impregnable North American stronghold of diesel traction, electrification of part of Canadian Pacific's transcontinental main line was under serious study in 1982. In the twilight of Jimmy Carter's Presidency, the US Department of Transportation came up with a scheme to capitalize a substantial mileage of US railroad electrification, since its first cost was beyond the prudent spending of the big companies then extracting a very low return on their railroad investment. The idea was that the railroads, which would have to buy their own electric rolling stock, would repay the Government's outlay on the fixed works over a period by handing over a per-tonne royalty on the traffic they hauled under the wires. But such a scheme was anathema to a Reagan Administration set on getting the Federal Government out of any involvement in railroading and as expected it was buried in 1982. Nevertheless several railroads, among them Southern, Southern Pacific, Burlington Northern and Missouri-Kansas-Texas (the 'Katy'), were still keeping a studious eye on the case for electrification with their own resources.

Other forms of traction have not shown such impressive advances. In mid-century gas turbine power was promising the accelerative punch of electric traction without the latter's high-cost burden of investment in fixed current supply plant, but its economy was destroyed by the oil price explosion.

From quite early in the century the turbine had appealed to rail traction engineers because of its minimum of moving parts and its theoretically superior efficiency as an energy producer, but only America's Union Pacific Railroad has ever successfully operated a fleet of turbine locomotives. These were gas turbine-electrics incorporating a single turbine, which UP employed first in a 4,500 hp then in an 8,500 hp development for freight haulage over its 7,230 ft (2,204 m) Sherman Hill summit between 1948 and 1969. When these UP machines were conceived their power/weight ratio was better than any on offer from US manufacturers' standard diesel catalogue, but by the mid-1960s diesel traction development had closed the gap. And even though the turbines characteristically thrived on cheap residual oil they guzzled far too much of it, even at the unbelievably low prices of the period, to challenge the improved economy of the latest diesels.

The Achilles heel of the gas turbine is its inability to reduce fuel consumption commensurately with power. Its economy is seriously diminished unless it is kept continuously at maximum effort. Thus UP found it paid to work its massive freight trains over the Sherman Hill route with one or two 2,000 hp diesels coupled

Union Pacific 8,500 hp gas turbine-electric locomotive; the third vehicle of the unit is a fuel tank.

behind a turbine locomotive the whole way, rather than stop the train and pick up assistant locomotives just for the steepest climbs, because of the fuel the turbine frittered away while it was at rest and idling.

A new rail role for the turbine was suggested in the mid-1960s by the aerospace industry's development of small helicopter and light aircraft turbines. These offered such high power from a very compact and lightweight structure that their potential in a high-speed passenger unit application looked striking, especially if their use was married to the latest techniques in aerospace body-building. Indeed, it was a North American aerospace firm, United Aircraft Corporation, which first consummated the alliance in Turbo-Trains that Canadian National introduced in the Toronto–Montreal corridor and the US Department of Transportation between New York and Boston as part of its North-East Corridor demonstration programme in 1968.

The Turbo-Trains were an ill-starred enterprise. UAC had sanguinely crammed the design with innovation that was untried in a rugged rail environment and a catalogue of flaws plagued and immobilized the units during the first six years of their Canadian employment. Unsurprisingly there were no follow-up orders after experience of the first seven Turbo-Train sets, though the last Canadian survivor of the prototypes was not retired until 1982.

In France the SNCF more sensibly and very successfully applied the new breed of aerospace turbine to 100 mph (161 km/h) railcar sets of perfectly orthodox design. Of the two types created by the SNCF the second, the five-car RTG with a 1,250 hp Turmo III turbine-hydraulic power car at each end, found export buyers as well as domestic fleet use. Amtrak bought six for its US network and had seven more built by Rohr of California under licence, while in the Middle East Iran and later Egypt were RTG customers (though the Egyptian train-sets have a decidedly individual outline and format).

No one else put a turbine-powered railcar into mass production, but in West Germany the DB experimented with turbine traction in a rebuild of one of its inaugural TEE diesel-hydraulic train-sets and also with a 900 hp gas-turbine booster, for extra short-term effort at starting and up-grade, in its 2,150 hp Class 219 diesel-hydraulic locomotive class. But the file on these essays was closed with the eruption of oil prices, as it was on the prestigious high-speed turbine train plans of British and French Railways described in Chapter 16.

The diesel traction industry has been incapable of matching the post-war improvement of the electric unit's power/weight ratio. An output

A French Railways RTG gas turbine train-set on the Paris-Caen line in the 1970s.

Top:
Spanish National Railways'
(RENFE) most powerful
diesel type, the Class 3,345 hp
Class 333 Co-Co, is built in
Spain by Macosa but has
General Motors' Type 645E3
engines and electric
transmission.

Above:
The 5,900 hp Class E1-16 Bo-
Bo electric. ASEA's version
of the Swedish Rc4 for the
Norwegian State Railways.

Opposite:
A pair of Class 7E electric
locomotives crossing the
White Umfolugi Bridge
behind electric power in
Natal.

of no more than 4,000 hp at most was the best on offer in the early 1980s for a locomotive weight of 100–120 tonnes (98·4–118 tons), assuming that the purchaser insisted on a power plant with an attested track record of reliability and with no liability to abnormal upkeep cost because of a riskily high rating that put undue stress on its components. On such provisos purchasers were more than ever adamant in a period of relentlessly inflating costs. Most railways, including those of North America, were content with six-wheel bogie machines in the 2,500–3,500 hp range which they could use in multiple for the heavier haulage assignments. But by 1980, one or two major systems, notably the French and German Federal, had ended all main-line diesel locomotive purchases because their exist-

ing fleets were sizeable and modern enough to see them through to almost total electrification.

Nevertheless, electronics has been improving diesel traction economy too, especially in North America where most railroads remain unconvinced that they can reap a worthwhile return from electrification of trunk routes predominantly traversed by infrequent but massive trains. A standard feature of 1980s ranges of the big US diesel manufacturers, for instance, is a creep-control device that electronically compares ground and traction motor speed, automatically adjusting power in the event of a discrepancy so as to sustain unvaryingly high adhesion. Coming into fashion, too, is an automatically-functioning 'fuel-saver' that adjusts the throttles of all locomotives.

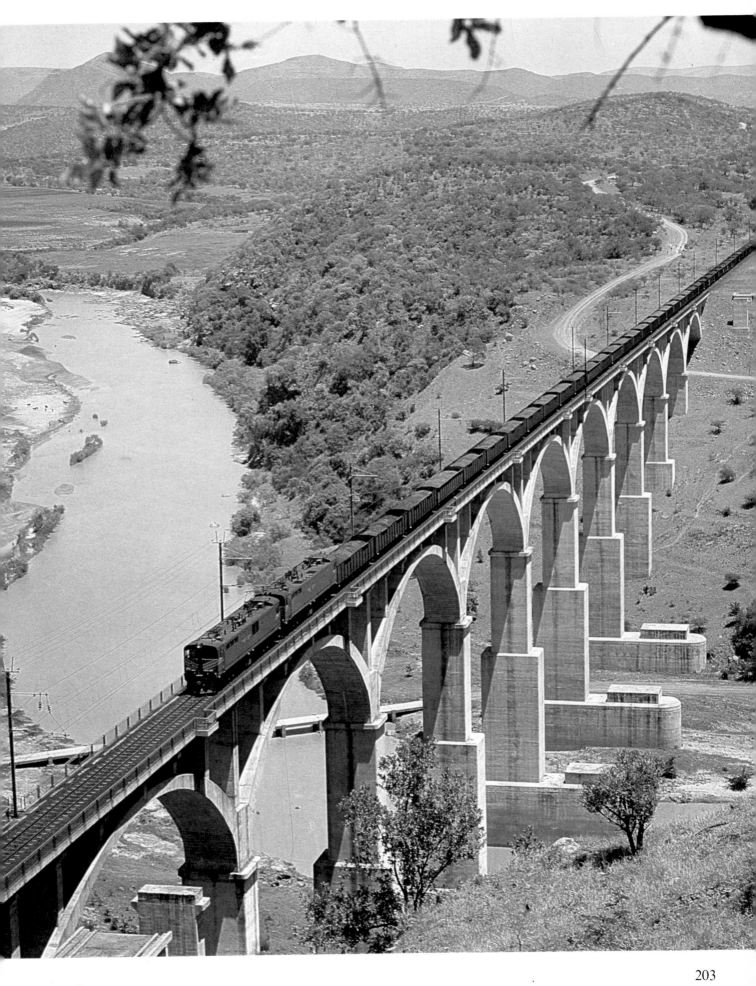

14

METRO, SCHNELLBAHN AND LIGHT RAIL TRANSIT

A PERCENTAGE OF THE MODERN WORLD'S public opinion might be found indifferent to the railway's eclipse as a trunk haulier, but the train would be pretty certain of unanimous endorsement as an indispensable bulk passenger carrier in the world's biggest cities. They have seen some of the most impressive rail development since the Second World War.

New Metros have been its centerpiece, proliferating at a rate unimagined before 1939. However, their social benefit would be less but for a concurrent drive by national and local administrations to better other elements of conurbation transport, including surface commuter railways, then to remould the whole as an inter-dependent system and market it as a persuasive inter-modal alternative to private transport for almost any journey within a conurbation's boundary.

Between 1907 and 1935 new Metro completions were averaging only two railways every five years. In the past 30 years the rate has jumped to roughly 12 every five years. Moreover, of the 71 city Metros operational in 1981 with an aggregate of 2,079 miles (3,346 km) as many as 51 were engaged in extensions totalling 475 route-miles (764 km) and cherishing plans for 995 more route-miles (1,601 km) besides. A further 16 cities were embarked on their first Metro construction, which when complete would swell the global sum by 270 route-miles (435 km). And yet 12 more had Metro schemes totalling 155 route-miles (249 km) either in the preliminary design stage or already into detailed engineering planning.

The US, which in the first century of railways had established only half a dozen metropolitan systems – more commonly termed rapid rail transit in North America – was the first to agonize over the post-war deterioration of the inner city environment. Few cities were anxious to follow Los Angeles' example and raze whole whole building blocks so as to carve wider freeways and bigger parking lots for the rapidly increasing use of cars: anyway that was to prove a negatory policy. The more road transport was indulged, the more it expanded, building up fresh pressure points that clamoured for additional road and parking space. To cite a notorious case of this on the other side of the Atlantic, post-war motorways to the fringe of inner London have stimulated an upsurge of motoring from the outer suburbs which has choked the areas immediately beyond the motorways' exits.

The first big post-war US rapid transit scheme pre-dated Federal initiative. As soon as the war was over the San Francisco Bay Area, fearing strangulation of the Bay's road bridges, moved to thread a sophisticated railway under the water from Oakland on one shore to San Francisco and the West Bay on the other through a $3\frac{1}{2}$ mile (5·6 km) immersed tube. Capital costs that had soared beyond $1 billion by the time the scheme had run a gauntlet of electoral and planning crises were to be funded entirely out of local bond issues and extra sales taxes. But even $1 billion was inadequate to cope with inflation and constructional miscalculation, and the project might have foundered without the enactment, just in time, of Federal support for US urban transport re-development.

Legislation to discourage the automobile's blight of US cities had been initiated under President Johnson in 1964 and the resources for it were greatly strengthened under President Nixon in 1970. The Urban Mass Transportation Administration (UMTA) was authorized to contribute up to 80 per cent of the capital cost of approved investment in properly integrated urban transport schemes, rail or road, and progressively voted funds that in the last year of President Carter's term would run to capital grants totalling $3·3 billions. UMTA was also empowered to subsidize operating costs so as to keep urban public transport competitively priced and at the start of 1980s it was disgorging about $1 billion a year under that head.

A lot of the operating bill subvention, unfortunately, was money ill-spent. Throughout the 1970s US big-city transport was ludicrously under-priced and its labour substantially overpaid and feather-bedded to the extent that a transit job in Boston, for example, was reckoned the next best thing to part-timing in paradise!

Another fillip to urban public transport development was the addition to the 1973 Federal Highway Act of an Interstate Transfer clause allowing cities to forego Federally-supported freeway extensions in their area and divert the money saved to local transit schemes. Thus Boston, which had halted construction of an expressway in 1971, had by 1980 drawn an extra $705 millions from the cash saved by that decision and still had $700 millions left to its account in Washington. Furthermore this sum was swelling with every year because the Act had tied any banked money to the indexed year-on-year rise in highway building costs.

Besides spawning extensions or improvements of existing rapid transit railways in Chicago, New Jersey and elsewhere, and handsome new systems in Washington, Atlanta, Baltimore and Miami, the UMTA legislation accelerated the trend to unify the entire public transport of a unitary socio-economic area under a single authority. The modern directory of US rapid transit management is a maze of these authori-

Opposite:
The last large-scale city centre 'Elevated' in the US is Chigago's: this is the intersection at Lake and Wells Street, used by Lake-Dan Ryan, Ravenswood and Evensden express routes.

Lake Merrit station on the San Francisco Bay area's BART system.

Piccadilly Circus Station, London Transport's Piccadilly Tube Line, which has been extended to connect London's Heathrow Airport with the centre of the city.

ties' acronyms. One such is MTA, the Metropolitan Transportation Authority which rules some 4,000 square miles (10,360 sq km) focussed on New York and oversees surface commuter train operation as well as the Subway of the New York City Transit Authority; another, SEPTA, the South-Eastern Pennsylvania Transportation Authority, runs the entire commuter rail system of five counties surrounding Philadelphia as well

as the city's bus lines; and a third, MBTA, the Massachusetts Bay Transportation Authority, like SEPTA, manages all the surface commuter, rapid transit and bus routes around its hub, Boston.

The size of some authorities' domains has thrown up the kind of problem which landed London's GLC in a devastating court case over its inner-city cheap-fares scheme in 1981. A chronic US sufferer has been the Chicago Regional Transportation Authority (CRTA), sovereign of 463 route-miles (745 km) of surface commuter train service operated on its behalf by seven different railroads and also the famous inner-city 'Elevated' of the Chicago Transit Authority and the latter's buses. CRTA is funded by taxes raised throughout its territory and is constantly slated by the city's outer-suburban taxpayers for spending too much of their money on inner-city CTA improvements. Right across the US, in fact, inner city mass transit is attracting far more interest and capital investment than suburban rail commuter operations, whose users are forced to pay steadily more for deteriorating, diminishing service.

CTA's adoption of the median strip of new freeways for its extension to O'Hare Airport, an ideal plan for creation of easy interchange between road and rail, exemplifies the attention to urban transport integration which the UMTA

era fostered. More significant still was Washington's reshaping of its bus service concurrently with the draft of its Metro, so that an area's buses would feel passengers into the trains for the downtown journey instead of paralleling the trains and aggravating city-center congestion. As for private cars, large parking lots and ample space for cars to decant or pick up rail passengers in station forecourts – the so-called 'kiss 'n ride' transfer – became a *sine qua non* of suburban station design.

Public authority is not only the begetter of an integrated urban transport system. Private enterprise is responsible for some impressively interlocked systems in Japan, where the quite numerous private railways include a number performing metropolitan commuter functions. In Greater Tokyo 40 per cent of the 10 billion rail passenger journeys recorded annually are on privately-owned trains, many of them owned by extraordinary conglomerates.

One of these is the Tokyu Corporation, which was launched in 1922 as a railway undertaking to stimulate residential development in one outlying area of the metropolis. Today the Tokyu Railway, running some 800 electric multiple-unit cars and logging around 750 million passenger journeys a year (at an operating profit, incidentally) over a 62 route-mile (100 km) network, is only one component of an incredibly

diversified concern. Its 234 constituent companies cover bus and taxi companies, road, air and sea freight, department stores and supermarkets, auto sales, rail vehicle manufacture, leisure activities, construction and real estate. Besides its rail car fleet, it owns 2,000 buses and 100 aircraft.

In 1953 Tokyu launched the Tama Den-en Toshi Garden City scheme in the south-western

Top:
Farragut North station on the Washington DC Metro's Red Line.

Above:
Close-up of a standard Boeing Vertol twin-car train-set of the Chigago Transport Authority.

207

A typical Japanese rapid transit train-set, used in the Tokyo area on the privately-owned Teito Rapid Transit Authority Hanzumon Line.

suburbs of Tokyo, still little more than half developed by the start of the 1980s but already counting 300,000 inhabitants. In 1966 Tokyu finished a 14-mile (22·5 km) line linking this development with the center of Tokyo (a Teito line was added in 1977) and this, operated by Tokyu-built train-sets, knits rationally with Tokyu bus routes in the Tama area. There, of course, commuters are also living in Tokyu houses, shopping in Tokyu supermarkets and quite possibly buying their cars from Tokyu and getting entertainment from Tokyu enterprises as well!

An influential factor in the post-war traffic designs of many Continental European cities was the tramway. Forced to reconstruct because of wartime damage, a number of city authorities seized the opportunity to rebuild tramway routes on segregated rights of way where there was space beyond the inner city itself. That created a tracked system with scope for operation of higher performance vehicles and inspired the train's sophisticated successor, the Light Rail Vehicle or LRV.

The standard Continental European LRV of the 1980s is an articulated unit of two or three cars (with the center car of a triplet invariably very short). This format is popular because it maximizes passenger/tare weight ratio, minimizes energy consumption, and at the same time eases the vehicle through the tight curves and clearances which prevail on most systems. Another virtue is the clear view from front to rear of an articulated unit's interior, which facilitate one-man operation, or OMO in the jargon of the day.

A typical LRV twin-unit, such as the Frankfurt U-Bahn's U2 devised by Düwag, one of the European majors in the LRV construction industry, has a power output of 400 hp for its 31

tonnes' (30·5 tons) total weight and boasts a top speed of 50 mph (81 km/h), but a 60 mph (97 km/h) capability is not uncommon. In the 1980s a growing number of LRV operators are asking for the refinement of thyristor control and rheostatic or regenerative braking in their LRVs, accounting the resultant energy savings of up to 25 per cent worth the extra cost and weight of the thyristor equipment. Hannover and Vienna are examples of cities already operating these more sophisticated vehicles.

With the LRV came the transmutation of the historic street tramway into Light Rail Transit, or LRT, and the decision of several Continental cities to lower their downtown tracks below ground. In some instances – Brussels was the best-known case – this was planned as a 'Pre-Metro' exercise: that is, uncertain both of the economic justification and of the funds to instal a full-blown Metro, the city bored underground tunnels and excavated subterranean stations to dimensions that would allow subsequent conversion of the LRT to an authentic Metro if and when demand solidified the case, as it eventually did in the Belgian capital.

In German-speaking countries one can be misled that all LRT systems are in a pre-metro phase. There it is common practice to term this form of urban railway a Stadtbahn when it is above ground on a segregated right-of-way (as distinct from a traditional street-bound tramway, which is a Strassenbahn), but a U-Bahn as soon as it dives below ground, whatever the tunnel size.

The other rail component of the big German cities' now highly-developed public transport system is the Schnellbahn, or S-Bahn, which is the main-line railway's contribution. In Munich, Stuttgart, Frankfurt and Hamburg the surface commuter lines on all sides of each city are being

progressively threaded into a new tunnel burrowing beneath the city center and en route making convenient connection with the U-Bahn in magnificent subterranean interchange stations. Besides conducting suburban travellers right to the commercial and cultural hearts of each city, and right to an escalator's length from its internal public transport, these S-Bahn tunnels vastly improve the economics of the main-line railway's commuter train operation by opening up through running between one suburban quarter and another on the opposite side of the city, and thus eliminating turnrounds in the main terminal stations.

The cost of these German city schemes is monumental. When their huge programme of S-Bahn tunnel building and suburban route extension, conversion of the Stuttgart Strassenbahn into a standard-gauge Stadtbahn and U-Bahn, and station improvement to create

over 16,000 parking spaces is complete, the authorities of Stuttgart and other communities governing the 1·5 million Germans affected by the enterprise will have spent at least £800 millions of public money. Over £1 billion has already been invested in Munich's S- and U-Bahn infrastructure since 1966. The greater part of these huge sums is disgorged by the Government, since a Federal grant of 60 per cent of the capital cost of all approved urban transport infrastructure improvement is mandatory under the country's Municipal Transport Finance Act (*Gemeindeverkehrsfinanzierangsgesetz*) of 1967. Between 1967 and 1980 Dm 22 billion, or some £5 billion, were advanced from the Federal Treasury for conurbation transport schemes under this legislation.

One should add that the S-Bahn networks of West Germany are not all focussed on a single city. The network embracing Frankfurt is the

A Hamburg U-Bahn train-set.

Australia's biggest urban rail transport scheme of the 1970-80s has been creation of a new Melbourne city-centre loop (here seen to the left of the historic tracks) to permit through running, obviate reversals at Flinders Street station, and greatly increase operating capacity.

Rhein-Main, which also takes in some neighbouring cities such as Mainz, while the mainly surface Rhein-Ruhr S-Bahn takes in a necklace of conurbations from Cologne to (ultimately) Dortmund and München-Gladbach. A sixth S-Bahn system is planned as a complement to Nuremberg's new U-Bahn.

In all the German territories covered by existing S-Bahnen – and in some others besides, such as Bremen – services of all public transport modes are integrated in function and marketed under a simple, impartial inter-modal fare scheme by a single public authority for which the operators work under contract. This arrange-

ment, pioneered by Hamburg in 1937, now has facsimiles in other countries – the Passenger Transport Executives of Britain's chief provincial cities, for instance, and the US area transportation authorities discussed earlier.

In recent years urban transportation improvement in West Germany has been partly funded – and sensibly so – by a percentage deduction of the national road fuel tax; Austria has done the same, so have one or two US urban authorities, but in their case by abstracting a proportion of local tax (others have applied part of a general sales tax). The only snag of this arrangement, and one that has lately furrowed some West German brows, is the side-effect of reduced use of road transport through the deterrence of rising fuel prices: that cuts the take for urban transport investment, yet the cause is paradoxically one which tends to greater reliance on public transport.

Several cities besides West Germany's have or plan a cross-city Schnellbahn or its equivalent. In Britain, Merseyside's railways have been interlinked beneath the heart of Liverpool. Oslo, Zurich, Philadelphia and Melbourne were examples at work on such schemes at the start of the 1980s, the Australian one a particularly ambitious project encircling the city center with four independent single-track loops. A plan has been tabled for London, though its hopes of execution are remote without a dramatic reversal of the niggardly British Government attitude to public transport investment at the opening of the decade. Meanwhile, one of the grandest of all inter-connections of outer suburban and inner-city rail transport is pursuing

a serene course to finality in Paris.

Paris toyed with the idea throughout the inter-war period. It was driven to positive action in 1960 by a post-war migration of population from the inner city to new dormitory suburbs on a scale only Italian cities like Milan equalled elsewhere in Europe. This exodus was mostly beyond the limits of the capital's historic Metro, which had been halted at the line of the old city walls (hence the 'Porte' or 'Gateway' in many of its terminal stations' titles), and matching extensions of the Metro lines would have been unfruitful for city-center journeys, because the Paris Metro stations are close-packed, every train is all-stations and long journeys by this means are very tedious.

So the 1960 plan's first step was construction of a new east-west, deep-level underground railway with limited stops. This, the first link in the Réseau Express Regional (RER), was completed by RATP, the French capital's bus and Metro operator, with a handsome infusion of public money in 1977. In the preceding four years, incidentally, the Government and the Paris authority in concert put up almost £1 billion for the betterment of the SNCF and RATP services in the Greater Paris area. From 1962 onwards rail transport was pre-empting on average a quarter of the total annual investment

budget of the conurbation authority, which became the Ile-de-France Regional Council in the local government reforms of 1976.

With the east-west RER Line A in place and affording several points of interchange with the

Above:
Paris RER system at Roissy–Charles de Gaulle Airport.

Top:
A class M179 electric multiple-unit of the RATP.

211

Metro in brilliantly-styled, cavernous stations suggestive of Kubla Khan's pleasure dome, the next stage of the plan involved the progressive tunnelling towards it of connections from the SNCF's surface network. The first phase of that was complete in early 1983 with the start of joint RATP-SNCF through multiple-unit working between the northern and south-western routes of the SNCF's surface suburban network via tunnels from the Gare du Nord and Gare de Lyons that debouch into a key stretch of the east-west RER Line A between the latter's Gare de Lyons and Châtelet stations.

Châtelet is quite probably the busiest and biggest Metro station in the world, with four tracks served by seven platforms at the deep RER level and as many as 34 separate escalators interlinking them with the Metro platforms immediately below the surface and the streets above. Châtelet needs its lavish layout at the RER level. By 1990, if present plans are fulfilled on schedule, 11 different services from the outer suburbs will be converging on it and merging in a dense peak-hour stream of 48 trains each way over the RER core between Châtelet and Gare de Lyons.

One product of this scheme will be a fast, direct and valuable rail link on a regular-interval basis between Paris' two airports, Roissy-Charles de Gaulle and Orly, both of which already have rail services to stations in the vicinity of their terminals. The post-war growth of air travel and in its most recent years the numbers of passengers a single jumbo jet can load or disgorge have made big city airports' customers a new and considerable ingredient of road congestion, rousing civic interest in airport rail links as much for environmental relief as for their promotional value (competition between city-owned airports is vigorous in many countries).

Some airport rail link design has been botched. The trains decant their passengers too far from terminal check-in counters, which can decide a luggage-laden passenger to stick with road transport that will ferry him right to the air terminal's doors. That goes for Washington Metro's service of the city's National Airport, where a planning imbroglio with no fewer than 18 different public agencies forced the station's siting a half-a-mile (approx. three quarters of a km) walk or an uncertain shuttle bus ride from the terminal. The train service to Paris Charles de Gaulle is extremely smart, but its quality is offset by a misguided decision to locate the station midway between the airport's original and prospective second terminal, now nearing completion, and a shuttle bus ride from each. London's Gatwick fortunately developed its terminal alongside a station on the main Brighton railway; but Heathrow, though its main terminal complex surmounts an underground station, is served only by an all-stations London Transport Piccadilly Line Tube operation, because the British Government of 1965 short-sightedly rejected the cost of building a fast BR link to the airport.

Frankfurt, Vienna, Amsterdam Schiphol and Zurich are the ideally served European airports, in a manner that is to be adopted soon at Geneva also, and in the USA at Chicago and Philadelphia. All four first-mentioned have had new offshoots of the main-line system tunnelled to stations right beneath their main terminals, with which they are comfortably connected by escalators. The Frankfurt and Zurich links have both been devised as loops off main routes, so that they can be served by long-haul as well as regular-interval local trains to and from the city center (which in Frankfurt's case already means that the city center's top-flight hotels are accessible in a 15-minute train hop straight from the airport to the Hauptwache station in the downtown S-Bahn tunnel).

Zurich Airport is a standard stop in the itinerary of a number of the Swiss Federal's Inter-City trains, besides which SwissAir has found it cheaper to charter one of the Swiss Federal's former first-class TEE electric multiple-units to ground-haul its transfer passengers between Basle and Zurich than fly them. As described in Chapter 16, Lufthansa has followed suit by hiring DB Class 403 electric multiple-units as a more economical medium than Boeing 737s for passengers interlining between the Rhineland airports and Frankfurt's intercontinental flights. Schiphol has been built on a new high-speed line from Leiden that gives it direct express service to and from Rotterdam and The Hague at daylong half-hourly intervals in each case; this airport's rail connection to the heart of Amsterdam was for long stymied by environmental haggling over route, but that has been stilled and by the mid-1980s it will also have a train service to and from Amsterdam Central station.

The Class M179 electric multiple-unit for the joint RATP-SNCF operation of cross-Paris services via the RER 'Interconnection' typifies the characteristics of the modern commuter electric multiple-unit. Each aluminium-bodied four-car unit is motored for a total output of no less than 3,785 hp, partly because of some severe gradients within its sphere of operation, partly to endow it with the sparkling acceleration rate of 2·8 ft (·85 m)/sec^2 essential in view of the eventual intensity of operation over the core underground section of the RER. Benefiting from thyristor control of its traction motors, it is

Netherlands Railway emu at Amsterdam Schipol Airport station.

fitted with both regenerative braking for use on the RATP's RER and for rheostatic braking under SNCF catenary. The M179's arrangement for dual-voltage operation, at 1·5kV under RATP catenary and on the SNCF south-west of the city, and at 25kV ac under the wires of the SNCF's north Paris suburban system, is of course not a common feature of contemporary multiple-unit practice.

Double-deck coaches have an obvious advantage in enlarging passenger capacity within the train-lengths permitted by station or signal-spacing parameters on a very busy surface commuter route, though their first cost is high. And unless adequate space is sacrificed to entrance vestibules and stairways the operators will be bothered by the extra station time needed to load and unload a bi-level train.

Double-deckers are almost as old as railways. The first recorded application of the concept was American, by the Baltimore & Ohio in the mid-nineteenth century, but it was between 1877 and the early years of this century that it attracted a number of European railways as a valuable medium for commuter operations. First practitioners were the Danes, for Copenhagen's services, followed towards the end of the century by the old Ouest Railway of France for its Paris suburban network, then the Berlin Stadtbahn. These early essays were stumpy four- or six-wheelers, but by the end of the inter-war period elegant bogie double-deckers were active in France, Germany (since the last war the East German Reichsbahn has operated a large fleet of bi-levels) and the US. Today the double-decker is in considerable vogue in Europe and a component of main-line commuter service in more than one North American city.

The amplitude of the North American gauge naturally makes it fairly easy to accommodate two levels in a body without sinking its floor between the bogies provided one adopts a 'gallery' interior layout: that is, on the upper level, seats with a side-passage access are ranged along each side of the coach body, leaving a central void for adequate headroom above the central gangway which serves the lower-floor seats. That is the format, for instance, of the considerable fleet of cars operated on Chicago's surface commuter routes in diesel locomotive push-pull trains. In contrast, the striking, lozenge-shaped, two-tone green and white bi-levels built by Hawker-Siddeley for the publicly-financed GO Transit services of the Toronto area dip their body centers to just above rail level so that two fully independent floors, each with decent headroom above their center gangways, can be accommodated. The Australian builders Comeng have managed likewise in the bi-level electric multiple-unit fleet which they have turned out for the New South Wales State Rail Authority.

Spreading Western European interest in the commuter bi-level has been fired by French Railways, which now deploys a fleet of well over 500 cars on the various suburban systems of Paris. Despite the constraints of the European loading gauge, the French too have maneuvered two entirely independent floors into a very low-slung body and have fitted as many as 175 seats into a single bi-level trailer.

The SNCF was driven to bi-level practice by the remorseless post-war growth of longer-distance Parisian commuting from new outer

Paris Metro rubber-tyred train set.

Driverless train of the fully automated Lille Metro (VAL).

suburban development, which has held a rate of around 6 per cent a year on the city's north side. A similar trend has exercised the Italians, especially around Milan; as a result the French design has also been mass-produced for that city's northern commuter routes. After sampling the French model, the Netherlands Railways are acquiring a bi-level fleet German-built to Dutch design for the rapidly-expanding traffic from North Holland to Amsterdam, where a congruence of inadequate parking space, congested road approaches, compelling rail fare offers and escalating petrol costs is converting more and more motoring commuters to train travel. Belgium's SNCB is having a derivative of the Dutch design built locally. Danish State Railways, on the other hand, are devising their own

bi-levels for the Copenhagen–Helsingor commuter run and the Swiss Federal is adopting bi-levels for its forthcoming Zurich S-Bahn.

Although the SNCF has lately produced an electric multiple-unit version of its bi-level, despite the tricky problems of locating a pantograph on an outsize car-body, which will be employed on the underground RER, most of the Parisian bi-level trains are push-pull. Now that running gear design makes propulsion of a coach-set safe and stable at 85 or even 95 mph (137 or 153 km/h), on BR's Edinburgh–Glasgow service, and that electronics have cut the cost of equipment for push-pull by making transmission of all controls from a driving trailer cab to a locomotive at the far end of the formation possible via coded impulses over a

214

single cab, push-pull with locomotives becomes a more considerable option to the self-powered multiple-unit. Besides, it may be profitable to have independent power which can be re-assigned to freight work outside the commuter peak periods, especially as the modern electric locomotive is so versatile. Consequently, a mix of multiple-units adequate for day-long basic timetable and of push-pulls for the peak extras is favoured by some operators. One qualification is that provision of a locomotive at each end of a push-pull rake may be found advisable for extra rheostatic braking power where the service is operated at high maximum speed within the characteristically short signal sections of a metropolitan rail network.

Provided that the seating of a majority of passengers is not socially essential, of course, the crush-load capacity of a single-deck body is surprising. Hong Kong's new Metro, the first 9·3-mile (15 km) stretch of which was inaugurated in the 1979–80 winter, is presently the prize example of design for volume movement. Its eight-car trains can each swallow as many as 3,300 passengers each in the rush-hour, but only 400 of them will be seated. At the moment no other railway, not even the horrendously crowded commuter lines of Tokyo and some other Japanese cities, aims to move so many passengers over a single track in the day's peak as Hong Kong's. Hong Kong Metro is expected to be handling 2 million passengers daily soon after the 1982 completion of its second 6·7-mile (10·8 km) section, and to be processing peak-hour passengers at the rate of 800 a minute in its key downtown stations.

Apart from traction plant refinement the chief development in post-war Metro train style has been the French enthusiasm for rubber-tyred running gear, with carrying wheels running on flat-headed concrete rails and guidance secured by horizontally-mounted wheels pressing against raised, lateral rails fixed at a constant gauge from each other outside the running rails. First installed on Line 11 of the Paris Metro in 1957, the system was subsequently applied to Lines 1, 4 and 6 – but no more, because RATP balked at the time each route had to be immobilized for conversion. The technique was sold to the new Metros of Montreal, Mexico City and Santiago as well as the new post-war Metros of France itself, in Lyons, Marseilles and Lille, but has not appealed to any of the cities around the world now drafting their first Metros. The high rate of acceleration attainable with the adhesive property of rubber is undeniable – and invaluable where stations are as closely spaced as on the Paris Metro – though it is not attainable without extra energy consumption; but the

A train of the Hong Kong Metro, note the concrete slab track bed.

friction generates excessive heat which demands abnormally high-powered ventilation of underground lines employing this form of running gear. A number of Japanese city systems also employ rubber-tyre technology, but of a different character to the French.

The peculiar aptness of the Metro railway to labour-saving automation, because of the repetitive routine of its working with standard trainsets over a segregated, classically simple track layout, has been outlined in the previous chapter. In the 1960s automation was eyed warily because of the endless malfunctions that harassed BART, the San Francisco Bay Area's Metro, but these traumas were the practically inevitable penalty of over-ambitious pioneering – a determined effort to create a fully automated railway with a phalanx of electronic devices, many of which were new and unsupported by proof of survival in rigorous daily use, and whose reliability was made the more critical by inadequate provision of standby systems to cover component failure in any of the tightly interwoven computer-controlled systems. Long-experienced operators like London Transport and Paris' RATP prudently took automation a well bench-tested step at a time.

With the cost of electronics reducing faster even than the science's advance – within the 1970s alone the price of a micro-processor dropped by a phenomenal 98p in the £1 – the scope for automation broadens by the year. For instance, a Metro train can now end its day's duty and arrive in its depot with the latter's staff already apprised of actual or incipient faults needing attention because the train's vital mechanisms are coupled to sensors which automatically transmit a performance report to the line's control center in coded current impulses

215

via the train-to-ground communication system.

One area of automation in particular where foolproof integrity has been prejudiced by pursuit of the ultimate in sophistication is automatic ticketing and revenue accounting, the latter achieved by connection of the ticket-issuing and validation machines to a central computer. The uncertain link in the process is the turnstile ticket-reader. This has to be quick-acting, childishly simple to use, insensitive to the most grotesque crumpling of a ticket by sweaty fingers, and above all almost superhumanly immune to failure, so that it does not block a peak-hour bull-rush of passengers. All this constitutes a taxing enough specification, but BART and the Washington Metro are two of the important and busy systems which have put reliability to a very severe test by embodying a 'stored-ride' facility in their automatic fare collection, or AFC. In this version of AFC one can buy a single multi-journey ticket; when it is submitted to an exit turnstile reader at the conclusion of a trip, the apparatus will assess the value of the journey from the point at which entry turnstile validation indicates travel was begun and engross the ticket with the cash balance of its cost still remaining for use.

The monumental expense of the superbly styled and technically elegant Washington Metro, forecast to top $7·5 billions if and when the remaining two-thirds of its planned 98-mile (158 km), five-line network are completed, had cooled Federal Government responses to proposals for UMTA-aided Metro building under President Carter. But under President Reagan funds for new Metro starts were at first completely frozen. Compared with the $3·3 billions of UMTA money the Carter Administration sought to make available in its last year (but did not get from Congress in entirety) Reagan's men aimed to reduce the total capital on offer from UMTA to $1·4 billions by 1986 and at the same time to taper off UMTA operating grant aid to zero.

That has kindled keener US city interest in Light Rail Transport, or LRT. LRT is one of the major growth areas of late twentieth-century railway industry, with new systems to show across the world from Japan, the Middle East, Algiers, Tunis, numerous European cities, and Calgary, Edmonton and Vancouver in Canada to several US conurbations. One US example will serve to illustrate its financial appeal. San Diego has completed a 16-mile (26 km) LRT route, largely by adapting a little-used main-line railway track that threaded the city's suburbs, for less than 10 per cent of the $1·2 billion bill of the Metro it originally contemplated. Moreover, it has met the capital cost without any UMTA help. Most of the bill has been financed by the share of California's public transport-oriented petrol sales tax to which the city is entitled.

Though it has been named the Tyne & Wear Metro, Britain's newest urban rail system is a model of LRT in operation. Its construction was begun in 1973 – or rather, so far as the major part of the system is concerned, its adaptation from an existing BR commuter network was put in hand. The latter had drifted into irretrievable decline after the Second World War. Because its Newcastle terminal, the Central station, no longer warranted the title and was remote from the city's commercial heart, and because outlying stations were not knitted into a convenient inter-modal public transport framework, road transport drained away the trains' off-peak traffic to such an extent that continuous electric multiple-unit operation became hopelessly unviable. In 1967 the lines' dc conductor rail was dismantled and the Tyneside commuter routes were relegated to less intensive diesel multiple-unit working.

The Tyne & Wear Council and its Passenger Transport Executive which had been established by the country's local government reorganization of 1973 and its 1968 Transport Act refused to tolerate more surrender to the private car. They accepted the premise of a 1971 land-use and transport study that Newcastle and its environs needed a thoroughly integrated public transport system, in which buses fed a conveniently frequent rail service penetrating to the heart of Newcastle. But the potential traffic volume could never economically sustain an intensive service manned, controlled and equipped with all the paraphernalia of a conventional railway. The only viable course was to convert 26 miles (42 km) of existing BR suburban routes to an LRT operation and weld on to them just over 8 miles (12·9 km) of new route, mostly underground but including an elegant new bridge over the Tyne, which would make downtown Newcastle directly accessible by rail from every station on the North and South Tyneside system. The scheme would also add several new stations to the historic total.

'Super-Tram', as the project was tagged in its youth, had a harassed pregnancy. Squabbles both with BR and with local railwaymen – in the latter case, bitter in the extreme – over the drastic changes of railway operating principle involved in the switch to LRT practice inflicted severe constructional delays that compounded cost inflation and helped to treble capital cost to £270 millions. Such daunting escalation horrified a Government committed to find 75 per cent of the amount under a clause of the 1968 Transport Act which, like the UMTA legislation on

A train of the Tyne & Wear Metro at Jesmond station.

Ticket Hall at Haymarket Station, Tyne & Wear Metro, Newcastle-upon-Tyne.

the other side of the Atlantic, had been framed to foster urban public transport improvement. For several critical months the half-finished Metro looked like staying that way, until a grudging Government agreed to its completion provided that its 75 per cent support was limited to a capital investment bill of only £167 millions.

The inaugural 12-mile (19·3 km) section was commissioned in the summer of 1980 and a year later the Queen formally opened the new Tyne Bridge over which the 'Super-Trams' head from South Tyneside to the city center. British-built by Metro-Cammell, each two-car 'Super-Tram' is single-manned, rheostatically-braked, has a 50 mph (81 km/h) maximum speed and seats 84 with standing room for 125 more. When the whole system is active, operation will probably be at a 2½-minute headway over the mid-town section, a frequency that would have been economically impossible with a full-scale Metro.

Tyne & Wear Metro working exemplifies the labour-saving simplicity of LRT working. The trains signal themselves automatically. Before a train starts a journey, its identity is set up on a cab control that actuates an underfloor transponder; and at strategic points on the system the code emitted by the transponder is interrogated by detectors which translate it, double-check it, then pass it to a microprocessor. The microprocessor thereupon route-sets as necessary, calls up the appropriate display on platform indicators at stations ahead and reports progress on the Metro control center's illuminated track diagram. Needless to say, all drivers have radio-telephonic communication with the control center, where the controller also has the means to take command of route-setting and signalling in an operational contretemps. No station platforms are permanently staffed, though a mobile force of inspectors is always riding the trains. In addition all the underground stations and the key interchange stations are continuously supervised from the control center through closed-circuit TV cameras, beaming to a bank of 18 monitor screens, and through bi-directional radio.

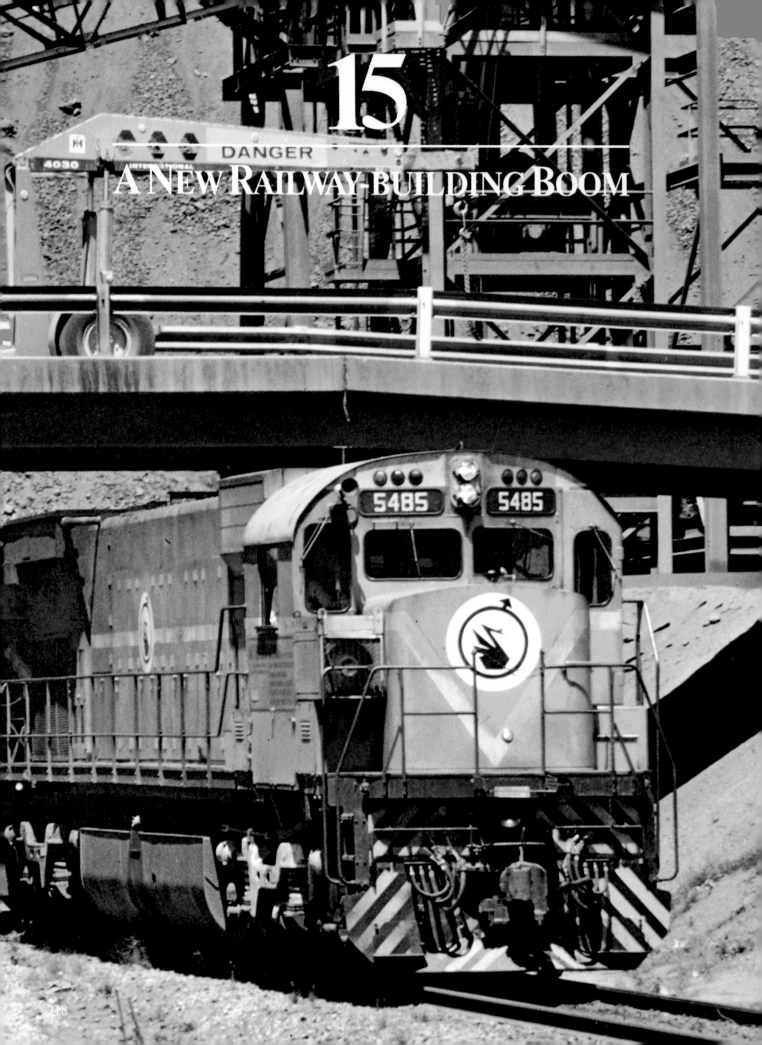

15

A NEW RAILWAY-BUILDING BOOM

DANGER

4030

5485   5485

A BOOM IN NEW TRUNK RAILWAY building looked one of the more improbable prospects in mid-century. Who needed new lines when the industrialized world's railways were locked in a rearguard action to halt the drain of tonnage from the networks they had, and when the air was heavy with the predictions by Jeremiahs that the decimation of the long-haul passenger train in North America would soon be re-staged in Western Europe? In several countries, too, existing networks were being trimmed as rural rail service crumbled in face of road transport's fast-improving economy and convenience.

Yet from 1960 to 1980 some 25,000 miles (40,233 km) of new line were added to the global total, quite exclusive of urban rail system expansion. Well before the Yom Kippur war explosively ended the halcyon years of cheap and free-flowing oil, some of the developed world's countries were recognizing that their railways' competitive debility was curable – and desirably so. The new strength of road transport derived as much from provision of new road systems as from technological advance; so the train would benefit equally if it were lifted out of the shackles of its nineteenth-century infrastructure. The science that would make it a highly effective and efficient bulk haulier in the new transport age was fast accumulating; and the marriage of that

to new infrastructure would tame the road transport growth which was seriously threatening the general quality of life. Some of the outstanding results, the Japanese Shinkansen, France's TGV, West Germany's *Neubaustrecke* and Italy's Rome–Florence *Direttissima*, are discussed in the next chapter.

A large part of the pre-oil crisis new construction was to be found in Eastern Europe, where most of the Comecon governments gave rail transport a higher priority than road freight in their post-war investment planning, in terms of equipment manufacture as well as infrastructure development. In 1956 the twenty-second Communist Party Conference of the Soviet Union focussed particularly on the USSR's rail needs and the Government responded with a massively increased allocation of funds to Soviet Railways (SZD) for dieselization, electrification and network extensions. Since then support has become even more generous. The 1981–85 Five-Year Plan, for instance, has hoisted the resources earmarked for SZD investment by as much as 29 per cent compared with its 1976–80 predecessor. In the past two decades more than 7,500 route-miles (12,070 km) of new railway have been laid, lifting the aggregate SZD route-mileage on the country's principal 5 ft (152·4 cm) gauge beyond 87,000

Opposite:
A pair of 2,600 hp diesel-electrics at the mine head on one of Western Australia's remarkable privately-owned ore railways, the Mount Newman, which regularly operates trains of 18,000 tonnes.

Below:
Chelyabinsk station in the Soviet Union.

A home-built Type 'Dong Feng 4' 3,300 hp diesel-electric Co-Co of Chinese Railways.

(140,009 km) – the USSR has some 1,600 route-miles (2,575 km) on narrower gauges. The 1981–85 Plan embodies a further 3,000 route-miles (4,828 km) of new railway building. Along with this route expansion SZD has been steadily double-tracking formerly single-track trunk routes at the rate of 200–300 route-miles (322–483 km) a year.

The most extraordinary Soviet feat of postwar construction is the second Trans-Siberian route, the 1,933-mile (3,111 km) Baikal–Amur Magistral (BAM), two-thirds finished and partly operational by the end of 1981. Electrified at high-voltage ac throughout, it will be opened in its entirety by 1986.

BAM has been built in as intimidating an environment as any rail pioneer has ever challenged, the permafrost area north of the Chinese border where temperatures can plummet to −60°C in winter but soar to +40°C in summer. Already a 700-mile (1,127 km) branch is reaching out from BAM northward to the hitherto rail-less area of Jakutsk.

BAM will tap huge deposits of oil, iron ore and coking coal which, with the eight industrial complexes created along its route, are expected to yield it 35 million tonnes (approx. 34½ million tons) of freight a year. This will be moved in trains of up to 9,000 tonnes (8,858 tons) gross, despite the new railway's sometimes severe gradients, for which SZD has created a new version of its standard twin-unit electric freight locomotive, the 1971-launched Type VL80. The BAM model, the 200-tonnes (197 tons) VL84 Bo–Bo–Bo–Bo, has a one-hour output of 10,330 hp. Shorter than the historic Trans-

Siberian Railway, BAM will also constitute an improved land-bridge for freight between the Far East and Western Europe, especially containerized tonnage that is less affected by the breaks of gauge.

Over half the world's entire rail freight tonnage movement is recorded by the SZD and it shifts 68 per cent of all freight in the USSR. The 1981–85 Plan aims to lift that percentage even higher. The *average* weight of an SZD freight train is as high as 3,500 tonnes (3,445 tons), but some gross as much as 12,000 tonnes (11,810 tons). A unique characteristic of SZD freight practice is its resort to four-bogie, eight-axle wagons for some bulk traffics, particularly petroleum products, so as to obtain 120-tonne (118 ton) vehicle payloads within an axle-load limit of 22 tonnes (21·7 tons). Construction of such vehicles has been restrained, however, since all key lines are being strengthened to accommodate 25-tonne (24·6 ton) axle-loadings.

Like North America's, Soviet track geometry is designed to absorb the punishment of intensive use by freight trains of wagons charged to the permissible extreme of individual axle-loadings, which are as high as 30 tonnes (29·5 tons) on numerous American roads, at minimum maintenance costs. That makes them unsuitable for traversal by high-speed passenger trains, except at considerable discomfort to the latter's occupants. So though SZD is eager to join the 100 mph-plus (161 km/h) club and has developed prototype electric train-sets designed for 125 mph (201 km/h) on the plum Moscow–Leningrad route, its passenger speeds are not scintillating. Since 1975, moreover, heavily subsidized Soviet airlines have creamed off some long-haul traffic, while expanding private car ownership, bus operation and a number of new city Metros have stunted short-haul rail growth. Nevertheless, SZD takes a 40 per cent share of all Soviet passenger travel and in high summer runs some 19,000 long-haul and 17,000 local passenger trains a day.

The most phenomenal rate of new railway building is China's. Since the founding of the People's Republic in 1949 the Chinese claim to have put down 107 new lines. As a result the system's route-length has already been increased by an incredible 150 per cent to more than 30,000 miles (48,279 km). The target for the century's end is 50,000 (80,465 km). At the start of the 1980s as many as 14 new railway projects were simultaneously active, five of them covering routes of at least 185 miles' (298 km) length and several of them in forbidding terrain.

The most daunting of all is almost literally pausing for breath. This is the 1,367-mile (2,200 km) line which is being projected from Xining, in Tsinghai province, to the Tibetan capital of Lasa, one of the schemes to introduce rail transport to the country's almost rail-less western provinces which complement those fashioned to relieve pressure on the heavily occupied trunk routes in the east of China. Construction has so far reached Golmud, about 520 miles (837 km) out from Xining. The rest of the planned route is almost entirely at 13,000 ft (3,962 m) or more above sea level, up to a peak of some 16,500 ft (5,029 m) in the Tangla pass. Here earthquakes are a constructional hazard as well as terrain permanently frozen to a depth of some 15–20 ft (4·6–6·1 m) and the Chinese have found more research into durable track structures a prerequisite for further advance. When the line is eventually finished, the thinness of the air over the remainder of the route will demand use of diesel locomotives with a special type of two-stage engine turbocharging and also of passenger cars with airliner-like pressurised interiors.

The Communist world has had no monopoly of new trans-continental railway construction. At the close of 1980 Australian National Railways, the 1975 reformation of the Federally-owned Commonwealth Railways, completed a new 516-mile (830 km) standard-gauge line northward from its Trans-Australian railway at Tarcoola to Alice Springs, that strangely isolated population center in the undeveloped – and uninviting – heart of the country. This new route supplanted Alice Springs' historic rail link, which was severely handicapped both by a transition from standard to narrow gauge for more than two-thirds of its distance and by its traversal of

Australian National Railways Class 900 diesel on the new Tarcoola–Alice Springs Line, now being extended to Darwin.

an area extremely vulnerable to destructive flash floods. Now projection of the new line beyond Alice Springs to Port Darwin, on the north coast, so as to establish Australia's first north-south transcontinental railway, is under way.

Chapter Ten noted some of the substantial investment in new railways undertaken in North America and South Africa to satisfy industrial hunger for coal and ores, from Japan in particular. But this has stimulated railway-building in several other resource-rich countries – Australia for one. Four different privately-built and operated lines, for example, ferry a huge tonnage of ore to Western Australia's ports from the State's Pilbara deposits, operating trains of over 5,000 tonnes (4,921 tons) gross in merry-go-round exercises under highly sophisticated CTC and track-to-train radio control.

In North Africa at the start of the 1980s Morocco was reserving three-quarters of its national transport investment funds for Moroccan Railways (ONCFM), chiefly to exploit the country's phosphate resources. Aiming eventually to double the size of its rail system, it was embarking first on a 594-mile (956 km) line from Marrakesh cross the Atlas Mountains – this initial stretch would involve 16·8 miles (27 km) of tunnelling and almost 10 miles (16·1 km) of bridgework – to Laayoun in the south, beyond which the line was then to extend a further 528 miles (850 km) to Lagwira, near the frontier of Mauretania.

Algeria, besides double-tracking parts of its existing system to serve industrial development, has embarked on its so-called High Plateau scheme, construction of a second rail route right

A 20,000 tonne ore train on another of the privately owned railways in Western Australia, the Hammersley Iron Railways.

Aleppo to Kamechlie, on the Turkish border in the north-east. However, the subsequent installation of a new 125-mile (201 km) line southward from Homs to Damascus, finished in 1981, could ultimately have a more striking repercussion – the rehabilitation of the whole 1,105-mile (1,778 km) Hedjaz Railway southward from Damascus to Medina, in Saudi Arabia.

This was the line the French built in the century's first decade to an idiosyncratic 3 ft 5$\frac{1}{4}$ in (104·8 cm) gauge, allegedly because of a clerical error that had the sleepers cut to the wrong length, and which Lawrence of Arabia's bands laid waste in the First World War. The damage he wrought at the line's southern end was never made good and for the next half-century that half of the line was left derelict, its flanks littered with the rusting shells of the trains which Lawrence's bands had wrecked. The Jordanians and Saudi Arabians agreed to rebuild the Hedjaz Railway early in the 1960s, but fell out in 1971 and abandoned the work already done, though the Jordanians subsequently appropriated some of their mileage for a new mineral route to the Red Sea port of Aqaba.

Later in the 1970s, however, the two nations and Syria jointly commissioned a fresh study, this time of a route completely redeveloped as a high-performance, standard-gauge line, upon completion of which in 1981 the Syrians declared intent to put their part of the job in hand immediately. As yet Saudi Arabia prefers to stand on the sidelines, even though it has lately embarked on a costly upgrading of its Dammam-Riyadh main line to reduce reliance on road transport, and an extension of this to a revived Hedjaz Railway at Medina would open its presently isolated rail system to through freight transits from Western Europe via Turkey. However, the Saudis may achieve that access less expensively via Iraq if the intervening State of Kuwait translates its talk of railway building into action.

The Russian involvement in Syria's post-war rail extensions, and the feasibility and subsequent detail design studies commissioned from European and North American consultancies which have prefaced the other Middle Eastern activity just outlined, hint at the rich market for which the world's biggest railway industries now compete. Practically all the State-owned railway systems have created their own multi-faceted consultancies to market experience-based advice, not only on the design of new railway development but on all branches of management and operation.

Each consultancy, naturally, is also a prime field salesman for its country's railway supply industry, implicitly if not overtly. That industry

across the country but deep inland, running more than 600 miles (966 km) from the phosphate deposits near Tunisia in the east to Sidi Bel Abbes, south of Oran. The recession has put a damper, at least temporarily, on a scheme to establish Algeria's second big steel plant in the west, at La Macta, near Oran (the first is in the east at El Hadjar, near Annaba, better known to Second World War North African habitués as Bône). If La Macta is developed, then Algeria aims to serve it with raw material from the far south-west of the country via a new 900-mile (1,448 km) ac-electrified line across the Saharan Atlas and Atlas North mountain ranges. This line would be designed to lift 45 million tonnes (approx. 44$\frac{1}{4}$ million tons) a year of ore, dolomite and limestone in 200-wagon, 15,000-tonnes (14,763 tons) gross trains on the South African and Australian model.

In the Middle East, war with Iran has not inhibited Iraq from launching construction of more than 1,650 miles (2,655 km) of new railway, to create high-capacity, standard-gauge links between all major cities. Centerpiece of the plan is a 735-mile (1,183 km) line from Baghdad to Basra and the port of Um Qasr. Here, too, Syria's determination to thread standard-gauge track to its Mediterranean ports from every industrial, raw material and agricultural center in the country has all but doubled its rail route-mileage since 1960. The centerpiece of the Syrian expansion to date is the 466-mile (750 km) transversal route built with Russian aid and opened in 1975 from the port of Latakia through

tends increasingly to attack the export markets as an integrated force, battling for national domination of every element of a new electrification or railway-building contract, from its civil engineering and its telecommunications to its traction and rolling stock. In many cases the struggle is also between sponsoring Governments, vying against each other with sometimes outrageously generous terms of credit, for the potential benefits to home industry, especially at a time of severe unemployment and domestic recession, are very inviting. In the non-Communist world alone the total market for new railway equipment in 1981 was assessed at around £17 billions.

Its value has risen substantially since the oil price explosion jolted Black African and South American countries out of their complacent dependence on road transport and neglect of railway investment. True, Africa's biggest new railway project, the 1,156-mile (1,860 km) Tazara or Tan-Zam Railway southwestward from Dar-es-Salaam to a connection with Zambia Railways between Lusaka and the Zambian Copper Belt, was begun before the Yom Kippur War in 1967 and finished in 1976. However, the catastrophic deterioration of almost half the line's mobile equipment into unserviceability within two years taught the Continent that there was a human as well as a physical aspect of neglect. For instance, Nigeria's grandiose aim of transforming its historic narrow-gauge system into a standard-gauge network fit for 100 mph (161 km/h) top passenger speeds, an objective set in a national 1975–80 Development Plan that abruptly reversed heavy emphasis on road transport, looked ridiculously premature until the country could muster a thoroughly trained railway staff from management down to shop floor.

The African Union of Railways founded in 1972 has sensibly made staff training a first priority. Then it hopes to set about some 10,000 route-miles (16,093 km) of new building to unify the various national systems built in the colonial era with no vision of today's Pan-African drive for economic solidarity, but solely to ferry raw materials from the interior to the ports. The problems are formidable. Finance is an obvious difficulty, but so is the mix of gauges and the conflicting operational methods inherited from the various colonial powers which originated the railways. Of Africa's 58,000 or so miles (93,339 km) of route 19 per cent is standard gauge (4 ft 8½ in, 143·5 cm), 60 per cent 3 ft 6 in (106·7 cm), 16 per cent 3 ft 3 in (meter-gauge) and the rest a variety of smaller gauges.

In South America, Mexico abruptly lifted its rate of investment in the national rail system,

NdeM, by 60 per cent in the closing 1970s and talked of reaching 1985 with an annual outlay on railways twice that of a decade earlier. A good deal of the money is going on a 10-year programme of new motive power acquisition at the rate of 100 units a year – the subject of a mouth-watering exclusive contract secured by the US manufacturer, General Electric – and on electrification. Though Mexico is a major oil-producer the Government prefers to sell its oil for foreign currency. Moreover, there is hydro-electric potential in the south of the country, so electric traction is a cheaper option for NdeM once the catenary is in place, and the capital cost can be funded by the earnings of exported oil. Besides these traction developments, however, NdeM is also building a substantial mileage of new railway to improve its route from Mexico City to the US border at Queretaro and has started two completely new main lines, one of 248 miles (399 km) along the country's Atlantic coastline to interconnect the ports of Vera Cruz and Tampico, the other of 161 miles (259 km) to establish a shorter route between Tampico and Mexico City. Unfortunately by 1983 this ambitious expansion was being crippled by the country's grievous financial difficulties.

Though Brazil still entrusts the bulk of its passenger movement to the roads, it has turned eagerly to rail for economic exploitation of its huge and still largely untapped mineral wealth. In 1979 the Government decided to build a new 460-mile (740 km) electrified railway through mountainous terrain – its first 198 miles (319 km) have entailed engineering 70 tunnels, including one of over 5 miles (8 km), and 95 bridges with an aggregate length of 16·8 miles (27 km) – to link its raw material resources with the steel industry in a triangular area bounded by Belo Horizonte, Rio de Janeiro and Sao Paolo. Operation of 12,000-tonne (11,810 ton) trains is in prospect. This so-called Steel Railway is likely to be followed by a project termed the Soya Line, to facilitate the export of agricultural products through the Atlantic port of Paranagua, and then by at least one new Coal Line.

Inevitably some of these breathtaking new railway projects were clouded by the prophecies of an imminent world banking crisis during 1982. A good many Third World rail development schemes are largely dependent on heavy credit financing by agencies in the industrialized Western countries, or else by the oil-rich countries of the Middle East, or by the World Bank and its affiliated International Development Association. And as the 1980s advance the World Bank is less flush with cash, because of reducing contributions from developed countries harassed by the recession.

16
THE QUEST FOR HIGH INTER-CITY SPEED

No special prescience was needed to guess that peacetime application of the last war's advances in transportation technology would make speed a more decisive factor in the passenger business. But in Europe only the French made not merely resumption but improvement of pre-war pace one of the immediate priorities in their reconstruction. As mentioned in Chapter 11, the electrification of the ex-PLM main line from Paris through Dijon to Lyons which the SNCF put in hand almost before the victory bells' echoes faded had a transformed passenger service as its focus. Thus France had an inter-city service in the 70–75 mph (113–121 km/h) average speed range operative as early as the winter of 1952.

Behind the scenes the SNCF also embarked at the start of the 1950s on the preliminary exercises of a methodical, continuous research programme to probe the ultimate speed potential of the orthodox steel-wheeled vehicle on steel rail. By June 1954 the French had spurred one of their newest Co–Co electric locomotives up to 140 mph (225 km/h) with a featherweight three-car load and satisfied themselves that the overhead-wire current system would withstand the purely mechanical stresses of moving locomotive pantograph contact at well over 100 mph (161 km/h). But a later test with a pair of Co–Cos and a 600-ton (610 tonne) train faced the engineers with a problem for their next two decades of research into extremely high rail speed with electric traction: the maintenance of smooth contact between pantograph collector strips and conductor wire, at unvarying pressure, without which there is vulnerability to severe and damaging arcing when the traction unit is demanding a maximum amperage of current.

In the succeeding winter laboratory and wind-tunnel work alleviated some of the current collection snags and in the following March the results were put to the proof at a rail speed that would not be surpassed for another 26 years. On 28 and 29 March 1955, on a near-dead straight and level 53 miles (85 km) of main line between Bordeaux and the Spanish frontier at Hendaye, and beneath catenary installed by the Midi Railway as long ago as 1927, two different locomotives were successively thrashed up to 205·6 mph (330·9 km/h). Precisely how and why the two protagonists, the six-axle No CC7107 and the four-axle No BB9004, were so exactly pushed up to and reined in at an identical speed – which in such a rarified range would be extra-ordinarily difficult to pinpoint the second time around – has never been disclosed. But no matter. Both machines undoubtedly exceeded the 200 mph (322 km) mark; and that was phenomenal enough.

However, those 1955 records did no more than identify a horizon of 200 mph. Apart from the fact that both runs culminated two or three years of careful preparation, and that both were made with an ideal racetrack specially fettled up, cleared of all other traffic and intently monitored, neither was completed without trepidating moments. Both finished with the locomotives' pantographs denuded of their collector strips, which had been swept away as molten metal in the trains' slipstream. And the trains had left a grotesquely mis-shapen track in their wake. In no way was the exploit an opening to immediate operation of daily, safe, mechanically foolproof and economically maintainable 100 mph-plus (161 km/h plus) passenger services.

The track distortion, for instance, dramatized a concern that was to preoccupy most railways as they sought to operate at three-figure pace: the fact that beyond 90 mph (145 km/h) the impact of traction units with conventionally-sprung motor bogies on the permanent way multiplied by a factor well in excess of the rate of speed increase. That was an addition to the fresh problems civil engineers were already confronting in the post-war environment.

On the one hand wage inflation was making the traditional manual maintenance of the track a burden on the balance sheet. On the other,

A complete tracklaying train removing old rail and laying new on the German Federal Railway; up to 3 km (1.9 miles) of track can be relaid in one eight-hour shift, with a staff of 50, a job which took 200 men five weeks in pre-mechanization days.

higher standards of upkeep were being dictated by the peculiar stresses of new diesel and electric traction, invariably employed more intensively than the steam it supplanted, and by the heavier axle-loadings freight managers were specifying to improve the payloads of their wagons. Stronger, more durable track and increasingly sophisticated mechanization, both of upkeep routines and of inspection, were the solution.

The change palpable by any rail traveller, of course, was steady transition to continuously welded rail on the busiest routes. But its eradication of the classic sensation of rail travel was gilt on its vital economic gain of longer track life under heavy and fast traffic (which there had to be to warrant its higher cost). The battering of rail-joints was a prime cause of general track wear and tear, but more importantly of at least a third of potentially hazardous rail failures. As for the rail joint's familiar function of providing for expansion of the rail's metal without distortion in rising temperature, that was covered by heat or hydraulic de-stressing of the welded lengths to the year's mean ambient temperature at each location just before the rails' installation. Thus the rails were fitted free of either compression or tension.

Except in North America, continuously welded rail was also laid on more costly concrete sleepers, or sleepers that were part metal and part concrete, rather than the traditional timber ties. That, combined with extra width and depth of ballast, achieved a more solid structure to contain expansion and avoid risk of track distortion in an abnormal rise of ambient temperature. At the same time rail weight was increased.

Installation of welded rail on open track still left discontinuity of surface at points and crossings. Rail strength there had to be reinforced by casting monobloc layouts in manganese steel, instead of assembling them from pieces of rail; and as speed climbed into the three-figure range, by resort to the expensive swing-nose type of switch. This leaves no gap in the rails whichever way the points are set, but at the cost of a pair of operating motors per switch, one to activate the blades, the other the movable nose.

The higher speed rose, too, the keener concern had to be for the depth and integrity of ballast cradling the track. Besides its stabilizing function, ballast spreads the load imparted by trains, which unless it is dispersed will set off progressive failure in the ground formation immediately below the sleepers. The ballast must not only be kept well-packed to a depth and width specified for the traffic characteristics of the route concerned, but also clean and efficiently drained.

In many cases an essential prelude to consistent daily operation at 100 mph (161 km/h) was complete dismantling of existing track and ballast and excavation of the ground below it to renew drainage. As for care of the ballast when track structure was restored, that was one of the chores taken over by the remarkably complex and still expanding range of permanent way maintanenace machines devised by specialist firms such as Matisa and Plasser & Theurer in Europe, and Canron in North America.

The precise alignment of newly laid track; the cleaning of dirty ballast in situ by a machine that passes an endless bucket chain between sleepers to scoop out unacceptable material;

An Italian State Railways
125 mph (201 km/h) Class
E444 Bo-Bo approaches
Rome Termini with the 06.18
express from Turin in June
1978.

German Federal 8,000 hp
Class 103 Co-Co and TEE in
the Rhine Valley.

227

the solid packing of ballast beneath sleepers by rapidly-vibrating tampers – these are just a sample of the tasks nowadays performed by self-propelled machines. The whole process of lifting life-expired track complete, depositing new sleepers in correct position and finally lowering on to them new lengths of long-welded rail, is now within the compass of a single machine; or rather, a cavalcade of inter-connected machines with motorized portal cranes that swing the discarded material back to flatcars in their rear and pass the new forward for installation. One US example of these con-trivances, measuring 220 ft (67·1 m) from front to rear of its various units, can remove con-demned track and deposit new for final fixing at the rate of 1,200 ft (366 m) an hour. In the design of modern track maintenance machinery a great deal of ingenuity has also been exercised to produce equipment that can deploy all its devices with minimum interference to normal traffic on adjoining lines – an important asset as traffic operation intensifies.

A good deal of the routine work to maintain a correct track geometry and a firm foundation is dispensable with the solid forms of track base that emerged in the 1960s. In these the rails are clipped directly either to a concrete pavement or a ladder-like concrete framework ballasted to a semi-rigid carpet of rolled macadam.

But paved track's long-lasting stability is offset by a number of debits. First, it is two or three times as expensive to instal as orthodox long-welded rail on concrete sleepers. Second, it takes much longer to lay and the job demands closure of the section to all traffic. Third, con-nection of a stretch of paved track to adjoining conventional track is tricky. And finally adjust-ment of alignment once paved track has been laid is not only very costly: quite likely it will be physically impossible. So as yet, with one out-standing exception to be discussed later, paved track schemes have been confined to locations with chronic problems of track stability or where track maintenance under traffic is peren-nially troublesome. Typical examples are the tunnels of BR's intensively used commuter lines at the approach to Glasgow Central and those of New South Wales on their Sydney bi-level electric multiple-units' descent from the Blue Mountains to Lithgow.

Most nineteenth-century railway builders had no conception of the speed that would be sought from their routes a century later. Brunel's visionary determination to drive his Bristol main line as straight and near dead-level as he could for the maximum mileage from London was almost unparalleled. There were cases where the flatness of the terrain and its dearth of townships presented engineers with a near-ideal alignment: the greater part of the route from Paris to Bordeaux, for example, and the crossing of the Po Valley plain from Bologna to Milan. On most trunk routes, however, the railways' founders bequeathed curvature that would be a brake on mid-twentieth century speed however refined the track that negotiated it.

On the railway a curve's speed limit is dictated by the mix of traffic it carries. If the track is used by a gamut of trains from low-speed freights with wagons imposing 20–25 tonnes' (19·7–24·6 tons) axle-weight fully laden to Inter-City flyers, the curve's degree of superelevation has to be a compromise between the ideal factors for trains at each extreme of the range. A measure of cant that favoured the fast passenger trains would have the lumbering freights bearing too oppressively on the curve's inner rail and subjecting it to intolerable wear. Once the compromise figure has been struck the speed restriction for passenger trains through the bend is set by considerations of passenger comfort. The safety limit is always higher than the ceiling beyond which centrifugal force gets the better of the superelevation and disconcerts a train's occupants.

The first successful attempt to lift passenger train speed through curves without prejudicing any of the precepts just described was Spanish. Animated by the particularly severe curbs on speed which the country's mostly tortuous and often indifferent track enforced on its inter-city trains, two engineers, Goicoechea and Oriol, devised the marriage of low-slung, ultra-lightweight coach bodies and patent wheel guidance which honours their ingenuity in the last two letters of its acronym, Talgo.

The first Talgo train-sets, put to public service by RENFE between Madrid and Irun in 1949, featured cars with bodies of only $34\frac{1}{2}$ ft (10·5 m) length and weighing no more than 10 tonnes (9·8 tons). With their floors sunk to a mere $2\frac{1}{4}$ ft (68·6 cm) above rail level for the lowest practicable center of gravity, each (apart from a two-axled car at one end of the set) was single-axled, its front piggybacking on a pivot above the axle of the car ahead. So close was the coupling between cars that internally each opened straight into its neighbour without a conventional vestibule connection. Flexible, zip-fastened diaphragms sealed the narrow gaps between the car bodies, giving a complete train-set the look of some unearthly metallic cater-pillar. The crucial element of the Talgo concept besides the minimal weight and extremely low center of gravity of its cars was a patent method of suspension and wheel mounting that was claimed to guide the vehicles into and through curves, thereby smoothing passage of the bend, curbing centrifugal forces and reducing material wear and tear.

Talgo never found adherents outside Spain. In the late 1950s the US Rock Island, New Haven and Boston & Maine Railroads each acquired a set when some Eastern railroads were under the spell of a galvanic little financier turned railway chief, Robert R. Young, who ultimately chaired New York Central. Young's doctrine, with which he bludgeoned his fellow rail executives through full-page press advertisements, was that cost-cutting investment in a new breed of weight-saving cars was the only way to stem the rising flow of red ink over passenger train operating balance-sheets; heavyweight Pullman sleeping cars, he snorted, had become obsolete 'rolling tenements'. But the Talgo and home-bred lightweights which Young's preaching spawned were soon derided by the railroads' customers as cramped and spine-jolting by comparison with the solid gait and stately interiors of traditional US cars. All were discarded within a year or two of their debut.

A distinctive feature of the Talgo rake which the Rock Island ran as its Peoria-Chicago 'Jet Rocket' was a TV camera in the locomotive's nose that transmitted to a screen in the train's lounge for what should have been the passengers' delectation. Instead it was someone's undoing on almost every trip. The driver up front was nerve-hardened to the frequent prospect ahead of lorries, school buses and other road traffic lazily and only just clearing the route's many ungated level crossings as he bore down on them at 90 mph (145 km/h). Not so passengers normally ignorant of each day's tally of near misses. Dead faints were not uncommon, terrified retreat from the TV screen to the lounge's bar for a stiff restorer the daily pattern of life in the car. The Talgo set did 'Rocket' service for less than a year, from mid-February 1956 to mid-August 1957, however, and was then dismissed with other Rock Island lightweight experiments to Chicago commuter operation.

In Spain Talgos not only prospered in their initial form but are now a cornerstone of RENFE's forward Inter-City service planning as a result of subsequent development. The first step, in the late 1960s, was perfection of a means to vary wheel gauge so that Talgo equipment could cross from the Iberian broad to France's

Top:
One of the German Federal
Railways prototype Class 403
Inter-City emus.

Above:
In German Federal Inter-city
trains of the 1990s passengers
may phone train staff as well
as the outside world.

standard gauge. Until then the limited number
of through-running vehicles – sleepers of the
Paris–Madrid 'Puerta del Sol' (complemented
from 1973 by Paris–Lisbon/Oporto/Vigo couchette cars of the 'Sud Express') and vans owned
by the Transfesa freight forwarding company –
had only negotiated the break of gauge by
pausing for a complete change of bogies or
axles. For that they had to be halted at the
border and lifted. Patentes Talgo SA, the company created to conduct Talgo business, contrived a way of adjusting Talgo wheel-gauge
simply by use of sliding stub axles: all that was
then needed was a guide-rail-fitted section of
track tapering from one gauge to another over
which the Talgo train was run to set its wheels to
the new parameter, to which they would be
securely locked.

In 1969 the technique was embodied in train-
sets which opened up a through service between
Barcelona and Geneva, the first class-only
'Catalon-Talgo'. This was later ennobled as a
TEE, though it was deprived of that status and
converted to a dual-class working in the summer
of 1982. An all-sleeper variable-gauge Talgo was
installed between Barcelona and Paris in 1974,
the 'Barcelona-Talgo'; and in 1981 that was

Italian State Railways are bit by bit improving their spinal whole route from Milan to the country's southern tip: here, in the far south a new double track has replaced the historic single line between Battipaglia and Reggio Calabria.

One of the latest Series 200 train-sets of Japan's Shinkansen.

complemented by the 'Paris–Madrid Talgo' sleeper, which has supplanted the 'Puerta del Sol' as the crack overnight train between the two capitals and links them in unprecedented time. Because of the laborious bogie-changing routine at the Franco-Spanish border station, Hendaye, the 'Puerta del Sol' had to leave Paris as early as 18.04 to reach Madrid by 09.00 next morning, whereas the 'Paris–Madrid Talgo' can start at 20.00 and still be into Madrid by 08.55.

The 'Paris–Madrid Talgo' exemplifies the latest mark of the Spanish equipment, which has a slightly longer body but more importantly features an automatic pendular body-tilting system; of that technology more will be said shortly. Enough to remark that the 'Talgo Pendular' are designed for 125 mph (201 km/h), that prototype tests in Spain have touched 144 mph (232 km/h) without, it is claimed, sacrifice of passenger comfort and that in 1982 RENFE was amassing a fleet of 132 day and 56 sleeping cars of this new model.

For the present RENFE confines Pendular trains to the ruling limit of 87 mph (140 km/h) on its metals. On the Paris–Madrid overnight service, though, they are licensed to run at 100 mph (161 km/h) within France. At that pace I have found their single-axle riding remarkably steady and serene, no way destructive of a sound sleep, despite the peculiar beat of a single pair of wheels beneath one's car. It has to be admitted, however, that the sleeping compartments of a low-slung Talgo car, its floor little more than 2 ft (61 cm) above the rail surface and its roofline more than 4 ft (122 cm) below normal, are palpably more cramped than those of a conventional European sleeper.

The event that fired a determined quest for higher rail speed on both sides of the Atlantic in the 1960s was Japan's stunning Shinkansen ('New Railway') premiere in October 1964. A railway world still struggling to establish 100 mph (161 km/h) as standard express train pace without being overwhelmed by high upkeep costs or operational complication was suddenly amazed by a train service of Metro-like frequency, running at 130 mph (209 km/h) from dawn to dusk day in and day out. And very lucratively too, to the extent that by the decade's end, despite the absurdly low floor to which the Government was then pinning Japanese rail fares, its phenomenal business was generating a healthy revenue surplus over and above capital and depreciation charges as well as running costs.

Driven to expand operating capacity between Tokyo and Osaka to cope with the intervening coastal belt's extraordinary post-war population and industrial explosion, Japanese National Railways and the Government had concluded that it was futile to pour new wine into old bottles. The inherent constraints of JNR's 3 ft 6 in (106·7 cm) gauge apart, the existing Tokaido main line was too continuously hemmed in by buildings and too frequently bisected by level crossings – almost a thousand of them – for speed-conducive improvement in the course of widening. Since passenger traffic potential far outstripped rail freight possibilities, because of the littoral industry's easy access for coastal shipping and its close-packed convenience for road service, the saner course was to drive a new high-speed and standard-gauge passenger railway from Tokyo to Osaka. This would cater only for key towns and cities en route, leaving the historic 3 ft 6 in gauge line to concentrate on intermediate passenger business and freight.

The new railway's limited function alleviated the daunting problems of equipment and infrastructure design for a leap ahead of contemporary rail speed standards. The track and curvature could be engineered ideally for a single type of train, a 25kV ac electric multiple-unit (and one of unprecedented power/weight ratio, with motors on every axle generating a total of 15,875 hp to shift 16 cars grossing 880 tonnes

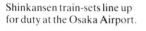
Shinkansen train-sets line up for duty at the Osaka Airport.

(866 tons), and an even more spectacular 23,600 hp for a total weight of 930 tonnes (915 tons) in the later, second-generation Shinkansen trainsets). A standard layout of two island platforms would serve for every intermediate station, so that even with the terminals and their ancillary depots only 230 sets of points would be needed in the whole 320-mile (515 km) route. Thus the whole line could be supervised from a single Tokyo center. And for such an uncomplicated network it was comparatively easy to devise an automatic train control system that activated a continuous multi-aspect signalling display on drivers' desks through transmission of coded impulses via the running rails and their reception and decoding by trainborne apparatus. The inaugural Shinkansen, the New Tokaido Line, was the first trunk route in the world to dispense entirely with lineside signalling.

At the peak of its popularity in 1976, after the New Sanyo line had been tacked on to the New Tokaido to forge a continuous 664-mile (1,069 km) route from Tokyo to Hakata in Kyushu Island, the first Shinkansen was operating more than 100 trains each way daily over all or part of its length; and its timetable glittered with almost 450 inter-station hops scheduled at average speeds in excess of 90 mph (145 km/h) start to stop. The uniform time allowance for the 320-mile (515 km) Tokyo–Osaka run by the higher-category 'Hikari' services, which made only two intermediate stops, was 3 hours 10 minutes. That constituted an end-to-end average speed demand of 101·1 mph (162·7 km/h) but between calls on route start-to-stop timings averages of over 110 mph (177 km/h) were exacted. On one epic 1976 day the railway counted over a million passengers.

In 1970 a euphoric Japanese Government called for six more Shinkansen and heralded them as just the first instalment of an 18-route network of some 4,350 miles (7,000 km) that would promote industrial development and population dispersal away from the teeming coastal belts. Not until 1982, however, were any fresh Shinkansen ready for commissioning. And even then the total of new lines that had at last made it to the starting line was two, not six. The rest of the 1970 vision had become badly clouded.

The post-1973 oil crisis inflation, searing Japan worse than many countries, was the first thing to dull Shinkansen lustre. Within a few years the already formidable costs of carving a new railway's elevated path through urban environments had trebled. The inflation's catastrophic effect on the finances of a railway hobbled by draconian political restraint of fares and freight rates was no help either. These chains were relaxed in the 1976–77 winter, when Government and Diet at last steeled a political will to decelerate if not arrest Japanese National Railways' helpless plunge into almost unfathomable deficit. JNR fares were hoisted 50 per cent overnight and from then on railway management was allowed to up-price in step with inflation (but not to overtake the damage already done through impotence to pace rising costs). The sharp fare jump, closing the price-gap between Shinkansen and parallel air services which new wide-body jets were simultaneously enhancing, drained away enough of the so-called Bullet Trains' traffic to counsel thinning out the timetable. And since road improvements too were making rail travel less of an automatic choice for the shorter inter-city journeys, the economic argument for more Shinkansen had become vulnerable on yet another count.

However, Shinkansen's worst beating was coming from Japan's rampant environment-alists. Bending to the new political wind, the Government enacted measures that forced JNR, at high cost, to erect sound-baffling walls and parapets at the lineside wherever Shinkansen passed within a specified distance of habitation. Meanwhile determination of routes for the two

new Shinkansen, the Tohoku northwards from Tokyo to Morioka and the Joetsu north-westwards from the capital to Niigata on Honshu Island's west coast, was being griev-ously harassed by environmental objection, especially within Tokyo and its environs. Even-tually JNR was forced to abandon concentra-tion of all Shinkansen on a single Tokyo station because of implacable resistance to any practic-able suggestion for the two new lines' access, either under or over ground, to the first route's Tokyo Central terminus. Totally divorced from the first Shinkansen, the Tohoku and Joetsu lines start from their own Tokyo station at Ueno.

Besides these political travails, some technical traumas had also set JNR back on its heels. The years of carefully orchestrated, multi-disci-plinary research and testing by the combined resources of Japanese industry, as well as JNR's own technicians, which prefaced completion of the Shinkansen specification had not proofed the first Shinkansen against all the stresses of an intensive 130 mph (209 km/h) train service. Quite soon rail breakages were rife and catenary wear an acute concern. The first problem per-suaded JNR not only to adopt heavier rail but to lay the New Sanyo Line entirely with concrete slab track – the major exception mentioned earlier to most railways' hitherto sparing use of the costly system. Furthermore, after a con-catenation of equipment failures that ravaged Shinkansen punctuality in the 1974 summer, JNR ruefully budgeted for total rebuilding of the New Tokaido Line's track and catenary in the next decade.

JNR has also embarked already on a progres-sive renewal of its entire first-generation fleet of Shinkansen train-sets. And though the Japanese were chauvinistically tempted by French Railways' 1981 inauguration of 160 mph (258 km/h) operation on the Paris–Lyons TGV, to be discussed later, to step up to the same pace in everyday working on the new Joetsu and Tohoku Shinkansen – they have been engineered for that speed and a Shinkansen train-set has been tested at up to 198·3 mph (319·1 km/h) – JNR eventually settled for retention of 130 mph. This prudence was partly influenced by fear of environmentalist reaction and is likely to be shortlived; by 1982 further test programmes had persuaded JNR that noise pollution problems had been licked and a step-up to 160 mph was foreshadowed before long.

In Europe the German Federal Railway (DB) was the first to operate a post-war train regularly at 100 mph (161 km/h) – its new 'Rheingold' of 1962 – and the first to essay 125 mph (201 km/h), between Munich and Augsburg in the autumn of 1965 with its then new 8,100 hp Class 103 Co–Co electric locomotives. In this exercise the DB was also the first in Europe to accept practically the belief that running in excess of 100 mph demanded more sophisticated driving safety aids than a basic form of automatic warning system such as its standard Indusi apparatus. This only emphasized passage of an adverse lineside signal aspect by sounding an alarm in the cab, then automatically applied brakes if the warning were disregarded. For 125 mph the Munich–Augsburg section was equipped with means to actuate inductively a continuous display of signal aspects in the 103s' cabs, and also to sketch on the driver's instruments an ideal deceleration curve in face of a cautionary aspect.

Within two years, however, the DB was recoiling from the much higher rates of wear and tear the 125 mph (201 km/h) operation of existing equipment was incurring. The West Germans were absorbing empirically what was soon an axiom of European railroading. Whereas a lift of everyday rail speed from 75 to 90 or 95 mph (121 to 145 or 153 km/h) had been fairly painless, each extra mile-an-hour's attainment above that level was matched by a disproportionately steep angling of the graph's cost line – if, that is, management was trying to squeeze more pace out of contemporary designs of traction and vehicle on existing main lines. Fifteen years after inauguration of BR's intensive 100 mph (161 km/h) electric Inter-City service from London to the West Midlands and the North-West, using locomotives of orthodox design, the route's track still wilts from its hammering.

Wear and more stringent maintenance requirements apart, 100 mph-plus (161 km/h) speed as already mentioned was held to demand more sophisticated and much more costly signalling and train control systems. Only BR regarded this last as dispensable until the 125 mph (201 km/h) mark was passed. And where higher passenger speed was introduced on a busy trunk route with a mix of traffic the widening of the speed band cost fixed asset productivity: since it was quite impossible simultaneously to raise the minimum line speed of the slowest-moving freight traffic, the faster passenger trains could only be found track room to sustain their new top speed by carving them a wider path through the timetable: in other words, by keeping a greater mileage ahead of them clear of other traffic and tolerating a greater mileage of empty track in their wake.

The DB reinstated a 100 mph (161 km/h) limit in 1967 and waited 10 years before it relicensed 125 mph (201 km/h) running between Munich Augsburg, then began a gradual upgrading for the higher speed of other well-aligned main-line stretches in the country's northern and southern plains. By 1984 it would have a 300-mile (483 km) aggregate of 125 mph railway.

During the decade of speed retreat the DB had formulated new parameters of track and running gear design detail to mitigate wear. Freight working had been remoulded to lift the speed of trunk inter-yard trains sharing tracks with the Inter-City service so as to stabilize as far as possible the breadth of the speed band. The DB had also evaluated and rejected a switch to multiple-unit self-powered trains so as to reduce stresses by dispersing traction plant weight to motored axles throughout the formation.

Test-beds for this latter appraisal were three prototype four-car streamlined units, the Class 403. They shared DB Inter-City workings with locomotive-hauled trains until 1979, when the multiple-units' first-class-only seating in an inflexible format made them quite incompatible with the DB's new intensive, dual-class Inter-City service reshaping. In the spring of 1982 the 403s were chartered to the West German airline, Lufthansa, to become ground-hugging Boeing 737 substitutes. In face of escalating fuel costs Lufthansa had realized that it had become much more economical to rail rather than fly interlining passengers from Dusseldorf and other Rhineland airports to the country's hub of long-haul air services, Frankfurt Airport, which has its own station directly accessible to main-line trains.

Though some of the DB's locomotive-hauled Inter-City trains are now timed to start-to-stop averages as striking as 104·3 mph (167·9 km/h) between calls in the Ruhr, end-to-end times of north-south journeys are shackled to unimpressive figures by the tortuous character of what, pre-war, were secondary Reichsbahn main lines through the central mountains, hills and up-lands of West Germany. In 1973 the Federal Government agreed that the worst bottlenecks must by supplemented by seven new double-track bypasses totalling some 590 route-miles (950 km), the *Neubaustrecke*, and others eased by realignment, installation of reversible signal-ling and addition of a third, relief track.

Initially the *Neubaustrecke* were conceived as Shinkansen-like passenger lines fit for speeds as high as 185 mph (298 km/h). But that ideal was abandoned in face of an increasingly critical need to accelerate freight train transits if the DB were to wrest a bigger share of the high-rated merchandise market from road and narrow the yawning gap between its operating surplus and its fixed costs. Now the *Neubaustrecke* will carry fast trunk freights as well as Inter-City trains, the latter held for the foreseeable future to a limit of 125 mph (201 km/h), which will be allowable almost throughout the vastly and expensively improved alignments of the new lines, so as to optimize operating capacity.

Sadly the *Neubaustrecke* have made miserably slow progress, and that despite Government anxiety since the late 1970s to see them realized as one of the vitally necessary tools for more productive rail operation to check the DB's horrendous deficit. Here again the stumbling-block is environmental. West Germany's politi-cally muscular environmentalists have fanned a

quite irrational antipathy to the noise of 100 mph (161 km/h) electric trains; and this, absurdly, in a country that has meekly submitted to far worse ravages from its *autobahn* builders. Moreover, until long-overdue legislative amendment in 1982 the country's planning processes allowed individual citizens seemingly interminable rights to object to new construction and enforce adjustment of plans even after lines of new route have been painfully resolved with their elected local authorities. At the start of the 1980s, consequently, no more than two *Neubau-strecke* – from Hannover to Würzburg and Mannheim to Stuttgart – were in progress and only the latter stood much chance of completion before the decade's end. Testimony to the strength of the environmentalists is the con-siderable mileage of the Mannhein–Stuttgart line which the DB has been forced to sink just below ground level in cut-and-cover tunnels purely to keep trains out of the landscape (a more incredible farce even than the newly-electrified line in North Germany which had to persist for some months with diesel traction because at the last minute protesters stymied the erection of pylons for its current feed).

Despite the brake on the DB's passenger speed aspirations for at least the next decade, West German industry, with the support of the Federal Research and Technology Ministry, is actively developing traction and rolling stock fit

West Germany's 'Super-IC' cars for the 1990s.

French Railways 270 km/h (167.7 mph) TGV (*Train à Grande Vitesse*) train-set.

for up to 300 km/h (186 mph). At the Hannover Industrial Fair of 1982 Thyssen-Henschel displayed its three-phase diesel-electric Bo–Bo prototype, bulbously streamlined at one end and tagged the 'Blue Streak', which is the test-bed for a new arrangement designed to relieve the bogie of the stresses of other gear at high speed. Whereas in previous designs the traction motor, transmission, axle drive and braking system have been treated as separate elements, in what Thyssen-Henschel calls its 'integrated power bogie' they are integrated in a block which is attached to the locomotive body by a swinging link on one side, and on the other is supported either on the bogie or on the body by a spring unit which is adjusted when the locomotive is on the move. At high speed this unit works so that the block's weight is fully borne by the body, but at slow speed the weight is automatically returned to the bogie.

Another West German firm, Messerschmitt-Bolkow-Blohm, is researching an elegant new design of 'Super-Intercity' car riding on a revolutionary lightweight bogie fashioned from fibre composite materials. One of the benefits claimed for the new technique is that the torsional elasticity of the fibre composite bogie permits use of a relatively hard primary spring, which will isolate flexural car-body vibrations from the bogie's pitching movement. Another novelty in the MBB design, calculated to enhance running stability and limit wheel/rail wear at very high speed, is the 'creep-controlled wheelset'. In this the axle is hollow and fixed to the bogie frame: each wheel rotates independently, fixed to its own shaft, and the two shafts meet within the center of the axle in a 'creep coupling' through which torque can be electrically transferred from one wheel to the other.

Italian State Railways' (FS) high-speed ambitions, too, have had to yield to the more prosaic need of enlarged freight operating

capacity. Handicapped like the DB by a viciously curved alignment on the heavily-occupied Rome–Florence core of their system's main north-south route, the FS secured Government approval at the start of the 1970s for construction of a third *Direttissima*. Moreover, it was authorized to build a gently-curved and modestly graded line fit for as much as 185 mph (298 km/h), even though the abrupt and irregularly-shaped succession of mountains and valleys between Rome and Florence would crucify the project on a mammoth bill for tunnelling and bridging.

A combination of Governmental foot-dragging over release of investment money (especially when the oil price explosion dealt Italy a particularly stiff dose of inflation and recession), environmental haggling over the line of route, engineering traumas and wildly optimistic forecasting has retarded completion well beyond the forecast date. In 1982 only 76 of the ultimate 145 miles (122 of 233 km) of new railway were in use, but without achieving any reduction of Rome–Florence journey times. Unbelievably the crack 'Settebello' was on a five minutes slower timing between the two cities than in 1980, allowed 2 hours 44 minutes for this stretch in stark contrast to the standard Rome–Florence of $1\frac{1}{2}$ hours the FS once euphorically forecast on the *Direttissima*'s completion; and taking almost half-an-hour more over its whole Rome–Milan run than it did before any of the *Direttissima* was usable! Presumably too much freight is being allocated *Direttissima* track room. A further 31·7 miles (51 km) of the new line was due for completion by early 1984, but the remainder was unlikely to be finished

British Rail 'Inter-City 125' HST, with a 2,250 hp Paxman Valenta-engined power car at each end, north of the Scottish border at Ayton on the journey from Edinburgh to Kings Cross.

A Class E656 Bo-Bo-Bo
hurries an express over the
completed section of the new
Rome–Florence Direttissima.

before 1987.

Year by year, in fact, the *Direttissima*'s bold engineering for such starry speed looks more of an inexplicable extravagance. Though the Rome–Florence expresses are already powered by locomotives with 125 mph (201 km/h) capability, the 5,600 hp Class E444 Bo–Bos, these machines are still limited to 112·5 mph (181·1 km/h) on the *Direttissima*'s commissioned mileage. The new line has been equipped with sub-station capacity that even at 125 mph would be strangled by trains threading one current feeder section at close headway. And the FS has so far been more intent on building new ranges of mixed traffic electric locomotive than on committing new special-purpose high-speed designs to production.

In 1982 American high-speed ambitions were very uncertain of fulfilment. They had flamed briefly when Amtrak was given suzerainty of the North-East Corridor main line from Boston through New York to Washington under the package of legislation which created Conrail in the mid-1970s, because Congressmen accepted the illogic of giving an essentially freight-oriented Conrail charge of a predominantly passenger route. The core of the Corridor line in and through New York was left in the hands of the local public transportation authorities in which it had been vested earlier, but the rest became Amtrak's first fully-owned railway. Conrail took the usual Amtrak role of track space lessee for its freight component of Corridor traffic.

Amtrak pressed for adequate funding to turn the Corridor into a Shinkansen. But the Ford Administration, which had only conceded Amtrak's Corridor takeover after a fight, particularly by its ill-disposed Transportation Secretary, flatly refused to give more ground. Amtrak had to be content only with intermittent rebuilding and re-alignment of the existing railway for 125 mph (201 km/h), with signalling modernization, and with renewal and extension of electrification north of New York from New Haven to Boston at 25kV 60Hz ac. The job was to have been finished by 1981 for $1·75 billion, but the time-scale had to be extended by at least two years and the budget topped up to $2·5 billions as a result of inflation and the project's ill-advised remission to incoherent and sometimes acrimoniously divided management by a combination of Federal and rail agencies.

Even this modest North East Corridor Improvement Programme (NECIP) was almost diluted following President Reagan's 1981 assault on subsidized public transport, which mounted the second attack on Amtrak's overall funding in two years. In 1979 the Carter administration had attempted as part of its drive for a balanced Federal budget to cut away 43 per cent of the Amtrak service network, reduce annual Amtrak train-mileage by a third and denude many Amtrak trains of their diners, sleeping cars and parlour cars.

The case against Amtrak was that though, with the aid of a steady infusion of new rolling stock, it had re-created a credible long-haul passenger service and though it had progressively increased business volume, its operations were still marketable only at a very uneconomic price. The New York–Washington Metroliners (since displaced to the New York–Harrisburg–Philadelphia service by locomotive-hauled trains using new Class AEM-7 machines based on the Swedish Rc4 design) and the popular New York–Florida vacation trains alone met even their direct running costs out of revenue. On average every Amtrak passenger was paying almost 10p less than his seat-mile running expenses; and very largely as a consequence Amtrak in 1978 was reporting an operating deficit swollen to over three times the figure of its inaugural year, 1971. Yet it was still catering for little more than 1 per cent of the total US travel market. Never mind the inter-city bus operators who fumed at the amount of Federal largesse Amtrak absorbed, many railroad managements publicly protested that the ratio of investment in Amtrak to the extent of its business outstripped anything they could manage for their entirely self-financed freight working.

However, Carter poised his axe just as the country was hit by petrol famine that crammed most of Amtrak's trains and jammed its reservation bureau lines with frantic appeals for space which had some services fully booked a month or more in advance. At that Congress reduced the White House economy plan to a 17 per cent surgery of the Amtrak network, at the same time doubling Amtrak's annual investment provision and lifting its operating subsidy by about 50 per cent.

In 1981 the new Reagan administration proposed a far harsher cutback. Had it been fully implemented, Amtrak could well have been left with only the North-East Corridor to operate. The rest would have been killed off by the attrition of a Federal funding so drastically reduced that there would have been inadequate money to run the trains unless fares were raised to a stratospheric level, in which event the passengers would have decamped and set off a destructive spiral of even worse fare inflation to offset diminishing load factors. Such a reaction would only have deferred the death throes.

As for the NECIP, contending that 'the costs of increasing train speed outweigh the benefits', Reagan sought to clip $310 millions from its budget. That would have cancelled the electrification from New Haven to Boston and pared the signalling plan to a titivation of existing apparatus. And in consequence ultimate 1983 journey times for the 231·8 miles (373 km) from Boston to New York and 224·6 miles (361·5 km) from New York to Washington would probably have to be set at 4 hours 10 minutes and 2 hour 50 minutes respectively, just 5 and 9 minutes less than the impoverished, decaying Penn-Central was offering on the eve of Amtrak's birth.

But Congress rolled Reagan's Amtrak offensive back from its full objective. Amtrak emerged only $36 millions short of the $853 millions it claimed as a bare minimum operating subsidy for 1982, not $240 millions poorer as Reagan's men had proposed, and with only 9·5 per cent of its timetable's annual train-mileage annulled, though it did have to accept stringent new financial criteria for continuation of each service. And the White House's threat to peg the aggregate of all Amtrak support, capital as well as operating, to $350 millions a year by 1986 still lay on the table. The NECIP programme also survived virtually unscathed.

Hope of other high-speed US railways has not been doused, either. Though Reagan's Department of Transportation has done its best to undermine the findings and the exercise was subsisting on very meagre Congressional funding, a study of the potential of other urbanized US corridors for passenger rail development was being kept alive by the legislature as the 1980s unfolded. It is possible that one or two Mid-Western states may proceed alone. In the mid-1970s, impatient of Federal parsimony and obsession with the Boston–New York–Washington corridor, Ohio set up a state Rail Transportation Authority (ORTA) with a remit headed by a charge to promote and establish a 600-mile (966 km) high-speed passenger railway interconnecting nine of Ohio's major cities. Republican capture of the state Senate from the Democrats later in the decade hobbled progress, and in the November 1982 mid-term elections the state's electorate as a whole sadly voted no to a 1 per cent sales tax aimed to raise some $500 millions a year to start the project, but the state's new Governor soon made clear that he favoured continued pursuit of the high-speed rail objective by other means.

Furthermore, four other Mid-Western states, Illinois, Indiana, Michigan and Pennsylvania, were associated with Ohio in a High Speed Passenger Interstate Compact, to map out an integrated strategy for a high-speed system covering their whole territory. In 1982 the first three states named were too pinched by recession and unemployment to think of high-speed rail investment, but Pennsylvania had got as far as funding a commission to advance its role in the scheme.

Amtrak's 'National Limited' leaves Pittsburgh for New York.

The oddest event of the early 1980s was the emergence, from the polyglot band of overseas railway industrial and consultancy scouts sniffing out export potential, of a philanthropic Japanese tycoon, Ryoichi Sasagawa, who was prepared to bankroll detailed engineering studies of the most promising US high-speed rail routes. Top of the list, ironically, was one in Reagan's own California, the heavily-populated corridor from Los Angeles to San Diego. Naturally enough, Sasagawa was pathfinding exclusively for Japanese Shinkansen technology. The findings of the Japanese study team, coupled with those of a market study financed by Amtrak, then prompted formation in early 1982 of the American High Speed Rail Corporation, a private enterprise confident of raising cash on the open market to build a US Shinkansen, and also of making it a profit-earner. Besides Los Angeles–San Diego, this ambitious body was eyeing possible routes from Miami to Disney World and Tampa in Florida, Dallas/Fort Worth to Houston in Texas, and one or more radiating from Chicago. European interests, too, were closely studying the Miami–Tampa–Orlando corridor. And the Budd Company was mounting a scheme for a MagLev line between Las Vegas and Los Angeles.

To the north Canada's Via Rail too confronted a 1981 threat of network amputation, despite its accumulation in three years' existence of 41 per cent more passengers than Canadian National and Canadian Pacific were recording just before Via Rail was born. But in this case Trudeau's Government was demanding a trade-

off, not a reduction of the entire envelope of Government aid. It was prepared to double Via Rail's capital allowance in 1983–4 provided a comparable amount were saved by thinning out the egregiously loss-making services in the timetable. That mostly postulated cuts outside the busy short-haul corridors in the east and in particular more mutilation of the transcontinentals, with abolition of the Halifax–Montreal 'Atlantic' and of through Montreal–Vancouver and Winnipeg–Vancouver operation.

Via Rail hungered for more of the new LRC diesel train-sets built in Canada by Bombardier-MLW. This low-slung creation, pairing an 84-tonne (83 ton), 2,900 hp locomotive with aluminium-alloy, tilt-body cars (vehicles of unimpressively heavy weight considering their body material – 52 tonnes/51 tons, compared with the 40 tonnes/39 tons of an orthodox French Corail car or the 33–36 tonnes/32·5–35 tons of a BR MkIII car), had been evolved by a consortium of Canadian industry after the first Trudeau regime's 1978 endorsement of a Government-funded revamping of inter-city routes in the 727-mile (1,170 km) Windsor–Quebec corridor for high speed. The 10 million population of the corridor looked a viable market for rail passenger investment.

Via Rail was initially authorized to buy a squadron of 21 LRC locomotives and 50 trailers and was anxious to double the fleet's size, not least because the average age of its inherited rolling stock was coming up to 25 years. The first LRC sets took up Montreal–Toronto service in the autumn of 1981, but at well below

their designed top speed of 125 mph (201 km/h). The route's present ceiling is 95 mph (153 km/h), but for a short distance only; over most of its length the prevailing limit is 75 mph (121 km/h). It would take at least a decade to execute all the infrastructure work needed – especially the replacement of numerous open level crossings – to allow sustained running at 125 mph and thereby to achieve Via Rail's goal of a 3 hours 40 minutes transit from Montreal to Toronto (335 miles/539 km), $2\frac{1}{2}$ hours from Toronto to Windsor (224 miles/361 km), 1 hour from Montreal to Ottawa (112 miles/180 km) and $1\frac{1}{4}$ hours from Montreal to Quebec (155 miles/ 249 km).

But even with thoroughly refurbished track and signalling these objectives could well be unattainable. Via Rail's management fretted over the problem of a distended speed band that has become a recurrent issue in this chapter: the Windsor–Quebec corridor's double-track main lines were too flush with freight for easy pathing of LRCs at their top speed. One solution propounded by Via Rail, given the comparative infrequency both of the passenger service and of the heavy-tonnage freight trains and also the effectiveness of CTC supervision of single lines, was that the double track might be converted to a pair of bi-directional single lines with passing loops, one for the LRCs, the other for the freight.

The Canadians are so far, along with the Japanese, the only mass practitioners of automatic body-tilting. The rationale of this technique is reduction of the effects of centrifugal force through means to increase the inward slant of a body beyond the angle imparted by the superelevation of a curve, plus any slight addition of cant resulting from movement of the swing links between body and bogie in a conventional suspension system. Consequently a coach thus equipped can take a curve faster than the latter's degree of cant normally allows with-

In 1978 South African Railways tested this temporarily streamlined class 6E electric Bo-Bo and a coach fitted with a new type of bogie at up to 153 mph (246 km/h). a world record for 3 ft 6 in; as a result a 125 mph (201 km/h) public service was to be test-marketed between Johannesburg and Durban in 1983.

243

Swiss Federal speed on the key Lausanne–Berne–Zurich route is severely restricted by curvature, as seen in this view of an Re 4/4 Bo-Bo and 'Inter-City' express: in 1983 Government approval was likely for major works, including almost 30 miles (48 km) of new route to bypass the worst curves, so as to allow 125 mph (201 km/h) over much of the distance.

on very sinuous routes where automatic body-tilting is justified by the transit time it saves through a fairly modest rise of speed over each of the many curves. But the Italians have been worried by chronic complaints of travel sickness from users of the Fiat-built prototype electric multiple-unit with passive body-tilting, known appropriately as the *Pendolino*, which the FS has operated between Rome and Ancona since 1975 for a saving of 45 minutes on previous best journey times over the 185·5 miles (298·5 km). RENFE was simultaneously running a Spanish-built facsimile, its *Tren Basculante*, but by 1982 was firmly declaring it unsatisfactory by comparison with Talgo Pendular equipment.

Other discouragements to adoption of automatic body-tilting are its extra cost and complexity: but above all the fact that on a purely double-track main line its lift of speed at the top end of the traffic range can reduce the route's operating capacity because of a widened speed band, for reasons already discussed. Alternatively the operators must renounce full exploitation of the device's speed-raising potential.

These disadvantages helped to dissuade French and Swiss Federal Railways from pursuit of tilt-body technology. However, Swiss disinclination to standardize the gyroscopically-actuated system devised for the SBB's MkIII air-conditioned coaches, distinctive for their inward-tapering body cross-section that was to allow for tilting without any infringement of neighbouring track clearances, was equally if not more influenced by signs of Government readiness to invest in ironing out the worst curves of the railway's axial route from Lausanne through Berne to Zurich.

The similarly cross-sectioned and very elegant 'Grand Confort' cars which grace some of French Railways' (SNCF) surviving domestic TEE services were also designed for body-tilting. These vehicles inaugurated the SNCF's second phase of regular 125 mph (201 km/h) operation on its existing infrastructure. The first phase, in 1967, had been restricted to 31·1 miles (50·1 km) of the Paris–Toulouse route and to just two of that line's supplementary-fare, first class-only *rapides*, the 'Capitôles', for the exclusive benefit of which the French installed a very complex cab signalling and automatic train control apparatus.

The 'Capitôles'' consistently high load factors demonstrated the market value of the higher speed. Moreover experience convinced the French that assured 125 mph (201 km/h) driving did not ineluctably demand such sophisticated and costly automatic controls; provision in the signalling of an extra cautionary aspect, flashing green, to give a driver an

out subjecting its passengers to a disagreeable excess of *g*. The prospective benefit, naturally, is the ability to sustain continuous high speed over original nineteenth-century alignments and their frequent bends without need to modify superelevation: and above all the scope for a substantial lift of end-to-end speed without the huge expense of building a Shinkansen.

But experience has balanced the advantages with a few considerable discredits. The simplest and cheapest forms of automatic body-tilting, known generically as passive systems, are broadly speaking pendular in their mode of operation: that is, the tilting mechanisms react *post facto*, inclining the body a degree or two further after they have taken the measure of the fixed cant. Except where bends have been prefaced by a fairly long and gentle transition curve, therefore, a passive system's reaction can be disconcertingly abrupt.

From the passenger comfort viewpoint that is not an embarrassment in the Class 381 electric multiple-unit fleet of Japan's 3 ft 6 in (106·7 cm) gauge system, because no more than 75 mph (121 km/h) is asked of them; they are employed

Thyssen-Henschel's experimental Um-An high-speed diesel locomotive, designed for 200 mph (322 km/h) trials on the German Federal, on preliminary trial with a test car and (at rear) a Class 103 electric Co-Co.

additional section's warning of a possible signal stop ahead would suffice, with the back-up of a simultaneous warning device in the cab. That minimized the cost of fitting the well-aligned two-thirds of the 359·8-mile (579 km) Paris–Bordeaux route for 125 mph almost throughout. But again the high-speed privilege was reserved for crack first-class-only trains, formed of Grand Confort stock and headed by new 8,000 hp Class CC6500 Co–Cos: first the 'Aquitaine' in the spring of 1971 and soon afterward the complementary 'Etendard', so as to furnish peak-hour flyers in each direction. One trip each way daily was non-stop in 3 hours 50 minutes, which represented an end-to-end average of 93·8 mph (151 km/h), the fastest required of any traditional locomotive-hauled train in the world over such a distance.

Like the 'Capitôles' these lustrous Paris–Bordeaux trains were created specifically to keep Air Inter, France's internal airline, at bay in the business market (competition between SNCF and Air Inter is a peculiar business: seen from the marketplace it does not noticeably bar many holds, yet SNCF has a 25 per cent financial stake in the airline and its chief is an airline board member). It took imminent completion of a continuous Paris–Bordeaux *autoroute* to goad the French to admit second-class passengers to the line's 125 mph (201 km/h) club with the autumn 1980 installation of two dual-class Corail trains timed to the higher speed limit.

By then the French had long since added up the balance sheet of selective high-speed operation on existing routes and set course for the new-railway alternative.

Addition of 125 mph (201 km/h) dual-class trains to the Paris–Bordeaux service had been resisted for so long on several counts: the difficulty of cleaving more abnormally high-speed paths through the rest of the route's traffic, already discussed; the lower margin of second-class revenue over the extra costs of high speed, such as the need under labour agreements to double-man the locomotives; and not least the capacity of the route's existing traction current supply system to satisfy the appetite of more than one 8,000 hp locomotive threading the same feeder section flat out. This last concern has forced the French to restrict the 125 mph dual-class trains to 12 cars instead of the normal 16-car Corail format on peak-period Paris–Bordeaux workings purely to avoid overtaxing the catenary; and as a result an extra normal-speed train or two had to be timetabled, at extra cost, to sustain the route's daily aggregate of seats.

So there was no longer any point in developing automatic body-tilting for routes less admirably aligned than Paris–Bordeaux. The Grand Confort cars, like the Swiss Federal's MkIIIs, have never demonstrated the technique to fare-paying passengers and undoubtedly never will. In both cases only one or two cars

France's fastest train the Paris–Toulouse 'Capitôle' was French Railways' first 125 mph (201 km/h) service, between Les Aubrais (Orleans) and Vierzon; this is the train in 1965, headed by a BB-9200 in the Vézère Valley near Estivaux.

were fitted with the device at birth and then stripped of it after conclusion of private tests.

That leaves Sweden's SJ and Britain's BR as the only European railways still intent on series production of automatic body-tilting train-sets. SJ is another system with no overweening high-speed ambition. Anything more than 100 mph (161 km/h) would be unacceptable without very costly action to accelerate reduction of the country's inordinate incidence of level crossings. But on most of SJ's trunk routes curvature is also recurrent. Ability to take it at even 25 per cent higher pace would achieve rewarding gains in transit time.

In conjunction with the Swedish electric traction firm ASEA, SJ evolved a prototype automatic tilt-body electric multiple-unit in the mid-1970s which was satisfactorily tested at up to 150 mph (241 km/h), and which demonstrated the possibility of paring the Stockholm–Göteborg journey time from 4 hours to 3 hours 20 minutes given an end-to-end average speed no higher than 85 mph (137 km/h). For the rest of the decade the Government's tight rein on SJ investment precluded development; but in the glow of a more benign Ministerial attitude to SJ's need of new and even additional coaching stock to satisfy the national cheap fare scheme's stimulus of inter-city business SJ was authorized in 1982 to order three more prototype tilt-body train-sets, this time for public service evaluation.

No tilt-body technology has been pursued with such transcendent expectations as Britain's. But sadly, none has been so dogged by delay and disappointment leading to disillusion among many of its putative operators.

The technology emerged from an early 1960s re-examination of wheel and rail inter-action from first principles by BR's Derby Research Centre that had been motivated by the often execrable riding of the nationalized railway's original standard coach designs. Many of the technicians deputed to this study were recruits from a contracting aerospace industry.

As the exercise progressed the commercial managers' files were thickening with refutations of the Beeching regime's belief that the British express train could never hope to increase its market share in face of air and automobile development, and that investment in higher speed would consequently be money down the drain. But with no practical hope of finding a path for a British Shinkansen, let alone the money, how could the commercial pressure for more speed be answered? Derby's solution was the marriage of lightweight aerospace construction methods and materials, the fruits of its exhaustive running gear research, and automatic body-tilting in an Advanced Passenger Train. This, Derby claimed, could be run at up to 150 mph (241 km/h) within the braking distances of existing signalling, would take curves up to 40 per cent faster than conventional trains, and because of its lightweight scientific undercarriage and suspension design would give a serene, wear-free ride over all existing track and pointwork.

First unveiled to a reverent press in 1967, the APT concept went through some drastic design revisions before its first hardware manifestation five years later as a four-car prototype with gas turbine-electric power. This was the APT-E which now reposes in York's National Railway Museum.

APT-E was the most audacious package of new techniques since the luckless Canadian-built UAC Turbo-Trains. Innovation permeated the design, from the long-wheelbase articulated bogies with their patent suspension that imparted a degree of positive steering through curves and their hydrokinetic main brakes, to a very sophisticated automatic body-tilting system. This last was the ultimate in 'active' body-tilting mechanisms: that is, instead of reacting retro-spectively like most of the systems described earlier in this chapter (Canada's LRC notably excepted) it employed sensors to detect and measure the deficiency of a curve's cant in relation to speed at the instant of entry into a transition from tangent track; thereafter the sensors automatically activated a degree of body tilt that was progressively graded to nullify the centrifugal forces.

At the APT-E's completion none was more enthusiastically bullish about its potential than the Transport Ministry's own scientific advisers. No need, they contended, to build any more orthodox Inter-City traction and rolling stock: APT should henceforward be the standard net-work product. And a wide and golden horizon of export sales for the technology, if not for complete trains, was seen among railways the world over thirsting for more speed at a fraction of Shinkansen cost, though the only positive score was a licensing agreement with Budd, the US car-builders, which eventually lapsed with-out any product.

Years passed without APT-E leaving the veiled confines of BR's private East Midlands test track. The project's lustre steadily faded through a depressing sequence of labour argu-ment over conditions of 100 mph-plus (161 km/h) driving, cash constraints, Government disen-chantment and yet more reappraisals of design, the most important of which was necessitated by the collapse of the case for gas turbine trac-tion. That started with failure of the British range of engines earmarked for the APT to pass the prototype stage and was complete with the post-oil crisis destruction of turbine traction's economy. Not least because no suitable and proven diesel engine meeting an APT specifica-tion was then available off the shelf, the APT had to be re-designed as an electric unit. This was also sensible because the APT's characteris-tics would be optimally exploited on the curves and long gradients of the electrified West Coast Route to Scotland rather than on the generally better aligned East Coast Route or Western main line to Bristol and South Wales.

By the end of the 1970s these last two trunk routes had 125 mph (201 km/h) trains of con-ventional type, diesel powered. An alliance of commercial managers dismayed at stagnation of Inter-City speed through APT's halting development and of BR's old school of mechani-cal engineers who bitterly resented the way they had been upstaged by the Research Centre's parvenus, drove the BR Board to give com-parative orthodoxy another run in the high-speed stakes. Fresh analysis showed that on the London–Bristol and London–Edinburgh routes at least a substantial cut in journey times was attainable if the track were fettled up and the worst curves realigned (but not those in very difficult locations, such as York station) to permit sustained 125 mph: and that this speed had become feasible in intensive daily service without special signalling safeguards or oppres-sive upkeep costs through the efficiency of modern disc braking and scientific bogie design. All in all, at least a 20 per cent gain in speed was within reach at much less cost than originally estimated.

The outcome was the High Speed Diesel Train, or HST. This was a push-pull set of two streamlined 2,250 hp diesel power cars enclosing seven or eight passenger trailers, boasting a high rate of acceleration to top speed by virtue of a power/weight ratio 25 per cent more favour-able than that of a 3,300 hp Deltic diesel loco-motive on an equivalent number of passenger cars. With these HSTs BR installed the world's fastest diesel service under the 'Inter-City 125' brand-name, first on the Bristol/South Wales main line from London then on the East Coast Route to the West Riding, North-East and Edinburgh.

Scheduling three HSTs each way every hour of the day between Paddington and Bristol or South Wales, plus peak-hour extras, the WR timetable of 1981 displayed 122 daily station-to-station HST sprints timed for an average of 90 mph (145 km/h) or more start to stop, up to a peak of 104·3 mph (167·9 km/h) between Pad-dington and the first call at Chippenham, 93·9 miles (151·1 km) out, of the 17.20 to Bristol. The subsequent East Coast Route 'Inter-City 125' operation was launched with even more demand-ing schedules, but before long they were eased – yet more evidence of hazards of high-speed timetabling over a mixed traffic main line – to safeguard reliability. Even so the 'Flying Scots-man' of 1981 was booked over the 268·3 miles (431·8 km) from Kings Cross to Newcastle at an average of 89·7 mph (144·4 km/h) whereafter it was due into Edinburgh within only 4 hours 43 minutes' travel time of the capital; and 88 station-to-station runs at start-to-stop averages ranging from 90 to 97·6 mph (145 to 157·1 km/h) figured in each day's working. The HST tech-nology has been bought by New South Wales State Rail Authority for what it calls an Inter-City XPT operation, but the limitations of NSW track restrict its Australian speed to

100 mph (161 km/h) at best.

BR had promoted the HST as the Inter-City network's standard equipment pending mass production of the APT. But after endorsing further HST construction for the Paddington–Plymouth–Penzance and North-East/South-West routes (in the latter case the number of sets sought by BR was severely clipped), an increasingly cash-conscious Government had the production line shut down at 95 sets. To contrive enough HST units for its investment-starved St Pancras–East Midlands–Sheffield Inter-City route in 1982–83 BR was forced to comb sets out of HST services already operating.

The Government's stance was that the rest of the Inter-City route system was not well enough aligned to allow HSTs long spells of running at peak speed. Consequently HSTs would not be able to cut end-to-end journey times as spectacularly as they had between, for instance, London and Newcastle: and therefore, it was argued, they would not reap the extra traffic needed to justify the inflated cost of their high power/weight ratio.

So for fresh advance in Inter-City speed BR was now totally dependent on more main-line electrification and on perfection of the APT. On electrification, however, the Government was stalling, professing an appreciation of its worth – which its own Department of Transport had proved by exhaustive evaluations – but delaying action by disingenuous revisions of its financial criteria for electrification investment. And APT was as far from public service in squadron strength as it had been a decade earlier.

Three prototype 25kV ac electric APTs, designated APT-P, had been completed in 1979. They were to be put through the year's probing in public service on which the Government had insisted before endorsing mass production: but even if that year's experimental service had been triumphant, series APT construction was impossible before the mid-1980s, since it was now realized that the APT-P format was an extravagance and that redesign was necessary.

APT-P was built to fulfil the 150 mph (241 km/h) potential of the concept. That demanded two power cars per train-set for a total output of 8000 hp. BR shared the French view that at the high speeds contemplated the traction current for both power cars was desirably drawn through the pantograph of one only. But unlike the French they were chary, for safety reasons, of running a 25kV line from one power car to the other through the intervening passenger vehicles. So in a full APT-P set the two power cars were marshalled in the train center, which debarred passenger movement between the

trailer-sets on either side of them and incurred the expense of furnishing each trailer-set with its separate buffet and kitchen.

Too late, BR grasped that 150 mph (241 km/h) was beyond economic reach without a drastic change in British political attitudes to rail investment. Footplate staff agreement to driving at much above 125 mph (201 km/h) was inconceivable without the very costly aid of continuous cab signalling as well as track-to-train radio links, not just the ground transponder-activated cab display of variations in fixed track speed limits which BR had provided for APT operation at up to 125 mph. And the traction current supply system would have to be reconstructed before it could cope with the flat-out operation of droves of 8,000 hp traction units, which would also raise energy consumption quite substantially. All this, moreover, for a fairly modest advance on the journey times attainable with the maximum speed set at 125 mph. Thus by the time the APT-Ps were ready to take the road BR was already redrafting the APT as a single power car push-pull with a power/weight ratio suited to 130 mph (209 km/h) operation at most.

By 1982 this redesign, too, was in the waste-bin as the result of embarrassing experience with the APT-Ps. In their private trials they succumbed so repeatedly to flaws in their components that it was found imprudent to launch even one of them in public Euston–Glasgow service before December 1981. That coincided with the most Arctic conditions to grip Britain for decades, which exposed other weaknesses. After the inaugural day's southbound run from Scotland scarcely a journey was completed unscathed by breakdowns of one sort or another. Confounding the euphoric prospectus of the 1970s, APT-P did not even ride as equably as the orthodox MkIII cars of an HST. Abruptly a red-faced management abandoned the whole exercise.

Bungled design or execution of straightforward components looked culpable for some of the chronic malfunctions, but the main source of trouble was clearly unreliability in the highly sophisticated body-tilting mechanism and its alliance with other running gear innovations in the hydrokinetically-braked articulating bogies. The concept had been far too ambitious and complex to develop and prove each device separately, and then as an integrated system, within the amount of money an impoverished BR could allow.

So in 1982 yet another and this time a simpler version of the APT was being worked up as the putative production model. Designated APT-U, it would have 10 body-tilting trailers,

non-articulated to improve ride quality and minimize tilt reliability problems, and with the high-performance hydrokinetic brake replaced by orthodox disc brakes, already proved adequate on the HSTs for 125 mph (201 km/h) running within the braking distances of existing signalling.

It would be back to two power cars in APT-U, because BR had found that with only one an APT was short of adhesion on the stiff Shap and Beattock banks either side of the Anglo-Scottish border. But they would enclose the trailers, because BR had also concluded that there would be no snags in deploying two pantographs simultaneously if the speed ceiling was 125 mph (201 km/h).

But will APT-U eventually materialize? Apart from the project's dismal saga to date, there are two reasons for scepticism. One is the likelihood that the curving speed limits which BR sets for orthodox Inter-City equipment are over-cautious and capable of some relaxation without detriment to passenger comfort. BR had realized before the 1981-2 APT-P fiasco that if the Paddington–Bristol and Kings Cross–Newcastle routes were electrified, it would be an extravagance to equip them with costly and delicate APTs. Their severest curves had been smoothed for the diesel HSTs, so that for 125 mph (201 km/h) operation under wires their

prime need was a purpose-built but basically orthodox high-speed passenger electric locomotive. Such a prototype was ordered in 1982.

At the same time the London Midland Region was preparing to test its West Coast main line's margin for increased curving speed with existing coaching stock. If it proved possible to achieve the equivalent of Eastern and Western Region HST schedules with a new 125 mph (201 km/h) electric Bo–Bo and MkIII passenger cars, then the case for more weary pursuit of a foolproof APT would be hard to sustain. Or at worst the new locomotive type could serve quite adequately as power cars for APT-U trailers.

APT's future was equally dubious because the case for investment in higher BR Inter-City speed had been dented by trends in rail traffic following the Government's late 1980 demolition of all constraints on direct road coach competition. The coach operators attacked on key routes to London with rock-bottom prices pitched as close as they dare to break-even point on full loadings. In the leisure travel market the Western Region's 'Inter-City 125' trains proved conspicuously vulnerable to this offensive. Yet when the LMR promptly counter-attacked – in an unresearched gamble – with equally cheap Liverpool–London fares on less glamorous services it picked up 111 per cent more passengers and an 18 per cent gain in net revenue

BR's 'Inter-City 125' Mk III
second-class car interior.

within six months. Clearly price counted for more speed. In the cut-throat competitive environment established by the Government it was looking, to take an analogy from the North Atlantic air routes, as though a Laker-like high-volume, low-cost policy would pay BR better than the Concorde-like pursuit of APT perfection. BR naturally responded by re-designing its MkIII second-class coach to a higher seating density.

The contrast with the same year's events in France was sharp-etched. There, at the end of September, President Mitterand was confident enough of the financial as well as the social benefit of the 160 mph (258 km/h) Paris–Lyons service he was inaugurating to call for definite moves towards creation of a similar operation from Paris to Britanny and South-West France.

The 160 mph (258 km/h) trains which the President was honouring, the world's fastest to date, were making that pace over brand-new railway engineered, like the Shinkansen, for exclusive use by standard passenger train-sets, but employing techniques that incurred far less capital cost than the Japanese enterprises. Like BR, the SNCF was initially prompted to investigate new possibilities for high-speed passenger train design in the context of the aero-space industry's early 1960s evolution of compact helicopter gas turbines that could endow a light-weight rail vehicle with high power at minimal

cost in power plant weight and bulk. Almost simultaneously the SNCF fell into talks with France's road-builders which established the feasibility of building a high-speed railway and an *autoroute* side-by-side on a shared infra-structure, with consequent reduction of both parties' engineering costs.

First fruit of this conclusion was the 1965 draft of a dual system on a common alignment most of the way from Paris to the Belgian border, with a rail offshoot to the prospective Channel Tunnel's mouth. However, the rail element of the project hung fire pending a positive decision to build the Tunnel and was then indefinitely postponed when Britain's Labour Government ditched its agreements on the Channel link at the end of 1974. That knocked the economic stuffing out of the rail scheme.

Long before that, in the summer of 1966, the SNCF had initiated the study of a similar high-speed railway between Paris and Lyons. The Paris–Lyons axis is the main artery of French social and commercial life, influencing as much as 40 per cent of the population because of its status as the main route to most of Southern and South-Eastern France. As far as Dijon it is also the capital's rail access to Southern Switzer-land and to Italy. Though much of the former PLM Paris–Dijon–Lyons main line is four-track, it is double where operation is most troublesome,

on the winding climb through the Burgundy hills north of Dijon. Here in particular the SNCF foresaw traffic strangulation in the century's last quarter if volume growth continued at the annual rate of the mid-1960s.

To quadruple the rest of the existing route's track would not obtain value for money because the sinuous alignment would have prevented *rapides* from taking full speed advantage of the room left by sidetracked freights. Better, the SNCF concluded, to leave the PLM line to slow-moving and intermediate traffic and create a new special-purpose high-speed line for the through passenger trains, especially as an environmentally unobjectionable route for the latter was not difficult to contrive in Central France's vast tracts of open country and the new-found technology would curb its capital cost to a fraction of the Japanese Shinkansen's. After ten years of detailed planning, exhaustive component research and development, and contention with some ecological and road transport lobby efforts to thwart the project, construction of France's first new LGV (for *Lignes Grandes Vitesses*), the Sud-Est (LGV SE), began with Government blessing in December 1976.

The enormous cost of building any new urban railway was avoided by branching the new line from the existing route 18·6 miles (29·9 km) out from Paris Gare de Lyons, then rejoining it to the historic system on the outskirts of Lyons. Between these two junctions the line's engineering was almost identical with that of a motorway, though it only shared infrastructure with *autoroutes* over a couple of sections totalling 44 miles (71 km). The LGV hugged the contours with an undulating profile featuring gradients as steep as 1 in 28·5, not far off the usual autoroute limit of 1 in 25, and curved on radii only slightly more generous than the *autoroute* norm, even though the TGV trains would have no artificial body-tilting mechanisms. With exclusive use by standard train-sets in view even curves this sharp could be made negotiable at 160 mph (258 km/h) because of the ability to cant them ideally and the science by now acquired in the design of low-center-of-gravity, lightweight vehicles and their running gear. The freedom to bend, dip and hoist the route as the terrain dictated not only reduced earthworks expense but obviated any tunnelling in the 242 miles (390 km) of new LGV.

Since the old line would cater for intermediate traffic the new could be kept exquisitely simple, with only two stations at Montchanin and Mâcon and three junctions en route, the latter to disperse some TGV trains to Dijon, Switzerland and the French Alps (compatibility with the historic system was a fundamental of the LGV concept, so that TGV trains could run beyond the new line's limits to Montpellier and Marseilles as well as Switzerland and Savoie).

A French Railways TGV crossing the Digoin viaduct on the Paris–Lyons high-speed LGV (Lignes grandes Vitesses).

The two stations each needed only two platforms both served by a loop; their entrances and exits, the divergences to the old line (built for negotiation at 137 mph – 221 km/h – incidentally), emergency crossovers between the two running lines installed at regular intervals and the access to a number of sidings provided to sidetrack failed trains were the line's only point work. That simplified the design of a continuous cab signalling and automatic train control system governed entirely by track circuitry-activated commands in normal working, and supervison of the whole route from a single Paris center.

The train-set design crystallized in a five-car gas turbine-electric prototype of 1972, the prolonged trials of which included 34,000 miles' (54,716 km) running at more than 125 mph (201 km/h) before its retirement in 1978. By the end of 1974, however, the oil price explosion had persuaded the SNCF to go electric, even though this would entail electrifying some routes in mind for TGV train service beyond the new line's limits, such as Lyons to Grenoble, and incur the weight penalty of multi-voltage traction equipment. Since the LGV would be electrified at 25kV 50Hz ac the train-sets would have to be adaptable to the 1·5kV dc of the historic PLM network; and though Geneva was accessible to 1·5kV dc, through service to Lausanne would predicate triple-voltage capability embracing Switzerland's 15kV 16⅔Hz ac.

The ultimate TGV train-set was a ten-car unit with power cars at each end (as already remarked, the SNCF had no qualms about running a 25kV line from one to another through the train) combining to achieve a continuous output of 8,650 hp under 25kV ac wires for 386 tonnes (380 tons) tare of train. On a large number of services two of these sets would be coupled under multiple-unit control, creating a formidable snake of 20 cars' length; that in-

tention forced the SNCF to make advance TGV seat reservation compulsory and tolerate the expense of two catering services on such workings, one in each set. The sword-point streamlining of the power cars, let alone the hazards of allowing passengers proximity to their high-voltage plant, would prohibit any communication between units once the train was on the move.

Prefaced by a stunning press demonstration on 26 February 1981, when a TGV set curtailed to seven cars and modified to jack its power up to a possible 13,410 hp for 302 tonnes (297 tons) of train was whipped up to a new world record of 236 mph (380 km/h), 169·7 miles (273·1 km) of the Paris–Lyons TGV was opened to public 160 mph (258 km/h) service the following September.

Standard journey time for the Paris–Lyons Brotteaux non-stop journey of 279·1 miles (449·2 km) was now set at 2 hours 40 minutes, representing an average of 104·7 mph (168·5 km/h) the whole way. That was only a curtain-raiser. In the autumn of 1983, when the residue of the new line was due for commissioning and the Paris–Lyons distance by LGV would be cut to 265·5 miles (427·3 km), the two cities would be an even two hours apart and by a considerably more intensive train service than in 1981. That would establish a phenomenal average speed standard of 132·7 mph (213·6 km/h), the world's best on rail by a handsome margin.

The LGV's first year was not without its traumas. The opening months were scarred by more than one instance of service interruption through damage to the catenary by trains' pantographs losing smooth contact with the current wires. Nor was the LGV operation unscathed by the vicious wintry weather which helped to humiliate BR's APT. Moreover, as 1982 moved through summer to autumn, the trains' riding at 160 mph (258 km/h) on their new track, which had seemed so soundlessly and silkily smooth in the inaugural weeks, was palpably losing some sheen. Right from the start they had been far less comfortably at home than SNCF Corail cars on the track and bends of the historic railway exit from Paris to the start of the LGV line proper, even at its 100 mph (161 km/h) limit, or on the sharply winding route through the Jura Mountains taken by two daily TGVs working off the LGV line to Geneva and back.

Within the trains first-class travel was unexceptionable, but second-class seating comfort had been somewhat sacrificed to economic pressures for a high passenger/tare weight ratio within a more cramped body cross-section than that of a Corail car. Only in first-class was a full meal service offered, pre-fashioned on terra firma and served airliner-style on trays from trainboard galleys. The part-car buffet-bar catering for other requirements proved seriously undersized and uncomfortable to patronize when a train was well-loaded (the SNCF has since conceded this to have been a design misjudgement).

Nevertheless, within its first year of operation the LGV carried 5·6 million passengers and its trains were notching an average load factor of 65 per cent. This was a level the SNCF had thought beyond reach until the whole new line was operational in the autumn of 1983, all 87 train-sets were delivered and the full, more intensive TGV train service was active. Around 40 per cent of the LGV's passengers in 1982 were reckoned to be new rail business.

The SNCF estimates that around 26 million of France's population will by 1984 have been brought within the marketing orbit of this first LGV, for its trains will range beyond Lyons over old infrastructure as far as Grenoble, Geneva, Marseilles and Montpellier (extension to Marseilles and Montpellier was launched on a limited scale in 1982). That convinces the SNCF that by 1984 the LGV's full regular-interval timetable will harvest as many as 20 million passenger journeys a year, a figure that will generate a fully acceptable pay-off on the £830 millions capital cost (at 1980 values) of the new railway and its initial 87 train-sets. Encouraged by initial results, the SNCF has not only ordered an extra 10 TGV train-sets but drafted expensive plans to make the existing route from Lyons to Marseilles fit for 125 mph (201 km/h) by the TGV trains through realignments, resignalling, installation of six additional sub-stations to beef up the traction current supply, and laying in some 35 miles (56 km) of extra single- or double-track where the main line's very busy freight can be bypassed by the TGV flyers.

The LGV's speed and first-class comfort score primarily in competition with air, whence the Paris–Lyons trains have snatched much of their initial new traffic. But even before LGV the railway was strongly competitive with the airlines; over such distances as Marseilles to Paris, 535·4 miles (861·6 km), the SNCF's passenger carryings were in fact superior. To fulfil its economic prospectus the TGV must clearly make a killing in the 60 per cent road sector of the market. Whether it will is a question made the more intriguing by Britain's 1981 hint that a sharply cut price counts for more in the leisure market than exciting pace.

Meanwhile, as remarked earlier, at presidential direction the SNCF is working up the plan for a second LGV in full engineering detail. This, the LGV-Atlantique, may be started as soon as the remainder of the Paris–Lyons LGV is commissioned in 1983, and could be operational by 1988. It would be a 160 mph (258 km/h) exit from Paris to junctions about 100 miles (161 km) out with the existing trunk routes to Britanny, Toulouse and Bordeaux, on which the TGV trains would complete their journeys at a maximum of 125 mph (201 km/h). From Paris Montparnasse the new LGV would adopt the handily available infrastructure of a never-completed suburban line to Chartres, then parallel a stretch of the A10 motorway, and beyond Chartres fork into connections with the Toulouse–Bordeaux routes near St Pierre-les-Corps and with the Britanny main lines near Le Mans. The new line can be more easily graded than the Paris–Lyons LGV, with a ruling slope of 1 in 67, so its train-sets, of which 95 will be needed, can be expanded to 12 instead of 10 trailers between each pair of power cars.

After that the LGV Nord scheme may be revived, but for the present with Brussels and Cologne as the only targets clearly in French sights. As for the British connection, President Mitterand, unlike his predecessor, has shown readiness to forget the Wilson Government decision on the Anglo-French Channel Tunnel agreement of 1974. But in 1982, though the Thatcher Government was keeping a wisp of breath in subsequent, scaled-down tunnel schemes, its dogmatic insistence that any fulfilment it might concede would be contingent on the project's entrustment entirely to private enterprise risk capital, with no Government guarantee back-up, left little room for optimism that the enterprise would soon be revived. And the outlook was dimmed yet more by the depressingly negative attitude to rail development permeating the report on BR of the Government-appointed Serpell Committee which, as already mentioned, was published early in 1983.

INDEX

All numbers in italic refer to illustrations.